Social *Movements*

Suzanne Staggenborg

OXFORD
UNIVERSITY PRESS

OXFORD
UNIVERSITY PRESS

70 Wynford Drive, Don Mills, Ontario M3C 1J9
www.oup.com/ca

Oxford University Press is a department of the University of Oxford.
It furthers the University's objective of excellence in research, scholarship,
and education by publishing worldwide in

Oxford   New York

Auckland   Cape Town   Dar es Salaam   Hong Kong   Karachi
Kuala Lumpur   Madrid   Melbourne   Mexico City   Nairobi
New Delhi   Shanghai   Taipei   Toronto

With offices in

Argentina   Austria   Brazil   Chile   Czech Republic   France   Greece
Guatemala   Hungary   Italy   Japan   Poland   Portugal   Singapore
South Korea   Switzerland   Thailand   Turkey   Ukraine   Vietnam

Oxford is a trade mark of Oxford University Press
in the UK and in certain other countries

Published in Canada
by Oxford University Press

Copyright © Oxford University Press Canada 2008

The moral rights of the author have been asserted

Database right Oxford University Press (maker)

First published 2008

Library and Archives Canada Cataloguing in Publication Data

Staggenborg, Suzanne
Social movements / Suzanne Staggenborg.

Includes bibliographical references and index.
ISBN 978-0-19-542309-9 (bound)

1. Social movements—Textbooks.   2. Social movements—Philosophy—Textbooks.
3. Social movements—Case studies—Textbooks.
I. Title.

HM881.S73 2007   303.48'4   C2007-902651-6

Cover Design: Sherill Chapman

Cover Image: Getty Images

1 2 3 4 – 11 10 09 08

This book is printed on permanent (acid-free) paper ∞.

Printed in Canada

Contents

(19) ch. 12 Snarr 4
(20) ch. 8 Snarr 14

(21) Ch. 7 War on Terror
Snarr 2

(22) Review Snarr 5 - Global Insecurity
"Why We Fight"
(23) Test II Snarr 8 - Poverty & Global
Tsbtsi
(24) Test II returned Snarr 9 - Pop + Migrat.
(25) Snarr 11/12 Children + Health
Constan
(26) Snarr 15 - Conflict / Co-op.

Preface and Acknowledgements

Social movements are important means of bringing about political and cultural changes through collective action. The study of social movements helps us to understand how movements achieve change, and how they are limited in doing so, by examining political and cultural opportunities and obstacles, organizational dynamics, resources, collective action frames, strategies, and tactics. The field of social movements is an exciting one, and scholars continue to produce new studies of a wide array of social movements in many different countries, while activists also regularly provide accounts of their experiences. Relevant to both activists and social scientists, the area is one that students find important and interesting.

Given the proliferation of social movement scholarship in recent decades, it is a daunting task to attempt to capture the field in a short book. Thus, my goal is simply to introduce students and other readers to some interesting history, ideas, and questions about social movements. No single researcher can be an expert on all of the many social movements that might be covered in such a book, and I have limited myself to some of the movements that I have followed for many years in teaching and researching in the area. Because this book is part of the Themes in Canadian Sociology series and because Aboriginal protest has been particularly important in Canada, I asked Howard Ramos to contribute a chapter on that movement. Hopefully, students will find this selection of contemporary protest movements interesting and will learn enough about theoretical ideas and approaches to movements to be able to apply this knowledge to other movements of interest.

I would like to thank Lorne Tepperman and the late James Curtis for inviting me to write the book for their edited series. I also thank all of the various editors that I worked with at Oxford University Press for their contributions to my work: Lisa Meschino, Roberta Osborne, Richard Tallman, and Dina Theleritis. I am very grateful to Howard Ramos for contributing a chapter to the book and for his very helpful comments on other chapters. Finally, I thank Rod Nelson for his advice and support.

Abbreviations

ACT UP	AIDS Coalition to Unleash Power
AFN	Assembly of First Nations
AIM	American Indian Movement
ATTAC	Association for the Taxation of Financial Transaction for the Aid of Citizens
CBC	Canadian Broadcasting Corporation
COC	Council of Canadians
CND	Campaign for Nuclear Disarmament
CUPE	Canadian Union of Public Employees
DAWN	Development Alternatives with Women for a New Era
EGALE	Equality for Gays and Lesbians Everywhere
ERA	Equal Rights Amendment
ETAG	Ethical Trading Action Group
EU	European Union
FFQ	Fédération des femmes du Québec
FLQ	Front de Libération du Québec
FTA	Canada–US Free Trade Agreement
FTAA	Free Trade Area of the Americas
GLF	Gay Liberation Front
ILO	International Labour Organization
IMC	Independent Media Center
IMF	International Monetary Fund
ITK	Inuit Tapiriit Kanatami
MAI	Multilateral Agreement on Investment
MNC	Métis National Council
MNSJ	Metro Network for Social Justice
MSOP	Movement for the Survival of the Ogoni People
NAACP	National Association for the Advancement of Colored People
NAC	National Action Committee on the Status of Women
NAFTA	North American Free Trade Agreement
NAIB	North American Indian Brotherhood
NCC	Native Council of Canada
NDP	New Democratic Party
NIB	National Indian Brotherhood
NIC	National Indian Council
NIMBY	not in my back yard
NGLTF	National Gay and Lesbian Task Force
NGO	non-governmental organization
NOW	National Organization for Women
PGA	Peoples' Global Action
PQ	Parti Québécois
REAL	Realistic, Equal, Active, for Life (Women)

SAP	structural adjustment program
SDS	Students for a Democratic Society
SMO	social movement organization
SNCC	Student Nonviolent Coordinating Committee
SQ	Sûreté du Québec
SUPA	Student Union for Peace Action
UFW	United Farm Workers
UN	United Nations
USAS	United Students Against Sweatshops
WRC	Workers Rights Consortium
WSF	World Social Forum
WTO	World Trade Organization
YMCA	Young Men's Christian Association

Introduction

Social movements around the world have used a wide variety of protest tactics to bring about enormous social changes, influencing cultural arrangements, public opinion, and government policies. Consider the following examples:

- At the beginning of the twentieth century British suffragists, impatient with the failure of their government to give women the vote, protested in Parliament, marched in the streets, chained themselves to the railings outside the Prime Minister's residence, and went on hunger strikes. Numerous suffragists were jailed and force-fed, and many were beaten by police when they participated in demonstrations. The militancy and bravery of the suffragists inspired movement activists around the world. By the 1920s suffrage movements had won the vote for women in many different countries, but struggles for a full range of women's rights continued. Today, the women's movement continues to combat problems such as violence against women and to fight for access to education, employment, and citizenship rights for women around the world.
- In the southern United States, civil rights activists in the 1950s and 1960s used boycotts, sit-ins, mass demonstrations, 'freedom rides' on public transportation, and voter registration drives to secure basic rights for blacks. Activists were jailed, beaten, and murdered as they combatted a society in which African Americans were denied service in many public establishments, forced to sit in the back of buses and give up their seats to whites, and disenfranchised by threats of violence when they attempted to vote. After the civil rights movement won battles over desegregation of public facilities and voting rights, blacks became a political force in the South and African Americans served as mayors of cities that once denied them basic rights, such as Atlanta, Georgia, and Jackson, Mississippi.
- In Canada, a group calling itself the Association for Social Knowledge formed in Vancouver in 1964 to begin the long process of creating a positive gay identity at a time when gays and lesbians were denied basic rights such as employment and often arrested simply for socializing together in bars and other public places. By 1971, the low-key approach of the early activists gave way to a gay liberation movement that marched on Parliament Hill to demand the 'freedom to love'. Since the 1970s, gay and lesbian rights groups have lobbied for inclusion

in human rights codes, filed lawsuits to secure legal protections, and staged numerous 'gay pride' parades and demonstrations. In 2005, after many years of equality-seeking work by the lesbian and gay rights movement, same-sex marriage became legal throughout Canada.

• In 1999, a seemingly new movement for global justice burst on the scene with large demonstrations against the World Trade Organization meetings in Seattle, which virtually closed down the WTO conference. In Quebec City in 2001, activists stormed the fence that had been erected to keep protestors from disrupting meetings to establish a Free Trade Area of the Americas (FTAA). These and other demonstrations around the world helped to raise public consciousness about the impacts of the trade and monetary policies of global institutions. The global justice movement works to unite local and international activists and organizations from a variety of different social movements and attempts to influence international labour, environmental, and human rights standards.

In all of these examples, individuals have banded together in collective efforts to create social change by presenting demands for justice and pressuring authorities to respond. Movements have organized to protect the environment, oppose wars, and advocate for the rights of more and more groups, including workers, women, gay men and lesbians, students, disabled people, senior citizens, and many racial and ethnic groups. Social movements are important vehicles for social and political change, yet it is not always apparent how it is possible to bring together a variety of groups and individuals with varying interests and ideologies to form a cohesive movement capable of effecting real changes. Thus, social movement theorists attempt to answer a variety of questions about the growth and impact of movements, which are relevant to activists and policy-makers as well as to social scientists. Key questions include why movements originate when they do, how they attract and maintain support, how they present issues and formulate strategies and tactics, how they structure organizations, how they change cultures, why they generate opposition and sometimes decline, and how and why they succeed or fail in achieving their objectives.

This book introduces students and other readers to the study of social movements by looking at some influential theories in the field, the issues they raise, and how they help to explain the mobilization and outcomes of social movements. I review major theories of social movements and collective action and identify important theoretical issues that we will explore in connection with a selection of substantive movements. I also discuss the cluster of protest movements that arose in many countries in the 1960s, creating strategies and changes that continue to influence collective action in the twenty-first century. Chapters on Aboriginal, women's, gay and lesbian rights, environmental, and global justice movements analyze general issues in the study of social movements as they apply to each movement, including how these social movements originate, mobilize participants, and bring about social change. In this introductory chapter, we consider the concept of social movements and related ideas, and place the study of contemporary movements in historical context.

THE ORIGINS OF THE SOCIAL MOVEMENT

The social movement, as we know it today, is a relatively recent means of organizing for social change. Charles Tilly, who has done extensive historical research on the origins of the social movement in the Western world, quotes from an account of a 'movement' in 1682 in Narbonne, France, to make this point:

> [T]here was a little movement in Narbonne on the occasion of the collection of the cosse tax, which had been ordered by an act of the royal council. Many women gathered with the common people, and threw stones at the tax collectors, but the Consuls and the leading citizens hurried over and put a stop to the disorder. (Quoted in Tilly, 1984: 297)

Although this seventeenth-century incident is referred to as a 'little movement', it bears scant resemblance to what we think of today as a 'social movement'. The term *petit mouvement* was part of the vocabulary of the time, used to refer to 'a localized collective action by ordinary people which the authorities considered necessary and proper to end by force' (ibid., 298). Tilly points out that today we would not consider this type of action a **social movement** unless it were more enduring, part of a series of collective actions rather than one incident, and enacted by participants with common interests and a distinct identity, who had broader goals than stopping a particular tax. He uses the concept of a **repertoire of collective action** to get at the idea that limited forms of protest are familiar during a given time. Our protest repertoire has changed dramatically since the women of Narbonne stoned their tax collectors.

Collective action in Western countries such as France and England (see Tilly, 1986, 1995, 2004a) was once localized and defensive. People got together within their communities to defend local interests, using protest forms drawn from local culture and typically directed at particular individuals. For example, the **charivari** was a traditional form of collective action directed towards individuals who had transgressed community norms, such as a married man who got a single woman pregnant. The guilty party would be subject to a noisy demonstration designed to humiliate him or her before the community. As historian Edward Shorter (1975: 219) describes, there were many variations of the charivari, based on local tradition:

> Sometimes the demonstration would consist of masked individuals circling somebody's house at night, screaming, beating on pans, and blowing cow horns (which the local butchers rented out). On other occasions the offender would be seized and marched through the streets, seated perhaps backwards on a donkey or forced to wear a placard describing his sins. Sometimes the youth would administer the charivari; on other occasions villagers of all ages and sexes would mix together.

Despite such variations, the charivari shared characteristics in common with other forms of protest in the traditional repertoire, which also included food riots, grain seizures, and land revolts (Tarrow, 1998: 32–6). All of these traditional forms of action were short in duration and local in scope; even when a national issue such as taxation was involved, the targets of the protest were local authorities and the actions were particular to the local community (Tilly, 1995: 45). In contrast to this traditional repertoire, a new repertoire of collective action, consisting of tactics such as large-scale demonstrations, strikes, and boycotts, began to develop in Europe and North America in the late eighteenth century and became firmly established in the nineteenth century. The new repertoire was cosmopolitan rather than parochial, with protests often targeted at national rather than local authorities. The tactics of the new repertoire were 'modular' (Tarrow, 1998) in that they could easily be transported to many locales and situations, rather than being tied to local communities and rituals. For example, the boycott and the mass petition were tactics that could be aimed at any target with regard to any type of grievance. The nineteenth-century abolition movement was one of the first social movements to use these tactics, organizing a boycott of sugar grown with slave labour and sending petitions signed by large numbers of supporters to the British Parliament (Tarrow, 1998: 38–9).

The story of how this shift in repertoires came about is a complicated one (see Tilly, 1995, 2004a, 2004b; Tarrow, 1998), but it involved the expansion of nation-states and the spread of capitalism. With the development of national electoral politics, special-purpose associations formed to represent the interests of various groups, including dissident aristocrats and bourgeois activists who sometimes formed alliances with dissatisfied workers. These coalitions adopted new means of making claims, such as mass petitions and disciplined marches, to replace the often violent direct actions, such as food riots and grain seizures, which had been central to the older repertoire and were more likely to be repressed by authorities. With the spread of wage labour, workers gained independence from particular landlords and masters, and were freer to engage in political activities (Tilly, 2004b: 27). The repertoire of collective action gradually changed, and the social movement became part of the new repertoire.

Thus, the social movement emerged in a particular historical period as a result of large-scale social changes and political conditions that made it possible. Although there have been some innovations in protest forms, social movements still select tactics from essentially the same repertoire of contention that became established in the nineteenth century. Tilly notes, however, that the social movement and its repertoire are products of historical circumstances and could change as political conditions change. For example, insofar as centralized nation-states are replaced with transnational bodies, the national social movement may become a less effective form of political organization (ibid., 14). Indeed, transnational movements and organizations are already significant, and new forms of action, such as Internet-based protests, have developed with new technologies and processes of globalization.

DEFINING SOCIAL MOVEMENTS

Research by Charles Tilly and others on the origins of the social movement has been influential in promoting a political view of social movements (see McAdam et al., 2001). In this view, social movements are one form of **contentious politics**:

Contentious politics

> contentious in the sense that social movements involve collective making of claims that, if realized, would conflict with someone else's interests, political in the sense that governments of one sort or another figure somehow in the claim making, whether as claimants, objects of claims, allies of the objects, or monitors of the contention. (Tilly 2004b: 3)

According to Tilly, social movements as they developed in the West after 1750 came to consist of sustained **campaigns** that made collective claims aimed at authorities. They typically created special-purpose associations or coalitions and engaged in strategies such as demonstrations, petition drives, public statements, and meetings —various tactics that make up the modern *social movement repertoire*. Movement actors attempt to represent themselves publicly as worthy, unified, numerous, and committed (ibid., 3–4).

Based on this contentious politics approach, Sidney Tarrow (1998: 4) provides a succinct definition of social movements as '*collective challenges, based on common purposes and social solidarities, in sustained interaction with elites, opponents, and authorities*'. Social movements are *sustained* in that they consist of multiple campaigns or at least multiple episodes of collective action within a single campaign. Movement campaigns consist of *interactions* among movement actors, their targets, the public, and other relevant actors. The targets of movement claims are often government authorities, but may also be other types of authorities, such as business owners or religious leaders (Tilly, 2004b: 4).

Social movements are not the only form of contentious politics. McAdam, Tarrow, and Tilly (2001) include in their definition of contentious politics various public and collective political struggles, such as revolutions, nationalism, and strike waves, as well as social movements. They also consider actions by established political actors within institutions as contentious politics, provided the action is episodic and departs from the everyday, non-collective action that goes on within institutions. For example, the activities of the National Commission on Terrorist Attacks Upon the United States (also known as the 9/11 Commission), backed by collective action on the part of family members of victims of the 11 September 2001 terrorist attacks, might be considered a form of contentious politics, though perfectly legal and using an established political forum. McAdam et al. (2001: 7–8) distinguish between *contained contention* by established political actors and *transgressive contention*, which involves at least some 'newly self-identified political actors' and/or 'innovative collective action' by at least some parties.

Although the distinction between social movements and other phenomena such as *political parties* and *interest groups* is not always sharp, movement scholars have generally regarded movements as *challengers* that are at least in part *outsiders* with regard to the established power structure (Tilly, 1978; Gamson, 1990 [1975]). Political parties and interest groups, in contrast, are *insiders* with at least some degree of access to government authorities and other elites. However, political insiders may engage in (usually) contained contention, and movements may become **professionalized** in the sense that they include fairly stable organizations, often headed by paid leaders, and may have memberships consisting largely of financial

Greenpeace

contributors, or 'paper members', rather than activists (McCarthy and Zald, 1973). It may be difficult to distinguish between a professional movement organization and an established interest group.

Some social movement theorists have distinguished between social movements and the organized entities that typically populate movements. John McCarthy and Mayer Zald (1977: 1217–18) define a social movement as 'a set of opinions and beliefs in a population which represents preferences for changing some elements of the social structure and/or reward distribution of a society' and a **countermovement** as 'a set of opinions and beliefs in a population opposed to a social movement'. In this view social movements are 'preference structures' or sets of opinions and beliefs, which may or may not be turned into collective action, depending on pre-existing organization and opportunities and costs for expressing preferences. Movements supported by populations that are internally organized through communities or associations are most likely to generate organized structures (ibid.; Oberschall, 1973). A **social movement organization** (SMO) is defined as 'a complex, or formal, organization which identifies its goals with the preferences of a social movement or a countermovement and attempts to implement those goals' (McCarthy and Zald, 1977: 1218). Movements differ from one another in the extent to which they are organized by formal organizations and in the extent to which they trigger organized opposition or countermovements. McCarthy and Zald refer to the collection of organizations within a movement as a **social movement industry** and to all of these 'industries' in a society as the **social movement sector**.

McCarthy and Zald's definition of the social movement as a preference structure differs from most other definitions, including the contentious politics view of movements as collective challenges, in that McCarthy and Zald separate preferences for change from organized collective action. They argue that this approach has the advantage of recognizing that movements are 'never fully mobilized' and that the size or intensity of preferences may not predict the rise and fall of the organized movement (ibid., 1219). Collective action may depend less on the grievances of unorganized groups than on social movement leaders who act as 'entrepreneurs' in mobilizing—and perhaps even creating—preferences (McCarthy and Zald, 1973). Moreover, McCarthy and Zald's approach leads us to focus on social movement organizations and the interactions of these organizations within the context of a particular social movement. Organizations have different structures, which affect their strategies and longevity, and they may co-operate or compete with one another. In some instances, organizational interests may interfere with the attainment of movement goals or preferences.

The distinction between a social movement and a social movement organization is important because major social movements typically include multiple organizations, and internal organizational dynamics and inter-organizational alliances are critical to movement strategies and outcomes. For example, the environmental movement in North America includes organizations such as Greenpeace, the Sierra Club, the Nature Conservancy, the World Wildlife Fund, and Earth First!, to name only a few of the many active organizations. These organizations have different ideologies and strategic approaches and may compete with one another for members and funding, despite their common commitment to environmental protection. Coalitions of movement organizations are often difficult to form and maintain, particularly among those with different structures and strategic preferences. However, many movements face organized countermovements, which increase the urgency of coalition work (Staggenborg, 1986). Movement–countermovement interactions, as well as interactions with the state, are an important topic for social movement research and often involve organizational dynamics (see Zald and Useem, 1987; Meyer and Staggenborg, 1996).

At the same time that analyses of social movement organizations are critical to social movement theory, scholars have recognized that movements consist of more than politically motivated organizations with an explicit mandate to seek change in public policy. The notion of a **social movement community** captures the idea that movements consist of networks of individuals, cultural groups, alternative institutions, and institutional supporters as well as political movement organizations (see Buechler, 1990; Staggenborg, 1998). Moreover, movements also consist of more than the public protest events emphasized by the contentious politics approach. Although the contentious politics approach recognizes that movements can target authorities other than the state, critics charge that movements such as religious and self-help movements tend to be neglected along with less visible forms of collective action, such as efforts to change institutions and create new forms of culture. Consequently, a number of theorists have called for broadening our conception of social movements.

Mayer Zald (2000) suggests that we should view **ideologically structured action** as movement activity. He argues that movement-related activity occurs within such organizations as political parties and government agencies, and that families and schools are important in socializing movement supporters. In short, action shaped by movement ideology can be found in a variety of institutions and structures of everyday life. David Snow (2004) argues that movements can be conceived as 'collective challenges to systems or structures of authority', including various types of organizations and institutions and also sets of cultural beliefs and understandings. These theorists and others argue that movement activity occurs in a wide range of venues, through a variety of forms of collective action. Movements consist of informal networks as well as formal organizations and they produce culture and collective identity as well as political campaigns (cf. Armstrong, 2002; Diani, 1992; Melucci, 1989, 1996; Polletta and Jasper, 2001; Rupp and Taylor, 1999).

The danger, as Tilly (2004b: 10) points out, is that 'one may see social movements everywhere.' He argues that it is better to stick to a definition of movements as consisting of sustained campaigns directed at authorities, which use the social movement repertoire and create public displays of worthiness, unity, numbers, and commitment. Then, movements can be compared to other forms of contentious politics such as conflict over policy within institutions. This approach has the merit of keeping the definition of social movements tied to the historical origins of the social movement that Tilly has so carefully documented. Nevertheless, studies of contemporary social movements such as the women's movement show that we cannot completely understand the maintenance and outcomes of important social movements without looking broadly at their cultural, institutional, and political manifestations (Staggenborg and Taylor, 2005).

As the above discussion shows, the area of social movement study is one in which there are disagreements even about the very definition of social movements. Rather than seeing this as a weakness, however, we can view it as a sign of a lively field in which new perspectives and ideas compete with existing approaches. Different definitions of social movements lead to different emphases in the study of particular movements. The contentious politics definition of the social movement as a sustained challenge to elites or other opponents by shifting coalitions of collective actors through a series of public campaigns points to the political nature of social movements and their role in putting issues on the public agenda and changing public policies. McCarthy and Zald's view of social movements as preference structures leads us to focus on how preferences get transformed into organized movements through the enterprise of leaders and the creation of different types of movement organizations. Conceptualizations of social movements as including ideologically structured action, social movement communities, and challenges to different types of institutional authorities all point to the multiple arenas in which movements operate. These different emphases are not necessarily incompatible, and their usefulness depends in part on the nature of the movement being studied.

OUTLINE OF THE BOOK

The field of social movements is an exciting one that contains a healthy mix of interesting theoretical ideas and empirical studies of real social movements. The best way to introduce the field is to look at some important movements, using the tools of social movement theory. The book highlights a few contemporary movements, including the Aboriginal movement, the women's movement, the gay and lesbian rights movement, the environmental movement, and the global justice movement. Although these are all progressive or liberal movements, they have provoked opposition in the form of right-wing or conservative movements, which I discuss as countermovements, particularly in the cases of the women's, gay and lesbian rights, and environmental movements. Because of its importance to Canadian politics, I invited Howard Ramos, an expert on Aboriginal protest, to provide a chapter focusing on the Aboriginal movement in Canada. My selection of the other movements discussed in subsequent chapters is based on my own expertise and interest, and I make no claim of providing a comprehensive survey of social movements. However, the book does attempt to equip readers with an understanding of the theoretical questions and issues involved in studying social movements, which can be applied to a wide variety of movements. The substantive chapters in this book provide examples of how several important movements have been analyzed by social movement theorists. Although a great deal of research has been conducted on these movements in the United States, I avoid focusing solely on this research, drawing also on studies from Canada and other Western countries, with some attention to global developments. It should be noted, too, that although there is a growing body of literature on movements outside the West (see Oliver et al., 2003), this book is limited largely to studies from North America and Western Europe, which still dominate the field.

Before delving into the specifics of particular movements, I discuss the theoretical approaches, and issues stemming from those perspectives, that guide social movement theorists. Chapter 2 provides a review of several major theoretical traditions in North America and Western Europe: collective behaviour theory; resource mobilization and political process perspectives; and new social movement theory. I note various attempts to synthesize ideas from these approaches, as well as efforts to go beyond them. My goal is to familiarize readers with the ideas in these perspectives and to highlight the contributions as well as limitations of each. Theories about social movements are important because they direct researchers to different types of questions regarding movements. Chapter 3 elaborates on the general types of issues studied by social movement theorists, which come out of the theoretical perspectives and guide studies of substantive movements. Because of the importance of the mass media to the movements described in the book, a section of the chapter is devoted to the role the media play in modern social movements.

In Chapter 4, before examining selected movements in detail in subsequent chapters, I discuss the historical importance of the cycle of protest of the 1960s for contemporary social movements. I describe the American civil rights movement, which had a worldwide impact on strategies of protest and political consciousness, and the New Left student and anti-war movements of the 1960s in North America and Western Europe. This discussion is important to subsequent chapters because the movements to be discussed were part of this cycle of contention or were strongly influenced by the 1960s protest cycle.

In Chapter 5, Howard Ramos analyzes the mobilization of Aboriginal protest, which gained momentum during the cycle of protest of the 1960s, and relates Canadian Aboriginal protest to broader trends in indigenous protest elsewhere in the world. He explains the importance of critical events, political opportunities, organization and resources, and collective identity in the mobilization of Canadian Aboriginal peoples.

In Chapter 6, I focus on the key question of what has happened to the contemporary women's movement since the 1960s. I examine the origins of the contemporary movement, the range of feminist activities, and how the women's movement has survived and changed over time, including its development within institutions, other social movements, and cultural venues. I also look at the role of anti-feminist countermovements in challenging feminist goals and channelling movement activism. The chapter demonstrates and explains the continuity and growth of feminism, as evidenced by recent developments such as third-wave feminism and expansion of the global women's movement.

Chapter 7 discusses the origins and strategies of the contemporary gay and lesbian movement and the role played by factors such as political opportunity, state repression, and countermovement campaigns. The chapter examines a variety of different movement approaches, including liberationist, equal rights, and queer politics, and the outcomes that have been achieved in Canada and other countries.

Chapter 8 takes up the problem of maintaining a movement that can deal with serious and ongoing environmental problems over many years. The chapter examines problems of winning and maintaining public interest and individual participation, combatting countermovements, and creating effective organizations and strategies. After discussing recent debates on movement strategy, the chapter looks at the mass-media focused efforts of Greenpeace, green lobbies and consumer boycotts, and grassroots direct-action campaigns.

In Chapter 9, I focus on the recent movement for global justice that came to public attention with the demonstrations against the WTO meetings in Seattle in 1999. In examining the origins of this new global movement, I discuss the importance of the Canadian anti-free trade movement in generating a model for cross-national movement organization. I discuss the strategic and organizational challenges facing the movement as it brings together local and international activists and organizations from a variety of different social movements and attempts to influence international labour, environmental, and human rights standards.

My conclusion, Chapter 10, ties together themes from the previous chapters and lays out important challenges for social movements. It stresses the importance of social movements in bringing about social and political changes.

Discussion Questions

1. Which definition of social movements is most useful for understanding contemporary movements such as the environmental movement?
2. How do different definitions of social movements focus our attention on different aspects of movements?
3. What are the major tactics within the contemporary repertoire of collective action? What explains the use of these tactics in our society?

Suggested Readings

McCarthy, John D., and Mayer N. Zald. 1977. 'Resource Mobilization and Social Movements: A Partial Theory', *American Journal of Sociology* 82, 6:1212–41. This is one of the seminal statements on resource mobilization theory.

Tarrow, Sidney. 1998. *Power in Movement: Social Movements and Contentious Politics*, 2nd edn. Cambridge: Cambridge University Press. This is an important synthesis of theoretical and substantive themes in the field.

Tilly, Charles. 2004. *Social Movements, 1768–2004*. Boulder, Colo.: Paradigm Publishers. This book provides a very good summary of Tilly's extensive historical work on social movements.

Chapter 2

Theories of Social Movements and Collective Action

Several major theoretical approaches have influenced the thinking of social movement scholars in Europe and North America. These theoretical approaches are important as perspectives that guide students of social movements to focus on particular issues, questions, and methods of inquiry. Often, researchers borrow from different theoretical approaches in carrying out their studies, and in recent years theorists have attempted to synthesize the major approaches. In the study of social movements, few scholars have aimed to build universal theories that attempt to make general statements about movements across time and place. Rather, researchers have generally recognized the importance of historical context and cultural differences, at the same time building a body of ideas about how movements operate within particular circumstances. Before the 1980s, European and North American scholars developed analytical approaches for the most part independently of one another, with 'new social movement theory' originating in Europe and 'collective behaviour' and 'resource mobilization' theories coming mostly from the United States. Many cross-national collaborations and influences between Europeans and North Americans have since resulted in extensions and integrations of these theories.

This chapter begins with overviews of collective behaviour theory, resource mobilization and political process theories, and new social movement theory, showing how each of these approaches raises different types of questions and points to different ways of describing and analyzing social movements. After summarizing these major theoretical approaches, I look at efforts to fill gaps in these theories, integrate approaches, and create new ones. In the following chapter, I discuss further some of the important issues raised by the theories.

COLLECTIVE BEHAVIOUR THEORY

A number of different perspectives are included in the category of **collective behaviour theory**, which is often referred to as the classical model of social movements. Collective behaviour theories have also been labelled *strain* or *breakdown theories* because they typically posit that collective behaviour comes about during a period of social disruption, when grievances are deeply felt, rather than being a standard part of the political process (see Jenkins, 1981; Marx and Wood, 1975; McAdam, 1999 [1982]; Morris and Herring, 1987). Collective behaviour theorists have studied a wide variety of phenomena, including crowds, panics, mobs, riots, crazes, fads, religious cults and revivals, social movements, and revolutions. The study of 'crowds' dates back to the late nineteenth century when European theorists such as Gustave Le Bon (1895) tried to explain crowd behaviour by analyzing the psychology of the collective or large gathering. Le Bon emphasized the irrationality and abnormality of crowds, and his work has often been invoked by scholars trying to disavow the supposed tendency of collective behaviour theory to treat social movement partici-pants as irrational and pathological. In fact, most collective behaviour theorists reject the view that collective behaviour is irrational, although many are concerned with the psychological states of participants and the spontaneous dynamics of col-lective actions outside established structures.

In general, collective behaviour theories share several assumptions (Morris and Herring, 1987: 145). First, they see collective behaviour as existing outside of insti-tutionalized structures, although some theorists note the linkages between institu-tional and non-institutional actions. Various forms of collective behaviour are connected insofar as they are all unstructured situations unbound by established norms. Second, collective behaviour theorists argue that social movements and other forms of collective behaviour arise as a result of some type of structural or cultural 'breakdown' or 'strain' such as a natural disaster, rapid social change, or dramatic event. Third, collective behaviour theorists assign an important role to the shared beliefs of participants in analyzing the emergence of social movements and other forms of collective behaviour. Although pre-existing organization and strategy are typically mentioned by collective behaviour theorists, they are not a major focus, whereas the psychological states of participants and emergent ideologies and forms of organization receive much attention. Beyond these similarities, there are major differences among collective behaviour approaches.

The Chicago School Approach to Collective Behaviour

The Chicago School approach to collective behaviour was initiated in the 1920s by Robert Park and Ernest Burgess (1921) and was developed by a number of other soci-ologists associated with the symbolic interactionist approach at the University of Chicago, including Herbert Blumer (1951), Ralph Turner and Lewis Killian (1957, 1972, 1987), and Kurt and Gladys Lang (1961). **Symbolic interactionism** is a social psychological theory that focuses on how actors construct meanings through social interaction. According to the Chicago School perspective, collective behaviour devel-ops in situations where established systems of meaning and sources of information have broken down, forcing participants to construct new meanings to guide their behaviour (Morris and Herring, 1987: 147). Collective behaviour theorists are con-cerned with how participants in social movements manage to act collectively, creating goals, new organizational structures, and new culture. Turner and Killian emphasize the role of the 'emergent norm' as a shared view of reality that justifies and co-ordi-nates collective behaviour. In the case of social movements, which are complex and sustained forms of collective behaviour, emergent norms may become 'highly elabo-rated ideologies such as the environmentalist's view of the consequences of ecological imbalance and the Marxist's view of class struggle' (Turner and Killian, 1987: 8).

Thus, Chicago School collective behaviour theorists focus on the emergence of social movements and the creation of new forms of activity and organization. Collective behaviour is a means of bringing about social change, and emergent forms of social order develop through the interactions of individuals in social movements. Ideology plays an important role in highlighting injustices and guiding collective behaviour, but the beliefs that govern this behaviour are not fixed; systems of belief emerge and develop as social movement actors interact with one another, the public, opponents, and authorities. Emergent norms may develop in response to a precipitating event or some type of extraordinary condition as individuals within pre-existing or new groups interact with one another and try out forms of action, revising their ideas and actions in response to changing events and opportunities (ibid., 10).

Smelser's Theory of Collective Behaviour
In his influential book *Theory of Collective Behavior* (1962), Neil Smelser presents a model consisting of six determinants. The model is 'value added' in that each condition adds value to the explanation; the conditions operate within the context of one another and together explain collective behaviour. First, conditions of *structural conduciveness* permit or encourage certain types of collective behaviour. For example, panics occur in money markets, rather than in financial systems where property is tied to kinship and cannot be easily transferred (Smelser, 1962: 15). Second, conditions of *structural strain* create real or anticipated deprivation; this strain, such as the threat of economic deprivation, combines with the condition of conduciveness. Third, the *growth and spread of a generalized belief* makes the situation meaningful to potential participants in collective behaviour; the generalized belief identifies the source and nature of the strain and suggests possible responses. Fourth, *precipitating factors*, such as a dramatic event, give the generalized beliefs a concrete target for collective action. For example, an incident of police brutality might provoke a race riot when it occurs in the context of conduciveness, strain, and a generalized belief (ibid., 17). Fifth, *mobilization for action* must occur, and Smelser notes that leadership is particularly important in mobilizing participants. Sixth, *social control* may act to prevent the collective behaviour, perhaps by minimizing strains, or to limit the scope of the collective behaviour. The potential or actual episode of collective behaviour will be affected by the actions of police, the courts, the press, community leaders, and other agents of social control.

Theorists have found the idea of a value-added model useful and a number of studies have shown the factors identified by Smelser to be important in predicting collective action. However, scholars have also raised a number of criticisms. Smelser's theory, along with other breakdown theories, has been criticized for relying too heavily on structural strains to explain social movements. Critics have argued that no clear criteria exist for identifying 'strain' in a society; once a social movement or other form of collective behaviour occurs, it is always possible to find some type of strain, making the argument tautological (Useem, 1975: 9; Wilson, 1973: 35). Moreover, the theory seems to assume that societies are normally stable and that strains, and the social movements that accompany them, are unusual. In fact, strains may be a fairly constant feature of societies and the rise of movements may be better explained by factors such as political opportunities, resources, and organization. Critics have also objected to Smelser's characterization of generalized beliefs as 'short-circuited' in the sense of bypassing normal routines and controls and 'akin to magical beliefs' insofar as expectations of the consequences of collective action may be unrealistic (ibid., 8). Smelser and other collective behaviour theorists have often been lumped with Le Bon and accused of treating participants in collective behaviour as 'irrational'. However, collective behaviour theorists have vehemently denied this charge, arguing that their approaches do not assume irrationality on the part of movement participants (see Killian, 1994; Smelser, 1970; Turner, 1981).

Mass Society Theory

One version of collective behaviour theory, **mass society theory**, does view collective behaviour as an extreme response to social isolation. Mass society theory takes off from the Durkheimian notion that social stability is maintained by the existence of common values that are transmitted and sustained through various social institutions. A 'mass society' is one in which there are few secondary or intermediate groups, such as religious groups or community organizations, to bind people together and keep them attached to the mainstream society. In *The Theory of Mass Society*, William Kornhauser (1959) argued that social changes, such as rapid industrialization and urbanization or economic depressions, uproot people from their normal associations, as in the case of new immigrants to cities or unemployed workers. Consequently, individuals become isolated from social and political institutions. This creates social 'atomization' and feelings of 'alienation and anxiety' that make people susceptible to recruitment by social movements such as the German Nazi movement. In a popular version of mass society theory, Eric Hoffer (1951) argued in *The True Believer* that alienated, fanatical, and irrational individuals participate in social movements as a means of finding an identity and sense of belonging in a rapidly changing society.

A large body of empirical research has challenged mass society theory, showing that the theory is essentially wrong (see Jenkins, 1981: 92–3). In fact, it is not isolated individuals who are most likely to be drawn into social movements, but just the opposite. Research shows that individuals who are tied into social networks, and who participate in organizations, are most likely to be recruited into social movements. Whereas mass society theorists viewed organizations as playing a conservative role in keeping individuals from participating in collective action, they failed to appreciate the role of pre-existing organizations in mobilizing participants for social movements (Morris and Herring, 1987: 155).

Relative Deprivation Theory

Relative deprivation theory is based on the observation, made by Alexis de Tocqueville and others, that people often rebel when things are improving; it is not the most deprived groups that engage in collective action, but those who seem to be improving their positions or who are among the best off within an aggrieved group. When conditions start to improve, expectations rise, but when the rate of improvement does not match expectations, people feel deprived. For example,

Freeman (1975) argues that support for the women's movement increased as women gained access to education but did not achieve commensurate access to high-paying occupations. Deprivation is *relative* because people feel dissatisfied with their situations relative to what they think they deserve, and they assess what they deserve by comparing their progress to that of other groups. Thus, college-educated women might compare themselves to men of the same educational levels in assessing their occupational satisfaction. Social changes such as large-scale economic shifts generate feelings of relative deprivation in that people's expectations rise, they experience change, and then they are frustrated by the gap between their expectations and their actual situations. When people become angry and frustrated, they rebel.

Relative deprivation theories were popular in the 1960s and 1970s (e.g., Davies, 1962, 1971; Gurr, 1970), but they have since been strongly criticized on a number of grounds (see Gurney and Tierney, 1982; Jenkins, 1981). One difficulty is that relative deprivation studies typically infer psychological states of relative deprivation from objective indicators such as unemployment rates. Studies designed to test the theory have found little evidence that such objective measures of relative deprivation are good predictors of various types of rebellions; instead, factors such as organizational capacities and governmental sanctions are better predictors of collective action (Jenkins, 1981: 100–1). Although feelings of relative deprivation may be present, they are not likely to generate collective action in the absence of other factors such as resources and organization. Moreover, feelings of relative deprivation may be generated through participation in a movement, rather than being a precondition for the movement (ibid., 103).

RESOURCE MOBILIZATION AND POLITICAL PROCESS THEORIES

In the 1970s, the focus of North American social movement research began to shift away from the concerns of collective behaviour theory to those raised by newly emerging **resource mobilization** and **political process** approaches (Gamson, 1990; McAdam, 1999; McCarthy and Zald, 1973, 1977; Oberschall, 1973; Tilly, 1978). These new models of social movements and collective action resulted in part from the experiences of social movement theorists with movements of the 1960s and their criticisms of classical collective behaviour theories for inadequacies in explaining the new wave of protest. Although the criticisms did not apply equally to all versions of collective behaviour theory, they helped to shape the new perspectives, which departed from past theories in important ways (see Jenkins, 1983). First, collective behaviour theory explanations for the rise of social movements and collective action were considered wrong or inadequate. Mass society theory, as we have seen, was not supported by empirical studies, and resource mobilization theorists argued that socially connected people, rather than social isolates, are most likely to be mobilized for collective action. Strain theories also failed to explain the rise of social movements insofar as neither large-scale strains in social systems nor individual discontents lead directly to collective action. The extent of movement mobilization and participation in a population cannot be predicted by the amount of frustration or suffering experienced by people. Second, resource mobilization and political process theorists rejected what they perceived as a sharp disjuncture in collective behaviour theory between 'normal' or routine actions and collective action. The newer perspectives emphasized the continuities between collective actions and institutionalized actions, as social movements were seen as a continuation of the political process, albeit by disorderly means (Gamson, 1990: 139). Whereas collective behaviour theories, by emphasizing the motivations of individuals, focused on social movements as psychological phenomena, the newer perspectives treated social movements as political phenomena (see McAdam, 1999: 11–19). Individual participants were seen as rational actors pursuing their interests and movements were argued to arise out of pre-existing organization, engaging in both institutionalized and non-institutionalized forms of action.

Resource Mobilization Theory

Early resource mobilization theorists argued that strains or grievances can nearly always be found; the mobilization of social movements requires resources, organization, and opportunities for collective action. As the name 'resource mobilization' suggests, **resources** are seen as central to successful collective action in this approach, and a wide variety of studies demonstrate linkages between resource availability and collective action (see Edwards and McCarthy, 2004). Resources include both *tangible* assets, such as funding, and *intangible* assets, such as the commitment of participants (Freeman, 1979). Edwards and McCarthy (2004: 125–8) identify various types of resources used and created by social movements: *moral resources*, such as legitimacy; *cultural resources*, including tactical repertoires and strategic know-how; *social-organizational resources*, including movement infrastructures, networks, and organizational structures; *human resources*, such as the labour and experience of activists; and *material resources*, such as money and office space.

In their seminal articles advancing an entrepreneurial-organizational version of the theory, McCarthy and Zald (1973, 1977) argue that **movement entrepreneurs** play an important role in defining movement issues by drawing on public sentiments and increasing public demand for change. While stressing the importance of resources such as skills, money, and time for movement mobilization, they note that resources do not necessarily come from aggrieved groups (the *beneficiaries* of a movement), but may come from **conscience constituents**, who contribute to movements but do not personally benefit from their achievements (McCarthy and Zald, 1977: 1221–2). In some instances, the ability to mobilize conscience constituents determines movement effectiveness. For example, Jenkins and Perrow (1977) compared a successful attempt to organize American farm workers in the 1960s and early 1970s with an earlier failed attempt, arguing that outside support from a coalition of liberal organizations was essential to the successful challenge. Other researchers, however, emphasize the importance of internal resources for oppressed groups. In the case of the American civil rights movement, Aldon Morris (1984) found that black churches and other community institutions provided indigenous resources that were critical to movement success.

Social movement organizations and their leaders are typically important in mobilizing resources for movements, whether from **beneficiary constituents** or conscience constituents. Resource mobilization theorists have called attention to the varying structures of social movement organizations, which influence their longevity and strategic choices. Studies have suggested that organizations with more formalized or bureaucratic structures are better able to sustain a movement over time, whereas informal organizations are better at innovating tactics and taking quick action in response to events (Gamson, 1990; Staggenborg, 1988, 1989). For example, in the environmental movement, loosely structured groups such as Earth First! have organized blockades to prevent logging and have engaged in other acts of civil disobedience to protect the environment, whereas bureaucratic organizations such as the Sierra Club are more involved in lobbying governments and are better able to raise funds to maintain a large organization with paid staff. In addition to political movement organizations, theorists have identified various other types of **mobilizing structures**, including formal and informal networks, groups, and organizational vehicles, which movements use to recruit participants and organize action campaigns (McAdam et al., 1996: 3). Morris (1984) shows the importance in the American civil rights movement of a type of mobilizing structure that he terms a 'movement halfway house'. For example, the Highlander Folk School was founded in the 1930s as a place where oppressed people could participate in educational programs that would draw on their own experiences and allow them to devise strategies of social change, and in the 1940s and 1950s many civil rights movement leaders attended the school and participated in developing a successful mass education program for the movement (Morris, 1984: 141–9).

Political Process Theory

The political process approach emphasizes the interactions of social movement actors with the state and the role of political opportunities in the mobilization and outcomes of social movements. Political process theorists argue that social movements are most likely to emerge when potential collective actors perceive that conditions are favourable. The concept of **political opportunity** refers generally to features of the political environment that influence movement emergence and success, but specific definitions of political opportunity differ considerably (see Meyer, 2004). Sidney Tarrow's (1998: 77–80) elaboration of the elements of political opportunity is perhaps the most widely employed schema. He conceives of political opportunity as including the extent of openness in the polity, shifts in political alignments, divisions among elites, the availability of influential allies, and repression or facilitation by the state. When opportunities expand generally, a variety of movements may mobilize, resulting in a **cycle of contention**, which is 'a phase of heightened conflict across the social system' (ibid., 142). For example, during the 1960s a large number of protest movements mobilized in Europe and North America, including the civil rights movement, women's movement, gay rights movement, environmental movement, and anti-war movement. Moreover, movements are not only influenced by political opportunities; they can also create opportunities for themselves and other movements. Tarrow (ibid., 77) suggests that movements that are 'early risers' in a protest cycle may open up opportunities for later movements by demonstrating that targets are vulnerable to collective action.

In addition to affecting the emergence of social movements, political opportunities may alter the strategies and outcomes of protest. However, opportunities for mobilization and opportunities to effect change are sometimes different (see Meyer, 2004: 136–7). Social movement theorists have recognized that *threats* are as likely as opportunities to mobilize activists by creating feelings of outrage and urgency. It may be more difficult to mobilize participants when authorities or other elites are sympathetic to movement goals because supporters may feel that there is no need for collective action. When threats arise or negative outcomes occur, there may be little opportunity for effecting change but great opportunity for mobilization as movement supporters become alarmed by unfavourable changes. When a countermovement mobilizes to oppose movement goals, movement supporters are likely to respond with heightened activity. For example, the rise of a strong anti-abortion movement in the United States helped to keep abortion rights activists mobilized, even after they had won victories such as legalization of abortion through the 1973 Supreme Court ruling in *Roe v. Wade* (Staggenborg, 1991).

A Synthetic Approach

By the 1980s and 1990s, resource mobilization and political process approaches dominated North American social movement theory. The two approaches were sometimes treated as distinct models (see McAdam, 1999) and sometimes as two variants of resource mobilization theory, with a political process version of resource mobilization theory associated with theorists such as William Gamson, Anthony Oberschall, and Charles Tilly and an entrepreneurial-organizational version of resource mobilization theory formulated by John McCarthy and Mayer Zald (see Perrow, 1979; McCarthy and Zald, 2002). Increasingly, however, resource mobilization and political process approaches could be seen as part of one evolving perspective, with many of the same theorists contributing to each and attempting to synthesize the model (see McAdam et al., 1988, 1996). Key elements of the synthetic approach became so essential to social movement studies that McAdam, Tarrow, and Tilly (2001) went so far as to refer to the synthesis as the 'classical social movement agenda'.

The synthetic resource mobilization/political process model views social movements as political entities aiming to create social change. Scholars have analyzed various features of the movement environment and of movement organizations and strategies that influence the mobilization and outcomes of collective action. The approach initially downplayed grievances and ideology, as these were thought to be overemphasized by collective behaviour theorists, who focused on individual discontent as the driving force behind collective action. As the newer approach developed, however, this lacuna began to be addressed. In particular, theorists sympathetic to resource mobilization/political process theory developed the concept of **collective action frames** as a way of capturing the importance of meanings and ideas in stimulating protest (see Benford and Snow, 2000). Collective action frames are interpretations of issues and events that inspire and legitimate collective action and *framing* is an important activity of movement leaders and organizations. The framing perspective emphasizes the role of movements in constructing cultural meanings, as movement leaders and organizations frame issues in particular ways to identify injustices, attribute blame, propose solutions, and motivate collective action.

In what is now a large literature on collective action frames, movement theorists have analyzed the role of framing in a variety of movement processes. Snow and Benford (1992) distinguish between **master frames**, which are generic types of frames available for use by a number of different social movements, and movement-specific collective action frames, which can be derived from master frames. They argue that the availability of an innovative master frame helps to explain the emergence of a protest cycle consisting of a number of different social movements. For example, they suggest that the 'rights frame' was a master frame used by the civil rights movement, which was adapted by a number of other movements such as the women's movement and the gay rights movement in the protest cycle of the 1960s. In addition to their role in the growth of a protest cycle, master frames can be used to bring different movements together in coalitions. Gerhards and Rucht (1992) analyze the ways in which organizers of multi-movement **campaigns** extended master frames dealing with peace and globalization to address the concerns of a variety of different movement activists such as feminists, environmentalists, and union members. In a study of cross-movement activism in Vancouver, Carroll and Ratner (1996) find that the use of a master frame stressing the 'political-economy of injustice' brought together activists from the labour, peace, and feminist movements.

Analysts of collective action framing have also looked at the *frame disputes* that often face social movements (Benford, 1993). Disputes over frames are common because social movements are not unified actors, but typically consist of many different types of groups and individuals with varying ideological and strategic perspectives. Framing disputes may occur either within or between movement organizations and their consequences may include the decline of some types of movement organizations, the depletion of resources that could have been used to accomplish goals, factionalism, and lack of cohesiveness in a movement (Benford, 1993: 694–7). Although the impacts of frames are often difficult to assess, movements that succeed in creating persuasive and coherent frames appear better able to attract movement participants, form coalitions, win public approval and media attention, and influence authorities. Moreover, effective frames may help movements to overcome a lack of political opportunities (Polletta and Ho, 2006).

The concepts of *political opportunities, mobilizing structures,* and *framing processes* became the core elements of North American social movement theory in the 1990s (McAdam et al., 1996). Attention to political opportunities reflected the state-centred approach of political process theory, and conceptions of mobilizing structures drew on the entrepreneurial-organizational version of resource mobilization theory. The concept of framing provided a means for resource mobilization theorists to bring ideas and cultural elements into social movement theory, but the strategic approach to framing did not satisfy critics who argued for a broader approach to culture and ideology. Consequently, there was a 'cultural turn' in social movement theory as scholars began to examine a variety of cultural processes. **Discourse analysis** became important as theorists looked at questions such as how actors construct frames and discursive strategies using the genres available in the

discourse analysis

contexts where framing occurs (Steinberg, 1998: 856). Expanding on the concept of political opportunities, Ferree et al. (2002) use the concept of a **discursive opportunity structure** to examine the factors, such as cultural context and mass media norms, that shape movement discourse in different countries. More broadly, a number of movement theorists have proposed notions of a **cultural opportunity structure** or 'cultural opportunities' to refer to elements of cultural environments, such as ideologies, that facilitate and constrain collective action along with political opportunities (McAdam, 1994; Noonan, 1995). This cultural turn in North American social movement theory has been influenced by European new social movement theories, which emphasize symbolic activities in cultural spheres as well as instrumental actions directed at the state (Buechler, 1995: 442).

NEW SOCIAL MOVEMENT THEORY

In Europe, the approach known as **new social movement theory** developed independently of North American theories, emphasizing the new types of social movements that have emerged in 'post-industrial' or 'advanced capitalist' society, including the peace, environmental, gay and lesbian, student, and women's movements. New social movement theorists have argued that these movements differ in structure, type of constituents, and ideology from the 'old' movements of industrial society, notably the labour movement. As is the case with collective behaviour and resource mobilization perspectives, however, a number of different views fall under the category of new social movement theory (see Buechler, 1995; Pichardo, 1997). Some theorists have been concerned with how large-scale socio-economic trends are related to the emergence of new social movements, while others have focused on changes in the sites of conflict and nature of civil society in an 'information society'.

Scholars concerned with the effects of modernization have argued that new movements mobilized because there are new grievances in a post-industrial society, resulting in new values, new forms of action, and new constituencies (Klandermans, 1986: 21). For example, German theorist Jürgen Habermas (1984, 1987) draws attention to the new goals and demands associated with movements in post-industrial societies. He argues that new social movements are concerned with defence of the 'lifeworld', that is, the sphere of life not governed by instrumental, economic concerns but where real debate and communication create normative consensus. Because political and economic institutions are interfering in this realm, new movements have arisen to defend against bureaucratic and economic intrusions and to raise issues related to quality of life, democratic participation, and identity. Although economic concerns remain important in new social movement theory, the nature of the economic concerns has changed and new concerns have been added. For example, new international movements have emerged in an era of global capitalism with new kinds of concerns such as the effects of world trade and environmental degradation. 'Post-materialist' values, focusing on quality-of-life issues, are central to new social movements (Inglehart, 1990).

Scholars who focus on the new sites of conflict that accompany large-scale transformations have stressed the various processes involved in the creation and ongoing construction of social movements. One important process emphasized by new social movement theorists is the creation of **collective identity**, which refers to the sense of shared experiences and values that connects individuals to movements and gives participants a sense of 'collective agency' or feeling that they can effect change through collective action (Snow, 2001). Alberto Melucci (1989, 1996) focuses on how collective identities are continually constructed by small groups in the 'submerged networks' of everyday life. He sees social movements not as collections of relatively stable movement organizations or as unified actors, but as fluid networks that can erupt into collective action from time to time. To understand how social movements are constructed, we need to look at the formation and maintenance of the cognitive frameworks and social relationships that form the basis of collective action (Melucci, 1988: 331). Before a movement becomes visible, there is a period of 'latency' when a new collective identity is emerging. For example, American women began to develop a feminist identity within civil rights and New Left student and peace movement networks (Mueller, 1994). Once a movement is underway, the 'collective' is continually constructed, and failure to maintain solidarity may lead to tensions in the movement and a decline in collective action (Melucci, 1988: 333). In the case of the women's movement, different organizations and networks formed around different formulations of movement identity (Mueller, 1994: 247–8). As relationships are formed within the submerged networks of new social movements and new collective identities are constructed, activists produce new cultural models and symbolic challenges. For new social movement theorists, these cultural innovations are a key contribution of social movements to social change.

This focus on culture and collective identity in new social movement theory has been influential in redirecting North American movement theory. A number of scholars attempting to fill in gaps in resource mobilization and political process approaches have adopted Melucci's (1988: 343) view of collective identity as a process that involves the formulation of cognitive frameworks, the activation of relationships among actors, and the investment of emotions. Recent studies have focused on collective identity to explain how interests get defined and movements emerge; how people are motivated to participate in collective action; how strategic choices are made; and what cultural impacts movements have (Polletta and Jasper, 2001: 284). Moreover, theorists interested in culture and collective identity have also begun to emphasize the role of emotions in protest, which help to explain such problems as why individuals participate, how collective identity is created, and why movements continue or decline (Jasper, 1998; Goodwin et al., 2001).

Along with these influences, however, new social movement theory has generated much debate among movement theorists. In particular, scholars have questioned how 'new' movements in post-industrial societies really are with regard to the forms of collective action employed, organizational structures created, and issues addressed. Charles Tilly (1988) argues that, from a historical perspective, recent social movements such as the environmental movement and the women's movement basically employ the same repertoire of actions as nineteenth-century movements, including forming associations, demonstrating, and petitioning. In response to the claim of new social movement theorists that new social movements are loosely structured, Dieter Rucht (1988) shows that in fact movements such as the environmental movement contain a mix of different organizational forms, including both bureaucratic organizations and grassroots collectives. And, disputing the idea that concerns with identity are new, Craig Calhoun (1993) shows that nineteenth-century social movements such as the labour movement were also concerned with issues of identity as, for example, they mobilized workers with different ethnic and regional backgrounds. Carroll and Ratner (1995) note both the historical importance of collective identity to labour movements and the need for contemporary unions to alter bureaucratic forms of organization and reconstruct collective identities in order to survive large-scale economic globalization and to attract workers such as women and visible minorities. In their research on labour organizations in Vancouver, they find that labour activists were involved in cross-movement coalitions, open to 'cultural politics' such as feminist music and gay pride events, and sensitive to the concerns of a variety of different groups.

Thus, the distinction between 'old' and 'new' social movements may be difficult to defend on the grounds of collective identity and organizational preferences. Nevertheless, new social movement theory has been valuable in directing attention to some central theoretical issues such as the connection between large-scale features of society and social movements and the importance of culture, identity, and everyday life in the mobilization and outcomes of social movements.

NEW DIRECTIONS IN SOCIAL MOVEMENT THEORY

Recent challenges to social movement theory come from different directions, yet voice surprisingly similar concerns. Some critics of the political process approach have argued that the theory is overly structural, focusing on the relatively stable 'political opportunity structure' that influences movement mobilization and outcomes (Goodwin and Jasper, 1999). According to these critics, the structural focus neglects the agency of movement activists, who respond to opportunities and in some cases create them, as well as cultural elements of movements and their environments. Social networks, for example, are treated as structures that mobilize participants, but the ideas and emotions transmitted through networks are often overlooked. Culture is subsumed under framing activities, while a broader understanding of how culture constrains and facilitates collective action is underdeveloped.

McAdam, Tarrow, and Tilly (2001) argue that the political process model, which they helped to develop, is too static, failing to capture the dynamic interactions of contentious politics. They argue for a new approach that will uncover the underlying mechanisms and processes of change. While political process theory works best in analyzing relatively unified movements in democratic polities, their dynamic contentious politics approach is developed by comparing different types of contentious politics—movements, revolutions, strike waves, nationalism, etc.—in a wide range of settings. To create a more dynamic model of contentious politics, McAdam et al. argue that opportunities and threats should not be treated as objective structures but as 'subject to attribution' so that the perceptions of activists are important. Mobilizing structures should not be treated simply as pre-existing organizational sites, but as structures that are actively appropriated by collective actors. Framing, similarly, is not just a strategic tool, but involves 'the interactive construction of disputes among challengers, their opponents, elements of the state, third parties, and the media'. Collective action involves interaction and mobilization 'occurs throughout an episode of contention' (ibid., 43–5). McAdam et al. aim to understand how collective actors attribute threats and opportunities, appropriate mobilizing structures, construct frames and meanings, and innovate collective action tactics.

In short, several of the major developers of political process theory agree with their critics that a more social constructionist approach to social movements and collective action is needed to focus on the perceptions and strategies of activists (Kurzman, 2004). Or, as Oliver et al. (2003) note, 'there is a growing appreciation for the need to integrate structural political theories of movements with constructivist theories rooted in social psychology and cultural sociology.' Klandermans (1997) discusses the interaction of structural factors, such as social networks, with social psychological factors, such as cognitive information processing, in the process of recruitment to social movements. Buechler (2000, 2002) proposes a 'structural approach to social movements' that recognizes the interrelationships of large-scale patterns and human agency. Polletta (1997, 2004) argues that social movement theorists have erred in treating 'culture' and 'structure' as distinct entities, tending to equate culture with agency and structure with politics. In reality, culture, defined as 'the symbolic dimensions of all structures, institutions, and practices' (Polletta, 2004: 100), constrains as well as enables collective action, and political opportunities have cultural dimensions.

Table 2.1   Major Theories of Social Movements

Theoretical Perspective	Origins of Movements	Important Features and Focuses	Key Outcomes of Movements
Collective Behaviour	Social disruptions, strains, grievances; precipitating events	Social psychology of protest; emergent organization and norms; protest outside institutional structures	New meanings and forms of organization
Resource Mobilization and Political Process	Pre-existing organization; resources; political opportunities and threats; master frames	Connections between social movements and political process; mobilizing structures; framing strategies; institutional and non-institutional forms of action	New resources, organizations, and frames; cultural and political changes
New Social Movement	Large-scale changes; everyday networks and organizational structures; new types of grievances	Collective identity; submerged networks; new types of structures, constituents, and ideologies	New types of values, identities, and organizations; cultural innovations

CONCLUSION

Theories of social movements and collective action continue to grapple with how best to integrate culture and politics, emotions and interests, macro-level changes and micro-level interactions. Ultimately, the theories are important insofar as they help us to understand the rise, development, and decline of social movements and to investigate key issues in the study of collective action. Despite efforts at synthesis, different theories focus on different aspects of social movements and lead to different research questions. Table 2.1 outlines the differing views on origins, focuses, and outcomes of the major theoretical approaches to understanding social movements. Collective behaviour theories are important in pointing to the grievances and breakdowns in routine that may result from critical events and social changes and the importance of ideologies in mobilizing activists around these grievances. They tend to see protest as occurring outside the normal political process and as resulting in new forms of organization and new social understandings. Resource mobilization and political process theories focus much more on the role of pre-existing organizational structures, resources, and political opportunities in explaining the origins of movements and they focus on the mobilizing structures, framing efforts, and opportunities that affect the maintenance and outcomes of movements. In this approach, social movements are an ordinary part of the political process, although they tend to employ disorderly protest strategies rather than the established practices of insiders with routine access to the political system. In the new social movement approach, theorists emphasize both how large-scale changes affect the organization and goals of movements and how movements create new cultural forms and identities and develop ideas and strategies within the structures of contemporary society. Their approach leads to an emphasis on the ongoing creation of movement identities and movement culture that sustain social movements and allow for periodic protests.

These major theories of social movements all contribute to the formulation of research questions by social movement scholars. In investigating different issues related to theoretical approaches, scholars add to a growing body of knowledge about the mechanisms and processes underlying movement mobilization and outcomes. In the following chapter, I identify some of the important issues that scholars have examined in studying various social movements and elaborate on some of the themes touched upon in describing the major theoretical approaches.

Discussion Questions

1. How might a theory of social movements influence how a movement is studied and analyzed?
2. What different questions about movements and ways of analyzing them are raised by collective behaviour, resource mobilization/political process, and new social movement theories?
3. How are large-scale social changes important to each of the major theories of social movements?

Suggested Readings

Jenkins, J. Craig. 1981. 'Sociopolitical Movements', in S.L. Long, ed., *Handbook of Political Behavior*, vol. 4. New York: Plenum Publishers, 81–154. This is a very good review essay detailing theoretical approaches to social movements.

McAdam, Doug, John D. McCarthy, and Mayer N. Zald, eds. 1996. *Comparative Perspectives on Social Movements*. New York: Cambridge University Press. This important collection of writings highlights the concepts of political opportunity, mobilizing structures, and collective action framing.

Pichardo, Nelson A. 1997. 'New Social Movements: A Critical Review', *Annual Review of Sociology* 23: 411–30. This is a good review essay dealing with New Social Movement theory.

Chapter 3

Issues in the Study of Social Movements and Collective Action

Theories such as those reviewed in the previous chapter aim to explain the origins, growth and decline, and consequences of social movements and collective action. In this chapter, I identify key issues and elaborate on theoretical ideas about these concerns, drawing on the major theories of collective action. The issues explored by social movement scholars range from macro-level questions about large-scale structural changes to meso-level organizational dynamics and micro-level questions about individual decisions and interactions. Table 3.1 lists the kinds of questions that are asked in each of these three levels of research. One of the challenges for theorists is to connect these levels of analysis in their explanations of social movements and collective action. The various issues to be covered are interrelated, and the following discussion is organized around the central categories of movement emergence, maintenance and decline, and outcomes. Under each of these broad headings, more specific problems are discussed. A separate discussion of social movements and mass media is also included because this topic is particularly relevant to several subsequent chapters dealing with specific movements.

MOVEMENT EMERGENCE: MOBILIZATION AND RECRUITMENT

Movements typically do not emerge suddenly, and new movements are often linked to previous ones. **Mobilization** is the process whereby a group that shares grievances or interests gains collective control over resources (Tilly, 1978: 54). The **recruitment** of individuals to movements is part of the broader process of mobilization, involving the commitment of individual resources, such as time, money, and skills, to a cause. Mobilization and recruitment are ongoing processes rather than one-time events, as groups challenging the social status quo need to continually maintain control over resources and keep individuals involved following their initial recruitment. We begin by looking at major factors in the mobilization of a social movement and then turn to the issue of individual recruitment and participation.

Influences on Mobilization

A number of factors are involved in mobilization, including large-scale socio-economic and political changes, opportunities and threats, critical events, pre-existing or emergent organization, leadership, resources, and frames. Collective behaviour,

Table 3.1   Key Issues in the Study of Social Movements

Macro (large-scale) level

- How large-scale changes and events alter resources and organizational structures and create grievances that stimulate collective action.
- How cultural and political opportunities facilitate the emergence of social movements.
- How cycles of contention arise and spread.
- How master frames originate and diffuse into a culture.
- How changing political, cultural, and economic conditions affect the ongoing strategies and growth, maintenance, and decline of a social movement.
- How social movements contribute to large-scale cultural and political changes, which affect subsequent collective action.
- How countermovements emerge in response to social movements.

Meso (organizational) level

- What resources are available to groups and what organizational structures tie group members together prior to movement emergence.
- How leaders use mobilizing structures, master frames, and cultural and material resources to organize movements.
- How leaders and movement organizations frame injustices and recognize opportunities for collective action.
- How collective identities are developed within structures of everyday life.
- How the organizational structures of movement organizations affect maintenance and strategies.
- How collective campaigns are mobilized and how they affect subsequent movement organization and collective action.
- How coalitions are formed and maintained within social movements.
- The impact of interactions of movement organizations with other organizations such as countermovement groups, established interest groups and institutions, government agencies, and mass media.

Micro (individual) level

- How social networks lead individuals to movement organizations.
- How individuals come to believe that collective action is necessary and effective.
- How outrage and other emotions are generated to motivate participation.
- How individuals decide that the benefits of collective action are worth the costs.
- How individuals take on collective identities and feel solidarity with a group.
- Why individuals sustain or terminate their participation in social movements.
- How individuals are affected by their participation in social movements.

political process, and new social movement theorists all have pointed to the importance of large-scale social changes in stimulating social movements. Urbanization, for example, creates social problems, such as poor housing conditions, that lead to grievances among particular groups. While grievances do not automatically lead to mobilization, large-scale changes can also affect the organization and resources of groups. Leaders can organize participants through pre-existing structures as well as new movement organizations, using the cultural and material resources associated with them. In the case of the American civil rights movement, studies point to the importance of socio-economic and political changes for the rise of the movement. The decline of cotton as a cash crop in the US had a number of important consequences that created favourable conditions for the emergence of a civil rights movement (McAdam, 1999: 77), including the migration of many southern blacks to cities, where they were concentrated in black neighbourhoods and could support indigenous institutions.

Both the resources controlled by a group and the extent of organization among members of a group or collectivity prior to movement mobilization are important factors. If individuals already share membership in some of the same organizations, they have a pre-existing communications network, resources, and leaders that can be mobilized; in some cases, blocs of people may be recruited rapidly through pre-existing organizations (Oberschall, 1973: 125). Numerous studies find that social networks help to recruit individuals into social movements. Leadership is also important, either in the form of indigenous leaders or movement entrepreneurs who define issues and create movement organizations (McCarthy and Zald, 1973, 1977). McCarthy and Zald suggest that entrepreneurs may even be able to mobilize movements in the absence of pre-existing grievances. Where grievances are long-standing and pre-existing organization exists, this type of entrepreneurial leadership is less likely to matter (Jenkins, 1981: 121), but leaders remain important in framing injustices and recognizing opportunities for collective action (Morris and Staggenborg, 2004).

Political process theorists suggest that political opportunities or threats lead to the emergence of a social movement. As Sidney Tarrow (1998: 71) argues:

> Contention increases when people gain the external resources to escape their compliance and find opportunities in which to use them. It also increases when they are threatened with costs they cannot bear or which outrage their sense of justice. When institutional access opens, rifts appear within elites, allies become available, and state capacity for repression declines, challengers find opportunities to advance their claims. When combined with high levels of perceived costs for inaction, opportunities produce episodes of contentious politics.

In this view, people are more likely to engage in collective action when they think they have a chance of succeeding. Moreover, social movement activists create opportunities for themselves and others by demonstrating the effectiveness of protest, in some cases spurring a cycle of protest.

Despite the existence of political opportunities, however, potential collective actors do not always take advantage of those opportunities. The framing activities of leaders and organizations are important in diagnosing problems and suggesting collective solutions. Collective action frames translate grievances into broader movement claims, and they help to create the sense of injustice and the emotional energy that make individuals willing to participate in collective action (Tarrow, 1998: 111). Frames point to collective solutions and encourage people to adopt a collective identity associated with a movement, which involves a shared sense of being part of a group and a feeling of 'collective agency' that invites collective action (Snow, 2001: 2213). Movements that frame issues in a way that resonates with the existing culture can sometimes mobilize support even in the absence of political opportunities. In a study of the American suffrage movement, McCammon (2001) examined differences between states where suffrage associations formed and those that lacked suffrage associations. Although some states offered political opportunities, such as a receptive legislature, McCammon found that culturally resonant frames, together with resources, were more important than political opportunities in arousing support for women's suffrage. In particular, suffrage associations were likely to form when activists used frames that emphasized the importance of bringing women's unique perspective to the political arena rather than arguments that emphasized women's rights as citizens.

Such studies suggest that mobilization is a complicated process, involving meso-level collective action framing and micro-level perceptions as well as large-scale opportunities and changes. The case of the gay and lesbian movement discussed in Chapter 7 provides a particularly interesting example of the relationship between large-scale changes and strategic actions; even in the absence of political opportunity, activists used the master 'rights' frame to raise the consciousness of constituents and build movement support, allowing the movement to take advantage of subsequent political opportunities.

Individual Recruitment and Participation

If movements need activists to mobilize, what makes individuals willing to commit their time, money, and skills to a social movement? The answer to this question may seem obvious in that participants typically believe in the particular cause and want it to succeed. Yet not all **adherents** to a cause, defined as those who believe in the cause and want to see movement goals achieved, become **constituents**, defined as supporters who contribute resources to a movement (McCarthy and Zald, 1977: 1221). Collective behaviour theories stress the importance of grievances and individual discontent in generating collective action, but not everyone who is aggrieved, upset, or even outraged about a problem becomes an activist. There are many more adherents of social movements than there are constituents. For example, as we will see in Chapter 8, many people support environmental measures, but few of them contribute to environmental organizations.

One important argument as to why this is the case comes from **rational choice theory**, which focuses on the costs and benefits of collective action for individuals. According to this theory, many latent groups have grievances, but few of them mobilize because the costs for the individual typically outweigh the benefits of participation. The problem of getting individuals to participate in social movements or other collective action is known as the **free rider problem**. In his influential book *The Logic of Collective Action* (1965), the economist Mancur Olson argued that rational individuals will be free riders because the goal of collective action is a **collective good**, such as clean air or water, which the individual will receive regardless of whether or not he or she works to achieve it. Olson argues that members of a latent group, such as women, may have a common interest in obtaining a collective good, such as pay equity, but they do not have a common interest in paying the cost of obtaining the collective good. Because the contribution of any one individual typically makes no difference to the outcome of the collective action, and because the collective good will be received—or not received—regardless of personal participation in efforts to secure it, the rational individual will be a 'free rider' and allow others to pay the cost of obtaining the collective good. Olson argues that rational actors will voluntarily participate in collective action only under two conditions: (1) if offered **selective incentives**, which are benefits available exclusively to those who participate in collective action, or (2) if they are in a *small group situation*, where an individual might be motivated to pay the entire cost of obtaining the collective good or where his or her contribution might make a significant difference. Otherwise, individuals will be free riders unless forced into participation through coercion.

This logic presented an important challenge to social movement scholars, who responded with various explanations of how the free rider problem might be overcome. Whereas Olson focused on **material incentives**, other theorists have broadened the notion of selective incentives to include less tangible rewards for participation in collective incentives such as **solidary incentives**, which come from associating with a group, and **purposive incentives**, which come from the sense of satisfaction at having contributed to the attainment of a worthwhile cause (Wilson, 1973). McAdam and Friedman (1992) argue that collective identity can act as a selective incentive, as when people participate in movements because they want to share in an identity (e.g., environmentalist) available only to movement activists.

Rather than broadening the definition of selective incentives, other theorists have addressed the free-rider problem by arguing that recruitment is affected not just by individual motivations, but by organizational arrangements and structures such as social networks. McCarthy and Zald (1973, 1977) argue that the free-rider problem may be less salient for modern social movements because many are becoming professionalized. That is, many movements have paid leaders who work full time for movement organizations and they often attract conscience constituents rather than beneficiaries. In the environmental movement, for example, many large organizations have paid staff and members who join by sending in financial contributions rather than by actively participating. When movements rely mainly on paid staff along with financial contributions from 'paper members', participation from large masses of people is less critical. Owing to the low-risk commitments required of conscience constituents, many of whom have discretionary income available, the free-rider problem is not particularly important.

However, not all movements involve low-risk activism and many still require participation from sizable numbers of people. Movements such as the civil rights, animal rights, Aboriginal, anti-abortion, grassroots environmental, and global justice movements have required *high-risk activism* (see McAdam, 1986). Theorists emphasize the importance of different types of organizational bonds and social ties in recruiting activists to movements. When members of an aggrieved group are tied together by various structural factors that generate group solidarity, individuals are more likely to participate in group actions (Fireman and Gamson, 1979). For example, a person who has friends in a group, or who participates in the same social clubs or other organizations with members of a group, is more likely to respond to a call to collective action by the group than someone who lacks such ties. Some individuals, such as visible minorities, may have 'no exit' from a group, insofar as they are identified and treated as group members whether they like it or not (ibid., 22). If an individual is closely tied to a group of people engaging in collective action, he or she has a big stake in the group's fate and may find it hard not to participate when everyone else is involved. When collective action is urgent, the person is likely to contribute his or her share even if the impact of that share is not noticeable. Critics of rational choice theory note that decisions about participation in collective action are made not by isolated individuals, but by people in group contexts, such as local communities and friendship networks (Klandermans, 1997; Marwell and Oliver, 1993).

McAdam, McCarthy, and Zald (1988: 707–9) identify several types of structural factors that increase the likelihood of activism. First, studies suggest that *prior contact with a movement member* makes an individual more likely to become an activist. Often, individuals are asked to come along to a meeting or activity with a friend, and this contact then leads to further involvement. Based on a study of recruitment to religious movements, Snow et al. (1980) argue that social networks are in fact more important than ideological motivations for participation; often, individuals become involved through networks and take on movement beliefs after their initial exposure to a group, through interaction with members. Second, *membership in organizations* makes people more likely to become movement activists insofar as their organizational memberships give them access to information and make them targets of movement recruitment efforts within organizations. Third, a *history of prior activism* increases the likelihood that individuals will participate in subsequent movements. People gain organizing skills that are transferable from one movement to another, and subsequent activism is a way of retaining one's identity as an 'activist'. Finally, *biographical availability* makes individuals more likely to be recruited to social movements. Individuals who have responsibilities such as young children and demanding jobs are likely to be less available for participation than people with flexible work schedules and fewer domestic responsibilities. Based on case studies of religious movements, Snow et al. (1980) propose a similar concept of *structural availability* to explain the recruitment of some individuals from the streets rather than through social networks. They argue that these individuals were structurally available insofar as they lacked commitments that would prevent their participation. Thus, network ties to activists can draw individuals into movement participation, and a lack of competing ties can also free people to participate.

MOVEMENT MAINTENANCE, GROWTH, AND DECLINE

Social movements, by definition, endure over some length of time, interacting with the broader public, mass media, supporters and opponents, authorities, and other targets. Once initial mobilization occurs, movements have to be maintained, and they may either grow in strength or decline. The commitments of individual participants need to be retained and new supporters must be recruited. As resource mobilization theorists have emphasized, social movement organizations are central to this process. Movement organizations and coalitions of organizations are typically the main organizers of movement campaigns, which are important to the growth of movements and their ability to bring about change. However, movements are not stable and unified entities. They consist of shifting coalitions of actors and, for long-lived movements, there may be periods without a great deal of visible collective action. Movements are maintained not only by formalized organizations, but by the more informal networks and cultural groups within social movement communities that keep people with a common collective identity tied together even during times when there is not much movement action going on. Movements can also endure within institutions, other social movements, political parties, and various other venues where ideologically structured action occurs.

The following discussion begins with movement organizations and the characteristics that help them to survive and generate collective action. We then consider collective action strategies and campaigns, and their importance to movement growth and decline. Finally, we examine other types of structures through which movements grow and sustain themselves.

Social Movement Organizations

Social movement organizations (SMOs) play an important role in mobilizing participants for collective action in most modern social movements. One important question is how the structures of these organizations affect their longevity and effectiveness. Scholars have identified some key dimensions on which SMOs vary, including the extent of **bureaucratization** or **formalization** in the organization and the extent of **centralization** (Gamson, 1990). Organizations that are more formalized or bureaucratic have established procedures for decision-making, a developed division of labour, explicit criteria for membership, and rules governing subunits such as standing committees or chapters. More informal SMOs have fewer established procedures, rules, and membership requirements and a less-developed division of labour. Decisions in informal organizations are likely to be made on an ad hoc basis and organizational structures are frequently adjusted. Centralized SMOs have 'a single centre of power' whereas power is dispersed in decentralized organizations (Gamson, 1990: 93). Although formalization and centralization tend to go together, it is possible to have decentralized formal SMOs and centralized informal SMOs.

These differences are important because they affect organizational maintenance, goals, and strategies. Some theorists have argued that formalization leads to a focus on organizational maintenance at the expense of protest, resulting in a decline of insurgency (Piven and Cloward, 1977). Others point to the benefits of bureaucratization in keeping organizations 'combat-ready' and of centralization in preventing internal conflict and factionalism (Gamson, 1990; Staggenborg, 1988). Taylor (1989) shows how a centralized, 'elite-sustained' organizational structure can keep a movement in 'abeyance' during a slow period when there is little collective action and it is difficult to recruit new members. With regard to strategies and tactics, a number of studies suggest that more centralized and formalized structures are associated with the use of institutionalized tactics, such as legislative lobbying, while decentralized and informal structures promote tactical innovation and direct action (Freeman, 1975, 1979; Gerlach and Hine, 1970; Morris, 1984; Staggenborg, 1988, 1989). Movements such as the women's movement and environmental movement succeed and endure in part because they include a variety of organizational structures with different capacities.

One of the important problems that SMOs face is how to encourage participation while avoiding internal conflict. Movements such as the civil rights, student, and women's movements have tried to develop forms of 'participatory democracy' whereby activists are closely involved in organizational decision-making. At its worst, this type of structure can degenerate into what Jo Freeman (1972) describes in her analysis of the 'younger branch' of the American women's movement (consisting of radical and socialist-feminist groups) as the 'tyranny of structurelessness'. Groups that shun 'structure', Freeman shows, may nevertheless end up with exclusive informal structures and unaccountable leaders. At its best, however, participatory democracy is a process that helps to build movements by involving participants and developing their political skills, creating solidarity, and encouraging the development of new tactics (see Polletta, 2002).

Studies suggest that successful movement organizations have structures that enable them to develop accountable and diverse leadership and to formulate innovative and effective strategies. In a study of efforts to unionize farm workers in California, Marshall Ganz (2000) shows how the United Farm Workers (UFW) succeeded in the 1960s and 1970s while a better-funded rival union failed. He argues that the UFW was successful because it developed better strategies as a result of access to information and through the ability to generate ideas based on salient information. Ganz finds that several features of organizational structures are important in expanding what he calls 'strategic capacity' (Ganz, 2000: 1016–18). First, organizations need to create forums for 'regular, open, and authoritative deliberation' among leaders so that they have access to information and the authority to act on decisions. Second, organizations have more flexibility when they draw resources from multiple constituencies rather than from a single source. Third, organizations that hold leaders accountable to their constituents are likely to have politically skilled and knowledgeable leaders. Ganz argues that strategic capacity increases when movement organizations, rather than relying on single leaders, promote interactions among members of a 'leadership team' consisting of both 'insiders' with links to constituencies and 'outsiders' with professional or value commitments. By including leaders with diverse backgrounds and repertoires of collective action, organizations have access to greater knowledge and more ideas about how to mobilize resources and create strategies.

Thus, one of the most important problems for social movements is the creation of organizations that are able to minimize internal conflict and develop effective strategies. SMOs are not the only structures within social movements, but activists often work through movement organizations to direct social movement campaigns. These strategic campaigns are critical not only for achieving movement goals, but also for the growth and maintenance of social movements.

Movement Campaigns

Social movements are loose and changing coalitions of groups and individuals that interact with opponents, bystanders, and targets through collective action. Marwell and Oliver (1984: 12) define the **collective campaign** as 'an aggregate of collective events or activities that appear to be oriented toward some relatively specific goal or good, and that occur within some proximity in space and time.' Social movements typically consist of a series of collective campaigns, which extend beyond single events and are aimed at government officials or other authorities (Tilly, 2004: 4). Through strategic campaigns, movement participants engage in dynamic interactions with authorities and third-party opponents and supporters; as these actors respond to movement strategies, movement actors in turn alter their strategies and organizational structures. The women's movement, for example, developed vehicles for new strategies, such as participation in electoral politics, in response to anti-feminist countermovements and unreceptive governments (see Chapter 6).

During movement campaigns, various types of interactions affect mobilization and outcomes. These include interactions with allies, countermovements and other opponents, and mass media as well as government officials and other authorities. Scholars have conceived of movement organizations as operating within **multi-organizational fields**, which include, in addition to SMOs, a variety of other types of organizations that might either oppose or support the movement (Curtis and Zurcher, 1973; Klandermans, 1992). Within and across movements, participants may form coalitions and engage in co-operative actions, compete with one another, or come into conflict with one another. Similarly, movements engage in a variety of different types of exchanges with non-movement adversaries, mediators, and audiences (Rucht, 2004). As the frequent targets of protest, government authorities or other elites may facilitate or repress protest campaigns through a variety of means. The *policing of protest* is a key aspect of state response to movement campaigns. Police handling of protests is more or less repressive or tolerant under different types of governments and in response to different types of collective action, and trends in the policing of protest have important impacts on collective action, in some cases reducing disruption and visibility (della Porta and Fillieule, 2004). In the case of the global justice movement (Chapter 9), movement activists have made numerous strategic adjustments in response to the policing of large demonstrations at the sites of international meetings.

Movement campaigns may occur in response to **critical events** and campaigns also generate such events. Critical events focus the attention of movement supporters, members of the public, and authorities on particular issues, creating threats and opportunities that affect movement mobilization and outcomes. There are various types of critical events, including large-scale socio-economic and political events, natural disasters and epidemics, accidents, policy outcomes, face-to-face encounters between movement actors and authorities or other parties, and strategic initiatives of movements, such as demonstrations (Staggenborg, 1993). Some types of critical events are completely outside of movement control, while others are orchestrated by movements. However, even when movements do not control the occurrence of an event, they may be in a position to make use of critical events. Depending on their organizational capacities, movements may be able to plan campaigns that take advantage of unforeseen events. For example, anti-nuclear power activists used the threat and publicity created by the 1979 accident at the nuclear power plant at Three Mile Island near Harrisburg, Pennsylvania, to attract many new supporters to their movement (Walsh, 1988). During campaigns, movements may be able to create events, such as dramatic confrontations with police, to call attention to movement issues and spread movement frames. In the case of Aboriginal protest in Canada, Howard Ramos (Chapter 5) assesses the impact of some critical events, such as the 'Indian summer' of 1990, on subsequent mobilization and protest.

Movements thrive when participants are engaged in collective campaigns, which allow them to mobilize previously inactive movement supporters and strengthen the commitments of activists to a movement community (Downton and Wehr, 1991). During a campaign, there are more ways for activists to become involved and more opportunities for participants to take leadership roles. Collective identities often undergo expansion during campaigns, incorporating the concerns of new actors, and individuals typically become more identified with the movement as they participate in its campaigns. Movements that are no longer capable of mobilizing public campaigns, or that find difficulty devising campaigns appropriate for achieving movement goals, are likely to have a hard time maintaining themselves.

McAdam (1983) demonstrates the importance of particular campaigns in the growth of the American civil rights movement. He shows that peaks in movement activity occurred with tactical innovations, which were then countered by opponents, creating the need for new tactics. Bus boycotts sparked movement growth in the 1950s, resulting in some victories but also some effective counter-tactics that limited continued use of the tactic. Next, the movement experienced dramatic growth with the sit-ins of 1960. After mass arrests helped to diffuse the campaign, movement activity declined until the freedom rides of 1961 revived the movement. When that campaign was neutralized by government action, community-wide protests again revived the movement in southern cities such as Albany, Georgia, and Birmingham and Selma, Alabama. After these campaigns, which resulted in many victories in desegregating public facilities, the movement faltered in devising non-violent tactics to address more entrenched and systemic problems of economic inequality. The urban riots of 1966–8 in northern US cities spurred calls for economic reforms, but the civil rights movement found it very difficult to devise campaigns to address issues of race and poverty, leading to a decline in the civil rights movement in the late 1960s.

Other studies also point to the importance of collective campaigns in expanding movements. Lofland (1979) shows how a religious movement achieved 'white-hot mobilization' in part by devising campaigns and public events that involved participants and created excitement about the movement. Kleidman (1993) demonstrates how the American peace movement ebbed and flowed in the twentieth century with several major campaigns that created peaks in the movement. Voss and Sherman (2000) show how some labour unions revitalized in recent years through innovative campaigns that encouraged member participation. Often, movements expand during such campaigns through coalition-building, as coalitions of organizations within movements and coalitions across movements often are needed to wage extensive campaigns. Particularly when cross-movement coalitions are involved, master frames are critical in providing a common language that can be used to address the concerns of a variety of groups (Carroll and Ratner, 1996; Gerhards and Rucht, 1992; Van Dyke, 2003). In the case of the global justice movement, for example, we will see how a master frame focusing on the consequences of neo-liberal economic policies helped to unite feminists, environmentalists, labour union members, and other activists.

In some instances, countermovement campaigns generate new movement strategies and new rounds of collective action. Movements and countermovements often respond to one another, and successful action by one side frequently spurs new activity by its opposition. For example, when Canadian abortion-rights activist Henry Morgentaler opened an abortion clinic in Toronto in 1983, anti-abortion activists launched an intensive campaign of daily protests against the clinic and abortion-rights supporters responded by organizing demonstrations to protect the clinic (Cuneo, 1989). When the militant anti-abortion group Operation Rescue mounted major protests of abortion clinics in the US in the late 1980s and early 1990s, the campaign stimulated a great deal of mobilization by abortion-rights groups in response. While countermovements arouse opposition to movement goals, they also help to fuel movement campaigns, as we will see in the cases of the women's movement and the gay and lesbian movement. In federal systems such as the US and Canada, there are numerous venues in which opposing movements can spar; when one side chooses a particular battleground such as the courts or legislatures, the other side may feel compelled to follow suit (Meyer and Staggenborg, 1996, 1998).

Collective action is clearly central to social movements, and movements survive and grow through their ability to generate action campaigns; as collective campaigns ebb, movements contract in size and become less publicly visible. Although no movement can sustain non-stop public campaigns, long-lived movements do not completely disappear between campaigns; they typically remain alive in less visible venues.

Movements within Institutions, Other Social Movements, and Culture

Beyond the visible faces of movements in political organizations and public campaigns, movements survive and grow in numerous other settings, including institutions, other social movements, and cultural groups and activities. A number of studies have examined movements within institutions as forms of ideologically structured action that expand movements and secure new advantages. Mary Katzenstein (1998) shows how feminism moved into the US military and Catholic Church in the 1980s and 1990s, as activists established 'organizational habitats' or spaces where they could meet and strategize within the institutions. In the case of the Catholic Church, feminist activism took the form of 'discursive politics' whereby feminists within the Church raised a broad range of social issues. In the military, activism took the form of 'interest group activism' as feminists lobbied Congress and used the courts to secure career advancement for women within the military. Nicole Raeburn (2004) examines lesbian and gay activism within corporations, showing how networks of employee activists influenced their employers to change their policies, winning gay-inclusive benefits from a number of major American corporations. In all of these cases, the movements within institutions were connected to the external movement, both drawing support from the larger movement and contributing to it. As movements gain footholds within institutions, new mobilizing structures are established, which can be used to organize campaigns both inside and outside institutions.

Movements also spread and maintain themselves within other social movements. Activists commonly participate in multiple movements with compatible ideologies, and movements influence one another in various ways. For example, Barbara Epstein (1991) describes how feminists became active in peace and anti-nuclear power movements in the 1970s and 1980s. Meyer and Whittier (1994) look at the 'spillover' of feminism into the US peace movement in the 1980s, showing how feminists contributed to the peace movement collective action frames, tactics, and organizational forms along with leaders and activists, while the peace movement helped to maintain and invigorate feminism at a time when there were few visible feminist campaigns. More recently, feminists in North America have become heavily involved in the global justice movement during lulls in feminist campaigns (Rebick, 2005: 256).

Cultural activities and the activities of everyday life provide additional venues for the spread of movement ideology and the maintenance of movement networks. In Alberto Melucci's (1989, 1996) view of new social movements, collective identity develops within the structures of everyday life and is transformed from time to time into political action. In her study of gay rights movement in San Francisco, Elizabeth Armstrong (2002) argues that the movement is sustained by a whole 'field' of cultural, political, and commercial organizations. A wide variety of groups such as gay pride parade organizations, gay and lesbian sports teams, gay bars, professional groups, religious groups, and service organizations have helped to create a 'gay identity movement'. Other researchers have similarly focused on social movement communities, which include cultural groups, alternative institutions, and other groups and events that spread movement ideas and provide spaces for activists to interact (see Buechler, 1990; Staggenborg, 1998, 2001; Taylor and Rupp, 1993; Taylor and Whittier, 1992).

One of the important issues raised by this conception of social movements is how submerged networks become activated for political campaigns. Depending on the context in which the activities take place and the intentions of participants, cultural activities might either support or detract from political activities. In some cases, cultural strategies are employed to promote political change, and political campaigns reinvigorate cultural rituals. In other instances, culture may be an end in itself. The relationship between cultural and political activities is thus an important topic for social movement research.

MOVEMENT OUTCOMES

Questions about the outcomes or consequences of collective action are the most important of all for social movement researchers; ultimately, we want to know what impact a social movement has on a society. Outcomes are also among the most difficult aspects to evaluate, for several reasons. First, movements produce numerous types of outcomes—intentional and non-intentional, long-term and short-term. Movements affect public policy, political access, culture, institutions, and opportunities for subsequent collective action. They may also provoke counter-movements or other forms of opposition that in turn have a variety of impacts. Second, because movements endure for some length of time, they don't produce single outcomes but rather multiple outcomes over time, such as court rulings and legislation. It is important to take into account how the outcomes of one 'round' of collective action influence future 'rounds' by affecting subsequent resources, tactics, and outcomes (Snyder and Kelly, 1979). For example, a positive political outcome at one point, such as the US Supreme Court ruling in *Roe v. Wade* for the abortion rights movement, is not necessarily good for mobilization in the next round as supporters may feel the goals of the movement have already been accomplished. Third, causality is difficult to determine; although social movements no doubt have impacts, other factors, such as large-scale socio-economic changes, also play a role in many social changes. Certainly, the women's movement helped to open up jobs for women and bring women into the labour force, but so did large-scale changes such as the shift from industrial to service-based economies in many countries. Much of the research on outcomes of social movements looks at political and policy outcomes, which are perhaps the most straightforward changes, whereas fewer studies examine the cultural and institutional effects of social movements, which are harder to assess (Giugni, 1998: 373).

To get a handle on the numerous outcomes of social movements, researchers have attempted to specify various types of impacts and to examine how movement strategies and organizational structures influence outcomes. In an influential formulation, Gamson (1990) offered two criteria for evaluating movement success: (1) *acceptance* of a challenging group as a legitimate representative of a constituency, and (2) *new advantages* or success in achieving particular goals, such as passage of legislation. Some theorists have expanded on this formulation by specifying other steps in the political process, such as getting issues on the political agenda, getting new policies implemented, actually having the intended effect, and transforming political structures (Burstein et al., 1995). Others have sought to identify broader cultural outcomes of social movements such as the creation of new pools of activists, new vocabularies and ideas (often disseminated by mass media), new cultural products and practices, and changes in public consciousness (Earl, 2004; Gusfield, 1981; Mueller, 1987; Staggenborg, 1995). Gamson (1998) amended his earlier categories to include measures of movement impacts on cultural change through public discourse. Arguing that the mass media are 'the most important forum for understanding cultural impact' (ibid., 59), Gamson suggests that impacts in this arena can be measured in terms of (1) *media standing* or acceptance as a legitimate source, resulting in opportunities to provide interpretations that are quoted in the media, and (2) *media discourse* as a reflection of new cultural advantages gained by a movement (see also Ferree et al., 2002).

Looking at movement impacts over time, scholars have examined how different types of cultural, organizational, and political outcomes influence subsequent collective action and outcomes. In a study of the influence of the women's movement on the election of women to public office in the United States, Mueller (1987) finds that the early women's movement did not initially have a direct impact on women's elections through means such as contributions of money and volunteers to campaigns. However, the movement helped to change the 'collective consciousness' about the appropriateness of women running for public office and the collective identities of politically active women. As a result of the change in their consciousness and identity created by the women's movement, women who previously would have played supportive roles in the campaigns of men decided to run for office themselves. Once elected, feminists helped to bring about changes in policies that benefited women and, as the movement developed, women's movement organizations began supporting feminist candidates more directly. Thus, challenges to existing ideas and cultural practices may be early outcomes of movements that later help to produce more substantive goals (Mueller, 1987: 93).

Movement outcomes are influenced both by organization strength and strategies and by ongoing interactions with opponents and elites. In a study of outcomes of the American civil rights movement in the state of Mississippi, Andrews (2004) looked at a number of different types of outcomes in different areas of the state, including electoral participation by blacks, social welfare policies, school desegregation, and election of blacks to public office. He finds that these outcomes are affected by the extent to which the movement has created a lasting infrastructure, by the strategies the local movement employs, and by countermovement mobilization and federal intervention. In places where the movement left behind a 'local infrastructure' consisting of networks of grassroots leaders, community centres, and other organizations, as well as a resource base of activists and money, it was able to have a greater impact. The creation of such infrastructures is one of the long-term legacies of a social movement, which affects its ability to respond to opponents and win support from authorities and other elites.

Movements and Media

The mass media are very important to social movements, yet it is quite difficult for social movements to get their messages across through the mass media because movements are typically less powerful than are media organizations in controlling images. Both social movements and media organizations frame issues, but the collective action frames offered by a movement rarely are presented just as the movement would like by mass media. Instead, media organizations have their own interests and routines that influence their coverage and framing of social movements. Movements generally need media coverage more than mass media need to cover movements, creating a 'fundamental asymmetry' in the relations of movements with media (Gamson and Wolfsfeld, 1993: 116). Often, movement activities are not covered at all, and when they are covered, movement messages are frequently distorted by media frames.

Organizational and resource considerations and journalistic conventions and values are among the factors that influence media frames (see Gans, 1979; Schudson, 2003; Sigal, 1973; Tuchman, 1978). News organizations in Western countries are bureaucracies, located either within public agencies such as the Canadian Broadcasting Corporation (CBC) or private profit-making firms, such as the American broadcasting networks and cable news channels, and they compete with other news organizations to attract audiences and sell air time, newspapers, and magazines. More material is collected by journalists than can be included in the news, and journalists working within news organizations have to sell their stories to their superiors. In developing stories, journalists work under organizational constraints and conform to occupational norms that do not necessarily work to the advantage of social movements seeking favourable media coverage (see Gamson and Wolfsfeld, 1993; Kielbowicz and Scherer, 1986).

Deadlines and resource considerations are among the organizational constraints that influence news coverage. One important consequence of limited time and resources is the *centralization of news gathering*. Because news agencies cannot afford to have reporters everywhere in the world and must produce news in a timely fashion, they rely on centralized sources, including news bureaus located in central places, such as large cities; agencies, such as the Associated Press, that collect and disseminate news; and news beats in established institutions, such as police headquarters and government legislatures, where reporters routinely are briefed and given press releases. Centralized organizations with accessible spokespersons get the most coverage because they make it easier for reporters to gather information and meet deadlines. Government agencies and officials are by far the most widely used sources, both because they have the resources to continuously provide news to the press and because they are generally seen as credible sources for news stories. The credibility of government officials as news sources does vary historically, however. In the United States, the Vietnam War and the Watergate scandal of the early 1970s both decreased the willingness of journalists to accept presidential statements at face value (Hallin, 1989).

The reliance of journalists on official sources creates an obvious problem for social movements in that they are not among the centralized, routine sources used by the media and therefore often do not get covered. In some cases, this results in a missed or incomplete story by news organizations. For example, during the conflict over the Canadian Meech Lake Accord in 1987, CBC news coverage focused heavily on in-fighting within the Liberal Party as a potential problem for the Accord. The reactions of women's, Aboriginal, and ethnic groups, which turned out to be the main opponents of the deal, received virtually no coverage because these groups were located outside the prime news locations (Taras, 1990: 105). Movement organizations that are more centralized and professionalized, and that learn how to conform to media norms and provide information or 'stories' in a format acceptable to media organizations, are most likely to get coverage.

Different types of movement organizations have employed different strategies for securing favourable media coverage, with varying degrees of success. In a study of movement organizations in Vancouver, Carroll and Ratner describe the dilemmas associated with the media strategies of different types of organizations. Greenpeace Vancouver put a great deal of effort into planning events that would attract media coverage and bring support to the organization through the free publicity garnered; although the strategy enjoyed some success, it detracted from grassroots organizing and resulted in the use of predictable 'media stunts' (Carroll and Ratner, 1999: 14). In contrast, a gay and lesbian community service organization used the media less to generate support than to combat homophobia by educating the public; in doing so, the group took a relatively conservative stance that alienated more radical elements in the gay and lesbian community. A third organization devoted to 'redistributive justice for the poor' had difficulty in getting across its leftist critique of government policies through the mass media despite use of standard practices such as issuing press releases and making contact with sympathetic reporters (1999: 24).

Often, movements resort to dramatic tactics that will secure media coverage, but the difficulty is that the standards for coverage may escalate. In a study of media coverage of the New Left anti-Vietnam War movement in the United States, Todd Gitlin (1980: 182) argues that, as the movement used increasingly flamboyant gestures, there was a rising threshold of rhetoric and violence needed for coverage; whereas 'a picket line might have been news in 1965, it took tear gas and bloodied heads to make headlines in 1968.' As Gitlin shows in the case of Students for a Democratic Society (SDS), movement organizations are often ill-prepared for dealing with the media, and media coverage can have extremely negative impacts on movements. Because the mass media have an 'event' orientation to deciding what is news (i.e., the 'news' is what is happening today), it is difficult for movements to secure coverage of long-term trends and conditions, such as poverty or environmental degradation. They have to stage events, such as an anti-poverty march or an Earth Day demonstration, to receive media attention, but even then there is no guarantee of coverage. Because the mass media are always looking for novelty, movements have to continually come up with new tactics to stay in the news, and this may not be helpful for the pursuit of many movement goals. Greenpeace, as Chapter 8 discusses, became adept at using dramatic tactics that attract media coverage, but found itself limited by its media-oriented strategies.

Thus, the issue of how movements can use the mass media effectively is a critical one for social movement studies. One important development is the availability of the Internet as a direct form of mass media for social movements. Movements have always used internal communications such as newsletters to convey their messages, but the Internet provides a quick, low-cost means of reaching a large number of potential supporters and of organizing events through e-mail and websites (see Ayers, 1999; Myers, 1994; Schulz, 1998). The global justice movement, for example, has made extensive use of the Internet to organize its international campaigns (see Chapter 9). In some instances, collective actions or 'e-movements' have been organized strictly on-line with little formal organization (Earl and Schussman, 2003; Peckham, 1988). The strengths and limitations of this type of organizing, which bypasses the mainstream mass media, are an increasingly important topic for social movement research.

CONCLUSION

Movements are faced with numerous obstacles and opportunities as they seek to mobilize and maintain themselves and to have a social and political impact. Large-scale political opportunities and cultural changes, meso-level organization and resources, and micro-level interactions and choices of individuals all affect the emergence, maintenance, and outcomes of social movements. The structures of social movement organizations and other mobilizing structures affect the ability of the movement to attract participants and to wage campaigns. Movement campaigns and strategies result in victories and defeats in achieving goals, and they also affect subsequent mobilization. Movements survive through and influence institutions, other social movements, and culture in addition to creating political changes by targeting the state. Social movement scholars study the numerous issues involved in mobilizing effective collective action, as we will see as we examine substantive movements in the following chapters.

Discussion Questions

1. How do large-scale changes, organizational structures, and collective action frames influence the mobilization of social movements?
2. Why do individuals sometimes participate in social movements rather than remain 'free riders'?
3. What conditions would be necessary for a new movement organization, such as a local environmental group, to get off the ground and engage in collective action? What conditions might lead to failure to mobilize and act?

Suggested Readings

Gamson, William A. 1990. *The Strategy of Social Protest*, 2nd edn. Belmont, Calif.: Wadsworth. First published in 1975, this seminal statement of resource mobilization and political process theory remains influential in its approach to studying movement outcomes.

McAdam, Doug, John D. McCarthy, and Mayer N. Zald. 1988. 'Social Movements', in J.S. Neil, ed., *Handbook of Sociology*. Newbury Park, Calif.: Sage, 695–737. This excellent review essay lays out important concepts and debates in the study of social movements.

Snow, David A., Sarah A. Soule, and Hanspeter Kriesi, eds. 2004. *The Blackwell Companion to Social Movements*. Malden, Mass.: Blackwell. This collection contains essays by well-known scholars on major theoretical issues and movements.

Chapter 4

The Protest Cycle
of the 1960s

The year 1968 became known as 'the year of the barricades', when turbulent demonstrations rocked many countries around the world, including France, Germany, Britain, Spain, Italy, Poland, Czechoslovakia, Mexico, and Japan, as well as the United States (see Caute, 1988; Fraser, 1988; Marwick, 1998). In France, students occupied an administration building at the Nanterre campus of the University of Paris on 22 March 1968 in response to the arrests of six members of the National Vietnam Committee; by May of that year, some 10 million students and workers were on strike. In Spain, students opposed the authoritarian government of General Francisco Franco, which closed down several universities; despite repression from the state, students joined with workers in a massive protest movement against the government. In the United States, students at Columbia University protested military recruitment on campus and occupied buildings, shutting down the university. Massive protests were held in Chicago at the site of the Democratic National Convention in August 1968, resulting in violent police response and the infamous arrests and subsequent trial of the Chicago Seven.

The world was experiencing a major wave of protest that would have aftershocks for decades to come. The Vietnam War was an important stimulus for the insurgency, both in the US and elsewhere, but the cycle of protest of the 1960s was more than a protest against the war and American imperialism. The protest wave consisted of numerous social movements with international appeal, including student, anti-war, women's, gay and lesbian, and environmental movements. The American civil rights movement, which began in the 1950s, helped to provoke the protest cycle by providing a model of effective collective action and a vision of freedom and equality that was emulated by movements worldwide.

This chapter begins by examining some arguments about the origins, decline, and consequences of the protest cycle of the 1960s. I then look at the American civil rights movement and the New Left student and anti-war movements that arose around the world in the 1960s and their influence on other movements of the time. A number of social movements that survived the decline of the mass movements of the protest cycle, including ethnic protests, the women's movement, the gay and lesbian movement, and the environmental movement, are an important legacy of the 1960s, as are some of the right-wing countermovements that also emerged in the 1960s.

The Rise, Decline, and Significance of the Protest Cycle

Why did so many people around the world take to the streets in the 1960s? What happened to that protest and what are the lasting consequences of the protest cycle? These are important questions that have occupied numerous social theorists. Many have pointed to large-scale changes such as the economic booms taking place in many Western countries, shifts in capitalism based on technological advances, and the dramatic expansion of higher education, which helped to nourish a youth culture (Fraser, 1988: 2–3). However, no single structural explanation can account for the variations in protest found in different countries. Sidney Tarrow (1989: 4) argues that, although the 1960s protest cycle 'originated in the general structural problems of advanced capitalism, its forms were conditioned by the particular political institutions and opportunities of each country and social sector.' The actors who mobilized and the course and outcomes of their protest differed greatly across nations, and numerous studies detail protests in France, Italy, Germany, the United States, Canada, and elsewhere (e.g., della Porta, 1995; Gitlin, 1987; Kreisi et al., 1995; Levitt, 1984; Tarrow, 1989; Touraine, 1971).

While recognizing that the course of protest varies from country to country, social movement scholars have nevertheless developed some theoretical ideas about the common features of protest cycles and the factors that lead to their rise and decline. Tarrow (1998: 142) characterizes a **protest cycle** or **cycle of contention** as:

> a phase of heightened conflict across the social system: with a rapid diffusion of collective action from more mobilized to less mobilized sectors; a rapid pace of innovation in the forms of contention; the creation of new or transformed collective action frames; a combination of organized and unorganized participation; and sequences of intensified information flow and interaction between challengers and authorities.

During a cycle of contention, collective action spreads to many different groups, beyond those initiating the cycle. Because so many new actors are mobilized and so many activists interact with one another, they commonly devise innovative tactics and new collective action frames. Innovations in repertoires of collective action and new collective action frames are widely diffused, allowing new groups to mobilize, including opponents of some of the initial movements. During the 1960s, it was not only progressive social movements that mobilized, but also right-wing opponents and groups that felt threatened by their demands and actions.

Explanations of the rise of protest cycles have focused on **political opportunities** for protest. A protest cycle occurs 'when the costs of collective action are so low and the incentives are so great that even individuals or groups that would normally not engage in protest feel encouraged to do so' (Tarrow, 1989: 8). Political opportunities such as increased access to political participation, realignments of power, splits among elites, and the availability of allies (see Eisinger, 1973; Piven and Cloward, 1977; Tarrow, 1998) make protest attractive because of the resources available and the increased chances of success. These opportunities are most likely to occur in democratic systems, though some theorists have extended the model to non-democratic contexts (see Almeida, 2003). Movements that arise early in a protest cycle, when successful, provide evidence to other potential challengers that elites are vulnerable and that protest is worthwhile. These 'early risers' (Tarrow, 1989, 1998) are also important in creating master frames that inspire protest and can be adapted by other movements (Snow and Benford, 1992), and highly visible models of protest tactics, which are often diffused by mass media. In some instances, the demands of early movements threaten the interests of other contenders, leading to the mobilization of countermovements. Thus, the protest cycle spreads through a variety of processes, as new contenders imitate early movements and extend or react to their demands (Tarrow, 1998: 145).

McAdam distinguishes between 'initiator' and 'spinoff' movements in explaining how protest cycles diffuse. He argues that political opportunities are critical to the emergence of the early riser or initiator movements, but that expanding political opportunities do not explain the rise of later, **spinoff movements**. In fact, later movements may be at a political disadvantage in that governments are already preoccupied with the demands of earlier movements and less receptive to new movements (McAdam, 1995: 225). Instead of being the result of political opportunities, spinoff movements may arise from the organizational, ideological, and cultural bases created by earlier movements. Networks created by one movement are often used as mobilizing structures by other movements. Collective action frames developed by early movements help to create new consciousness for other movements. And long-lived movements such as the women's movement create communities that spawn subsequent collective action and help to maintain movements after a protest cycle declines (Staggenborg, 1998). During slow periods in between visible movement campaigns, collective identities are maintained within the submerged networks of cultural groups, institutional spaces, and other elements of movement communities. As McAdam (1995: 230) notes, 'enduring movements such as feminism never really die, but rather are characterized by periods of relative activity and inactivity.'

While individual movements maintain themselves in various forms, periods of intense protest activity by multiple movements do not last forever. Cycles of protest decline because they eventually 'produce counter-movements, violence, and political backlash, new repressive strategies, and thence demobilization' (Tarrow, 1989: 9). Tarrow (1998: 147–50) identifies three sets of processes involved in the decline of protest cycles. (1) Activists simply become exhausted, but not all activists drop out at an equal rate. Those who are more extreme in their beliefs, and less likely to compromise with authorities, are most likely to remain active despite exhaustion. Moderates are more likely to scale back their participation, and as they do the movement may become more polarized between those who are willing to compromise and those who are not. (2) Splits between moderates and radicals lead to two tendencies. On the one hand, radicals may become more violent in their behaviour while, on the other hand, moderates turn to more institutionalized actions. (3) Governmental authorities selectively repress some movement actions and facilitate others. When governments encourage the actions of moderates and repress those of radicals, they are likely to push the latter to further extremism while shrinking the movement as moderates turn to institutionalized action.

Despite the decline of intense periods of collective action, protest cycles continue to influence subsequent collective action in various ways. Many leaders and other participants who become active during a protest cycle remain involved in new social movements both inside and outside of institutions after the protest wave subsides. Tactics created during the protest cycle continue to be used by movements that persist or form after the cycle declines. For example, many activists, including gays and lesbians and environmentalists, continued to employ variants of the sit-in tactic devised by the civil rights movement. Master frames and new cultural understandings endure, influencing new generations of activists. Organizational bases created during the protest cycle often remain as submerged networks, which can be mobilized for subsequent collective action. And opponents aroused during the cycle of contention may also endure as countermovements or submerged networks. In some cases, countermovements keep particular movements alive beyond the decline of a protest cycle as the two opposing movements continue to do battle (see Meyer and Staggenborg, 1996).

THE AMERICAN CIVIL RIGHTS MOVEMENT

The American civil rights movement provides an example of an initiator movement during the 1960s cycle of protest, which has had a lasting influence on social movements worldwide. The civil rights movement played an important role in the rise of the New Left and the diffusion of protest in the 1960s. The movement has been studied extensively by historians and social scientists (e.g., Andrews, 2004; Branch, 1988; Carson, 1981; Fairclough, 1987; Garrow, 1986; McAdam, 1988, 1999; Meier and Rudwick, 1973; Morris, 1984), and here I provide only a very brief account that highlights key factors in the origins and impact of the movement and the protest cycle.

Large-scale socio-economic and political changes, including both international and domestic pressures, were critical to the emergence of the civil rights movement in the US (see Jenkins et al., 2003; McAdam, 1999; Skrentny, 1998). Internationally, the Cold War exerted a strong influence on American policy in the post-World War II era, and civil rights violations at home left the American government vulnerable to international criticism that its record on human rights was no better than that of the Soviet Union. With the establishment in 1946 of the United Nations Commission on Human Rights and the subsequent creation of its Subcommission on the Prevention of Discrimination and Protection of Minorities, the US record was open to challenge (Skrentny, 1998: 256). This concern prompted some American officials to support various civil rights measures, resulting in domestic tensions between the federal government and the political elite in the American South, which was committed to racial segregation. Socio-economic changes in the US, including the decline of cotton as a cash crop and the large-scale migration of southern blacks to urban centres, also facilitated the emergence of the civil rights movement (McAdam, 1999; Morris, 1984). Many blacks moved to northern industrial states, where they had a national electoral impact, causing both major political parties to become concerned about the black vote and creating political opportunities for blacks. Blacks also migrated to southern cities, where their concentrated numbers allowed them to support their own institutions and organizations and where the black vote also became a potential political force.

These political opportunities fuelled perceptions that change was possible, and organizational shifts related to these opportunities helped to mobilize the black community. Significantly, urban black churches, unlike rural ones, were able to support their own ministers. Although not all black ministers committed their churches to the movement, a sizable number of the new urban ministers were educated middle-class devotees to a radical theology stressing social activism, and these ministers became key leaders of the civil rights movement (Fairclough, 1987; Morris, 1984). The black church provided critical support to the emerging civil rights movement, including leadership, meeting places, and numerous cultural resources. Culturally, civil rights leaders were able to build on the participatory tradition of the black church, together with its theological emphasis on freedom, justice, and liberation (Morris, 1984, 2000). Ministers who became leaders of the civil rights movement adapted the traditions of the black church to draw members into participation in the movement, and they also used their social networks to share information about strategies and tactics. Thus, pre-existing organizational and cultural bases, together with large-scale changes, were key factors in the origins of the movement.

Based on perceptions of political opportunities, organizational resources, and cultural understandings, the civil rights movement developed a repertoire of strategies and tactics that was critical to its growth, success, and influence on other social movements. In framing movement concerns and devising tactics, movement leaders and their allies deliberately took advantage of global concerns about human rights (Skrentny, 1998), and they also emphasized themes of freedom and justice in the tradition of the black church (Morris, 2000). Movement tactics, including bus boycotts, freedom rides, sit-ins, and community-wide protests, mobilized participants, produced victories, and helped to spread the ideas of the movement by creating dramatic confrontations (McAdam, 1983, 1996). Worldwide media coverage showed images of heroic, non-violent protestors facing police brutality and racist resistance, in some instances forcing federal intervention and resulting in movement victories. Tactics such as the sit-in have since become part of the contemporary repertoire of collective action (see Morris, 1981).

The themes of human rights, freedom, and social justice employed by the civil rights movement became part of a master frame adopted by women's, gay and lesbian rights, and ethnic and nationalist movements around the world. Although several scholars have suggested that the civil rights movement created a 'rights' frame that was subsequently adopted by other movements (Snow and Benford, 1992; Tarrow, 1998), Morris (2000) disputes the characterization of the central frame of the movement as one of 'rights' growing out of legal court challenges and instead emphasizes the 'freedom and justice' frame rooted in the traditions of the black church. However, both types of themes seem to have been important in influencing other social movements, and the rights theme draws on global concerns about human rights as well as legal efforts to secure civil rights.

The civil rights movement was exceptionally influential for other social movements because its activists promoted a global vision of human rights. As Gay Seidman notes, a number of civil rights movement leaders were involved in framing issues in global terms, creating linkages with activists in other countries, and speaking to international audiences about global issues of justice and freedom as well as issues specific to the United States. Many participants in the civil rights movement 'viewed their struggle in terms of an international campaign to end racial inequality globally' and connected their movement to larger issues such as pan-Africanism and decolonization (Seidman, 2000: 345–6). Indeed, the philosophy and tactics of the civil rights movement were influenced by Mahatma Gandhi, who began his career fighting non-violently for the rights of workers and 'coloured' peoples in South Africa and then India and who was a central figure in the Indian independence movement.

In addition to the influence of its ideological frames and tactical models, the civil rights movement was important in mobilizing students, who were critical to the international movements of the 1960s. In 1960, large numbers of black students participated in waves of sit-ins that galvanized the civil rights movement and stimulated increased participation by white and black students in the northern US. Black students founded the Student Nonviolent Coordinating Committee (SNCC) and organized numerous campaigns, including Freedom Summer, which brought hundreds of northern white students to Mississippi in 1964 to register black voters and fight for civil rights in the state. The project had a huge impact on both the civil rights movement and the American student movement. For many black activists in SNCC, Freedom Summer ended in disillusionment owing to racial tensions on the project and to a lack of immediate success in influencing American politics (McAdam, 1988). Some turned away from non-violent protest and became committed to the emerging 'black power' movement, which emphasized black pride, strength, and identity rather than racial integration (see Bush, 1999; Van Deburg, 1992). For many white volunteers, Freedom Summer was a life-changing experience, and many of them returned in groups to their university campuses to become leaders in the emerging student movement (McAdam, 1986, 1988).

The Rise of New Left Student and Anti-War Movements

In the 1960s, students were at the centre of protests around the world (Caute, 1988; Fraser, 1988; Owram, 1996). The large student cohorts of the 1960s developed 'an entirely new student consciousness', which led them to focus on their condition as students and on transformation of the larger society (Ricard, 1994: 114). Their concerns varied in different national contexts, but included reforms of the university, calls for free speech, demands on governments, support for civil rights, and protests against the Vietnam War. Student movements emerged in several Western countries in the 1950s in response to issues such as the Cold War, nuclear threats, colonialism, and racism as part of a New Left. The New Left consisted of the radical movements of the 1960s, which dissociated themselves from existing Communist and democratic socialist parties and failures of the Old Left (see Caute, 1988: 33–8; Owram,

1996: 226–33), and attempted to create a new kind of politics that would criticize capitalism and advocate meaningful forms of democracy. In Britain, the New Left was closely associated with the Campaign for Nuclear Disarmament, which mobilized many students through its youth wing. In Canada, students first mobilized around the anti-nuclear issue in 1959, developing a view of 'the common welfare over partial interests, of humanity over politics' that would become central to the larger university movement of the 1960s (Levitt, 1984: 40–1). Students in Quebec were influenced by the nationalist movement there and aimed for 'a sweeping change in the conduct and organization of their society' (Ricard, 1994: 119). In France, massive mobilizations of students began during the Algerian War, which lasted from 1954 to 1962, to support the Algerian National Liberation Front. In the United States, students began organizing on campuses in the late 1950s to support the civil rights movement and to protest US Cold War policies. In many countries, a post-war boom in student enrolments put university students in a position of strength and also created grievances as to the dehumanizing nature of the 'multiversity' and its role in producing workers for the capitalist elite.

At the University of California at Berkeley, what became known as the Free Speech Movement erupted in September 1964 when the university administration attempted to ban on-campus organizing and fundraising for off-campus political causes (see Heirich, 1968). Students who had been organizing on campus in support of the civil rights movement, some of whom had recently returned to campus after participating in the Freedom Summer project in Mississippi, led a protest against the policy. Highlights of the protest included the spontaneous surrounding of a police car to prevent an arrested student from being carried off, a student strike, and use of the sit-in, a tactic learned from the civil rights movement, to occupy the administration building. By January 1965, after the arrests of over 800 students, the university relented and agreed to allow organizing and fundraising for outside causes on campus once again. The Free Speech Movement gave a huge boost to the student movement, both in the US and internationally.

Student concerns about the nature of the university were linked to their concerns about the nature of society. In complaining about student alienation, overcrowded and irrelevant courses, distant professors, and university bureaucracy, students were also critiquing the large corporations and meaningless work of capitalist society (Levitt, 1984: 33). While protesting against university restrictions on their freedoms and demanding greater student involvement in university governance, students connected their struggles to larger issues of civil rights, racism, and democracy. In the US, Students for a Democratic Society (SDS) used the slogan 'A Free University in a Free Society' to connect the Berkeley movement to these larger concerns (Sale, 1973: 168). In Canada, the Student Union for Peace Action (SUPA) worked with disadvantaged communities and championed Native rights in addition to organizing on campuses (Owram, 1996: 221). In Britain, students protested government policy in the colony of Rhodesia (later Zimbabwe) and, in 1967, 100,000 students demonstrated in protest of the government's plan to raise foreign student fees, a move that particularly affected Third World students and was considered racist by the student movement (Fraser, 1988: 109). In Italy, students in overcrowded universities protested lack of access to higher education for the working class as well as antiquated curricula, examination methods, and university hierarchies (Caute, 1988: 77). While students organized around their own grievances, they also questioned the policies of governments and the nature of the larger societies in which they lived.

The Vietnam War became an important focus of student protest in many countries. In the US, student concern about the war increased greatly after the war escalated and the draft was enlarged in 1965. SDS held a national protest against the war in Washington in April 1965, and, at Berkeley, the Vietnam Day Committee emerged out of the Free Speech Movement and sponsored a massive teach-in about the war in May 1965. Throughout the country, SDS and the New Left expanded as concerns about the war mounted. In Britain, teach-ins about the war were held at the London School of Economics and at Oxford in the summer of 1965 in support of the American anti-war movement (Caute, 1988: 23). In Canada, a teach-in on Vietnam was held at the University of Toronto in October 1965, and, following the event, student anti-war activists began raising the issue of Canada's complicity in the war through armament sales and other actions (Kostash, 1980: 46–8). SUPA became heavily involved in anti-war activities, in part as a way of radicalizing students who might not otherwise be drawn to the New Left (Owram, 1996: 221). In West Germany, the first major anti-Vietnam War demonstrations were held in Berlin in 1966, and opposition to the war was linked to anti-authoritarianism and concerns about German society (Fraser, 1988: 101–7). As demonstrations against the war spread to many countries, including France, Italy, and Japan, student movements linked criticisms of American imperialism to critiques of their own societies and the need for greater democracy.

Movement activity in the United States clearly influenced activists in other countries, even as movements in each country had their own particular concerns. Both mass media and personal contacts among individuals and organizations in different countries are important to the international diffusion of protest (McAdam and Rucht, 1993). In West Germany, a student New Left organization called the Sozialistischer Deutscher Studentenbund (SDS) arose in the early 1960s at the same time as the American SDS was organizing. In the mid-1960s, writings of American New Leftists and descriptions of American tactics were published in the journal of the German SDS. Several activists from West Germany visited the US, some as exchange students, and returned home to organize demonstrations in support of the Black Panthers and against the Vietnam War. The German New Left adopted tactics such as sit-ins and teach-ins, styles of dress, and their own versions of slogans from the American New Left and black power movements. For example, activists in Berlin turned the black power cry 'burn, baby, burn' into 'burn, warehouse, burn' to inspire firebombings of warehouses and other symbols of capitalism in Germany (McAdam and Rucht, 1993: 69).

In Canada, the influence of the American civil rights and anti-war movements was extensive, but Canadians also created their own unique movements. Some Canadians who became involved in the New Left had gone to the United States and participated in civil rights campaigns, and many Americans who fled to Canada to avoid the draft were activists in the civil rights and anti-war movements who continued their activism in the Canadian anti-war movement (see Hagan, 2001; Levitt, 1984). Writings of the American New Left circulated widely in Canada, including a famous essay by Jerry Farber, 'The Student as Nigger', which even influenced high school students in Winnipeg who lobbied for a student bill of rights (Vipond, 2004). Canadian groups such as the Labour Committee for Human Rights had ties to American organizations such as the National Association for the Advancement of Colored People (NAACP), and activists in Canada were inspired by Martin Luther King's leadership of the American civil rights movement. In a collection of his writings published in 1968, Pierre Trudeau used the language of the US Supreme Court ruling *Brown v. Board of Education*, which found the 'separate but equal' principle of racial segregation in education unconstitutional, to discuss the need for linguistic equality and the integration of Quebec in Canada (Vipond, 2004: 96–7). By the late 1960s and early 1970s, American-influenced 'rights talk' had become widespread in Canada. However, the frame was modified in line with a more collective Canadian perspective; the American vision of individual rights and equality of opportunity became, in Canada, 'a notion of rights that focused on the state's obligation to ensure equality' (ibid., 95).

LEGACIES OF THE PROTEST CYCLE OF THE 1960S

The civil rights, New Left, and anti-war movements mobilized large numbers of participants for a period of intense collective action. By the late 1960s, however, these movements began to disintegrate for a variety of reasons, including internal weaknesses in movement organizations, an escalation of violence by radical factions, backlash from right-wing groups, and repression by governments (see Caute, 1988; Gitlin, 1980; Oberschall, 1978). Nevertheless, the protest cycle of the sixties had an enduring influence, both in spawning new social movements that survived beyond that period and in challenging the dominant culture. As Fraser (1988: 317) argues, 'one of the major effects of the student rebellion has been a generalized disrespect for arbitrary and exploitive authority among the 1968 and succeeding generations in the West, a lack of deference toward institutions and values that demean people and a concomitant awareness of people's rights.' Women, gays and lesbians, Aboriginals, animal rights activists, disabled people, environmentalists, and many others were inspired to question authority and organize during and after the 1960s.

Among the movements that continued to advocate for new rights after the 1960s were numerous ethnic and nationalist movements. Although such movements often originated prior to the 1960s, many grew in strength and changed in character along with the protest cycle. In some instances, government affirmative action policies provided incentives for new groups to organize around their ethnic identities. In the United States, a variety of ethnic groups such as American Indians, Latinos, and Asian Americans were inspired by the successes of African Americans and encouraged by new government policies; as African Americans developed a new collective identity and a new rhetoric of black pride, other ethnic groups followed suit (Nagel, 1994: 166). At the same time, white ethnic mobilization occurred in response to affirmative action and desegregation efforts in the 1960s and 1970s, resulting in backlash movements such as anti-busing movements (ibid., 158).

In Canada, the contemporary Quebec independence movement picked up steam in the late 1950s and 1960s as a result of a number of social and economic changes occurring in the province (Coleman, 1984; McRoberts, 1993). In the early 1960s, Quebec society underwent a period of modernization and secularization of its educational system, culture, state, and economic structures known as the Quiet Revolution. Significantly, French-Canadian nationalists embraced economic and social development and became confident of their own capabilities (McRoberts, 1993: 129). Despite these changes, francophones in Quebec faced limited economic and cultural opportunities, and disaffected members of both the working class and the middle class were attracted to the sovereignty option. Inspired in part by anti-colonial and anti-imperialist movements in Algeria and the Third World, various organizations promoting independence formed and activists developed 'a vision of a new Quebec that would be independent, secular, and social democratic' (Coleman, 1984: 218). Quebec labour unions, which grew in strength during the 1960s with the organization of public-sector workers, moved to the left politically and strongly supported the separatist movement. In 1968, sovereignty movement activists came together to form the Parti Québécois, which first won power in Quebec in 1976.

The Quebec independence movement provides an example of the tendency of some movements to split into militant and institutionalized factions; while part of the sovereignty movement became institutionalized, a radical element of the movement also emerged. Activists linked the Quebec struggle to the international protest movement of the 1960s (Krieber, 1989: 218), and one supporter of the Front de Libération du Québec (FLQ), Pierre Vallières, employed the American race analogy in his book *White Niggers of America*, which was widely read by radical Quebec nationalists (Vipond, 2004: 95–6). Owing to its use of political violence, the FLQ remained marginalized, 'directly involving perhaps no more than 100 people in its various waves of bombings and vandalism during the 1960s' (McRoberts, 1993: 200), and was strongly discredited by its 1970 kidnapping and murder of a Quebec cabinet minister, Pierre Laporte, and kidnapping of James Cross, a British trade commissioner. However, the struggles for liberation of the 1960s remained one source of inspiration for the larger, non-violent Quebec separatist movement, which became centred in the Parti Québécois.

Aboriginal protests also intensified in Canada and other countries around the world in the 1960s. In the United States, the American Indian Movement experienced a resurgence of activity as a result of the precedent of the civil rights movement and opportunities created by new government policies and programs (Nagel, 1996: 121). Ethnic identification became a source of status rather than stigma in the 1960s and 1970s, and American Indians organized around the goal of 'red power' in an effort to regain their cultural heritage as well as to settle various land claims (ibid., 124–5). In Canada, as Howard Ramos describes in Chapter 5, mobilization by Aboriginals also accelerated for the first time in the late 1960s in response to the federal government's 1969 White Paper, which proposed eliminating previously held indigenous rights, and to changes in opportunities and resources (Ramos, 2006).

The protest cycle of the 1960s provided organizational bases, communications networks, and experiences that created new skills and new consciousness among activists. In the case of the women's movement, discussed in Chapter 6, women who were active in the civil rights movement and the New Left began to think about their oppression as women as a result of their new consciousness about the oppression of other groups and they also developed grievances about their treatment in other movements. Women easily applied organizing skills gained in earlier movements to the new feminist movement. Gay and lesbian movements, the subject of Chapter 7, similarly expanded their consciousness and their organizational bases as a result of their experiences in New Left and other movements of the 1960s. As described in Chapter 8, the protest cycle of the 1960s also inspired a new wave of the environmental movement as activists applied frames and tactics learned in previous movements to the urgent problem of saving the environment. These and other movements survived the decline of the protest cycle of the 1960s, and their ongoing activism and accomplishments are an important legacy of the period. Subsequent movements, such as the global justice movement discussed in Chapter 9, continue to draw on the frames and tactics of the protest cycle.

CONCLUSION

The protest cycle of the 1960s mobilized large numbers of activists in many countries for numerous causes. Early movements, including the civil rights movement and anti-nuclear and nationalist movements, created collective action frames and tactical models that inspired massive New Left, student, and anti-war movements around the world. These movements generated change and conflict, and helped create new and lasting social movements, including the women's movement, gay and lesbian movement, and environmental movement. Although the cycle of protest of the sixties declined, a number of movements survived, continuing to perpetuate the values, organizational forms, and strategies of the 1960s protests. Many activists from the movements of the sixties continued their activism in other social movements for decades to come. In some instances, the movements of the sixties also created countermovements, as we will see in examining the ongoing efforts of feminists and other activists. The following chapters examine the origins, organization and strategies, and outcomes of several ongoing social movements.

Discussion Questions

1. Why do numerous social movements emerge during a cycle of contention?
2. Why did the protest cycle of the 1960s decline? How did some movements survive beyond its decline?
3. How has the protest cycle of the 1960s influenced the social movements of today?

Suggested Readings

McAdam, Doug. 1995. '"Initiator" and "Spin-off" Movements: Diffusion Processes in Protest Cycles', in M. Traugott, ed., *Repertoires and Cycles of Collective Action*. Durham, NC: Duke University Press. This article uses a political process model to analyze the influences of movements that come early in a protest cycle on later ones.

Morris, Aldon D. 1984. *The Origins of the Civil Rights Movement: Black Communities Organizing for Change.* New York: Free Press. This excellent book on the civil rights movement demonstrates the critical role of indigenous resources and local organizations, including the black church, in the mobilization of the movement.

Tarrow, Sidney. 1989. *Democracy and Disorder: Protest and Politics in Italy, 1965–1975.* Oxford: Oxford University Press. This book examines a cycle of protest in Italy, which ended in both institutionalization and violence in the mid-1970s.

Chapter 5

Aboriginal Protest

Howard Ramos

Social movements often face the problem of uniting diverse groups into a cohesive movement and this is true for Canadian Aboriginals.[1] Their mobilization is characterized by plurality and difference among actors rather than homogeneity. In fact, this is especially the case in Canada because the term 'Aboriginal' refers to a number of different peoples, including status Indians (First Nations), non-status Indians, Métis, and Inuit.[2] Among these groups a number of additional legal, linguistic, cultural, urban/rural, and geographic differences at times come in conflict with one another, creating divergent interests.

Yet, despite diversity among Aboriginals, all have faced common problems and have been forced to engage in long-standing resistance against colonization. For example, all have struggled against appropriation of land and material property, resisted displacement to reserves (Miller, 1989), disenfranchisement (Indian and Northern Affairs Canada, section 9.12), residential schooling (Haig-Brown, 1988: ch. 6), the banning of cultural practices (Indian and Northern Affairs Canada, section 9.5), being transferred from state to state without consultation (Grand Council of the Crees, 1998), and discrimination in employment and daily life (Fleras and Elliott, 2003: 175; Langford and Ponting, 1992; Ponting, 2000). Thus, despite differences among Aboriginals, government policy, practice, and social attitudes have created common grievances.

This chapter will examine tensions between divergent interests and the roles that resources, political opportunities, and collective identity play in engaging critical events. We first examine the concepts of community, bystanders, and critical events and then consider their dynamics by looking at Canadian Aboriginal mobilization in the post-World War II era. The chapter examines how three specific events—the announcement of the White Paper in 1969, patriation of the Constitution in 1982, and the 'Indian summer' of 1990—affected patterns of contention. The discussion of these events is made with comparison to the broader international context and indigenous protest in the US and Mexico. As will become apparent, despite many differences, critical events demand similar responses, which increase the potential for mass mobilization and the generation of common frames of resistance.

COMMUNITIES, BYSTANDERS, AND CRITICAL EVENTS

As Chapter 3 and many social movement scholars suggest, social networks play a significant role in mobilizing people (Diani, 1997; Gould, 1993; Klandermans and

Oegema, 1987; McAdam et al., 2001; Melucci, 1989; Snow et al., 1980). Nevertheless, just knowing someone does not translate into social action, and thus a focus on networks alone can be misleading (Snow et al., 1986: 468). Instead, people and communities define issues and mobilize, and if they are unable to generate bonds with other communities that share similar concerns, the outcome of their efforts will be minimal. This is because movements tend to be defined by supporters rather than by members per se (Staggenborg, 1998: 181). This is particularly the case for Aboriginal peoples because their traditional communities are often small, with limited resources; consequently, it is difficult to mobilize more resources or exploit political opportunities alone. To achieve social change, small communities need to act with wider institutions, address grievances that have broad salience, and gain the support of bystander publics in other Aboriginal communities and the dominant society.

It is thus important to examine how communities, and the social movement organizations that represent them, interact with bystanders outside them. Turner and Killian define a **bystander public** as 'a public that defines issues strictly from a bystander's perspective'; bystanders are people who have no stake in the outcome of a conflict, issue, or protest but may be affected by the dynamics that play out between political interests or mobilized groups (Turner and Killian, 1987: 216). They go on to note that mobilization does not occur in a void, and actions by political elites, or those who engage them, affect others who are not directly involved in the political process. Because of this, it is worth examining how bystanders respond to mobilization by supporting, fighting against, or remaining apathetic to it.

At a local level, community, identity, and support are constructed through basic group interactions. These allow people to share time and space, cultivate common interests, and in turn create bonds that can be drawn upon to generate resources, form organizations, engage political opportunities, defend identities, or even challenge grievances. Nationally and internationally, however, such interactions are difficult to foster because of regional and temporal differences that inhibit shared interactions that create common frames of reference. Because of this, commonality is constructed through processes of *imagining communities* or creating new collective identities. This involves producing common symbols of who *belongs* and *what* binds communities together (Anderson, 1991), for example, the use of common images, narratives, or events that create shared experiences. Large masses of people rarely share time and space together and thus national and international communities, as well as support for them, are built through the engagement of frames of reference that transcend differences.

As a result, the question of importance for small local communities, such as those found among Aboriginals, is how to generate support from bystanders in other communities and gain national and international attention? Dayan and Katz (1992) offer partial insight by examining the role of 'media events', including coverage of celebrity and sporting events as well as national tragedies. For social movements, instances of political crisis should also be considered. That is, we need to consider what role **critical events**, or opportunities that affect widespread contention, play in generating yet more mobilization. As Staggenborg (1993: 320) argues, 'social movements are event-driven insofar as critical events alter expectations and perceptions of threats, focusing or distracting the attention of movement constituents and other important actors on or away from movement issues.' In other words, critical events provide opportunities to create a common political environment, frame of interest, and support for a given issue (Pride, 1995).

Others have examined similar phenomena. Ganz (2000: 1019) highlights how 'focal moments' result in sudden changes that alter organizations' strategic capacities to mobilize. McAdam and Sewell (2001) show that critical events act as poignant transformative instances that alter the trajectory of contention and negotiation of social order. Yet others, such as Khasnabish (2004), illustrate how 'moments of coincidence' align the mobilization of indigenous struggles to other movements. He illustrated this with the Zapatistas' struggle for autonomy and support from the labour movement in Mexico. Such moments create common experience and in turn generate support from other movements and bystanders.

Critical events, by any name, are thus 'signalling opportunities' that contribute to frame alignment. This is because they affect all actors in a given context simultaneously. However, unlike political, legal, or economic opportunities, which re-emerge in later cycles and involve institutions that continue to exist after the opportunity is gained or lost, critical events are defined by their immediacy and significance. This is why they gain the greatest salience, offer the ability to garner widespread response, transcend differences across a movement spectrum, and in turn demand engagement from bystander communities. Because of the shared experiences created by reaction to critical events, they in turn lead bystanders to focus on issues embedded in them. In some cases this facilitates the renegotiation of dominant ideologies and social change. Before this occurs a mobilized group must be able to influence the way an event is interpreted and how bystanders interact with it (Gamson, 2004; Staggenborg, 1993). The ability to do that is largely dictated by the availability of resources, political opportunities, and the strength of movement identities. As a result, if a given community or social movement organization is able to tap into a critical event, it can be used to bridge differences among other movements, communities, and bystanders.

The following sections will examine these dynamics through an analysis of Canadian Aboriginal mobilization from the end of World War II to the present. As noted above, one of the biggest obstacles facing Aboriginal mobilization is the lack of solidarity that fosters support among communities. Consequently, much Canadian Aboriginal social action lacks widespread engagement and is difficult to sustain (Ramos, 2006; Wilkes, 2004a, 2004b). However, there have been notable exceptions, such as protest against the White Paper, engagement of the patriation process, and the 'Indian summer'. Each acted as a critical event for Canadian Aboriginal mobilization, intersecting local communities, protestors, national movement organizations, and bystanders across the country and around the world. The following section will also compare them to international events as well as American and Mexican indigenous contention.

The Rise of Contemporary Canadian Aboriginal Mobilization

The post-World War II era was an unprecedented period of social change in North America and Europe. It ushered in human rights and anti-colonial discourses that forced existing nation-states, such as Canada, to reconsider their treatment and recognition of ethnic and national minorities (Niezen, 2000; Tennant, 1990: 121). At the same time, large numbers of Aboriginal servicemen returning from World War II were becoming increasingly politically active and questioned their treatment by the dominant Canadian society (Fleras and Elliott, 1992: 42). They began to demand better educational opportunities, sought resources to develop communities, demanded the federal government respect and honour past treaties, and pressured it to amend the Indian Act, which governed the lives of Aboriginal peoples (Cardinal, 1999: 85). An example of such mobilization can be seen when Andrew Paull, Grand Chief of the Squamish, in British Columbia, and president of the North American Indian Brotherhood (NAIB), criticized the 1951 amendments to the Indian Act, calling them dictatorial (Canadian Press, 1951). Similar trends were also apparent in the US, where returning indigenous servicemen also sought similar social justice (Cornell, 1988: 130; Nagel, 1996: 118).

However, formally organized contention, representing a broad range of Aboriginal interests, was the exception rather than the norm during the 1950s. Paull's actions were not followed by a surge of Aboriginal protest or support, as was the response to later proposed changes to the legislation. Moreover, NAIB actions were 'hindered by a lack of nation-wide support and suppressive government actions', which eventually led to internal administrative problems and the organization disbanding (www.afn.ca/article.asp?id=59). Instead, during that decade much Canadian Aboriginal protest came from specific First Nations and local communities, and because of this it tended to occur around local grievances. When outsiders supported Aboriginal causes, they were largely from neighbouring communities or members of the same First Nation who were jointly affected. For instance, Mohawk communities in Ontario and Quebec were politically active in the 1950s, engaging in internal disputes between traditionalists, who wanted their communities to adhere to Mohawk practices, and elected band councils, recognized by the federal government. In one case 40 traditional chiefs of the Six Nations Reserve and 1,000 supporters took over the band council office. They ousted the elected council and sent telegrams to the Queen, Prime Minister John Diefenbaker, and American President Dwight Eisenhower declaring the reserve a sovereign and independent nation (*Globe and Mail*, 6 Mar. 1959). Mobilized communities thus reacted against issues affecting only their immediate interests, a limited number of neighbouring communities, or a specific First Nation. As a result, many actions during the period had little resonance for outside communities and yielded little broad-based support.

Few formal Aboriginal organizations emerged in the 1950s. Instead, the emphasis of Canadian Aboriginal organizing at this time was on creating clubs and informal meeting places that promoted indigenous culture and getting to know people rather than politics. A prominent example of this can be seen in the founding of the Indian Club at the 'Y' (YMCA) in Toronto. The urban Aboriginal community felt it was poorly represented and wished to establish a meeting place to generate a sense of pride and reflect an Aboriginal cultural presence (Obonsawin and Howard-Bobi-wash, 1997: 29). However, although organizations were able to foster local identities and mobilize immediate communities, they faced difficulty in extending their concerns to outside bystanders, both Aboriginal and non-Aboriginal. As a result, the scope of their mobilization was limited by their small size and local focus. They faced many obstacles when trying to recruit support across Canada or internationally.

In part, these trends are explained by a general lack of resources available to promote widespread mobilization. Most of the organizing that took place was informal and focused on specific community interests rather than larger pan-Canadian issues. This further limited the pool of resources that could be drawn upon and in turn muted the potential for mass mobilization. By the late 1960s state funding became available (Miller, 1989: 329–30) and organizations began changing their mandates from fostering meeting places to also becoming service providers and eventually engaging the state through political action. Among the first contemporary national political organizations to emerge was the National Indian Council (NIC), established in the early 1960s (www.afn.ca/article.asp?id=59). It sought to create a movement of status Indians, non-status Indians, and Métis. Because it was predominantly urban-based, when the majority of Aboriginal people lived on reserves or in rural communities, it failed. The organization also faced obstacles because it did not have stable funding and because of tensions stemming from divergent interests. In particular, status Indians did not want to be grouped with the Métis for fear of losing their treaty rights. The NIC dissolved in 1968 and its failure led to the creation of the National Indian Brotherhood (NIB), which represented status Indians alone (Cardinal, 1999: 92–3; Young, 1969).[3] At the same time, national-level Aboriginal organizations emerged in the US and Mexico. The American Indian Movement (AIM) was founded in 1968, representing all indigenous peoples there (Wilkes, 2006: 512). The same can be observed in Mexico with the formation of a National Indigenous Movement in the early 1970s (Brysk and Wise, 1997: 94). In all three national contexts, indigenous peoples were responding to changing attitudes towards human rights, colonization, and national minorities.[4]

The emergence of the NIB in Canada signalled a shift in how Aboriginal organizations were funded. Unlike earlier organizations, which gained much of their core resources through private means, the NIB would be almost entirely financed from government grants (Young, 1969). The shift in organizational funding structures and access to resources moved organizations away from community donations, volunteerism, and local community building towards government grants and paid lobbyists. Many feared the shift would alienate the very communities they wanted to represent and in turn weaken the potential for resisting colonial policies of the federal government.

THE WHITE PAPER

The 1960s ended with the Canadian government's proposed 1969 White Paper on Indian Policy and intense mobilization against it. The White Paper was a federal policy brief proposing the elimination of Indian status and the assimilation of the

Aboriginal population into dominant Canadian society (Cairns, 2000: 163). The federal government wanted to overcome the disparities among Aboriginals as well as respond to changing international discourse prizing human and civil rights. This became a significant political opportunity that many believe acted as a critical event marking the birth of contemporary Aboriginal mobilization (Long, 1992: 121). Status Indians were concerned about losing their treaty rights as First Nations; at the same time, however, the paper also affected all other Aboriginal peoples, including non-status Indians, Métis, and Inuit. Because of this, it resonated beyond the critical mass of communities that initially opposed it. The White Paper provided a common collective action frame, aligning goals and grievances among Aboriginal peoples.

The first signs of opposition came from Alberta status Indians, who responded by drafting their own legislation, which they called the 'Red Paper'. This document was presented to the federal cabinet in Ottawa in June 1970. It was based on the findings of the 1966 Hawthorn Report[5] and demanded 'citizenship plus' (Cairns, 2000: 67). The Red Paper sought recognition of Aboriginal rights, as well as the rights of basic Canadian citizenship. Opposition emerged because the government refused to accept Aboriginal perspectives on the Indian Act. A month before the White Paper's unveiling, Aboriginals met with the Minister of Indian Affairs, Jean Chrétien, in an unprecedented conference at which they adopted a resolution seeking the establishment of regional and provincial committees to investigate their rights (Morris, 1969a). However, the federal government was interested in constructing a single policy that would incorporate Aboriginals into Canadian society rather than preserving a multiplicity of First Nations, non-status Indians, Métis, and Inuit (Morris, 1969b). The government thus released its policy paper and most Aboriginal leaders reacted with shock and outrage—apparently government consultations were merely symbolic. The announcement of the White Paper created a common grievance and frame of resistance that garnered support among different communities. It became a critical event that generated widespread protest, as seen in Figure 5.1, and it signalled a new era for contemporary Canadian Aboriginal contention (Ramos, 2006: 223; Wilkes, 2006: 513).

At the same time, in the US, the AIM became increasingly active. During the same year, a group of indigenous students from San Francisco State University began a 19-month occupation of Alcatraz Island. They declared themselves 'Indians of All Tribes' and claimed the island on grounds of treaty rights granted the Sioux in 1868 (Cornell, 1988; Johnson, 1996; Nagel, 1996: 131; Wilkes, 2006: 513). Like the White Paper, this event sparked much support. Nagel even argues it was of central importance as '*the* symbolic icon of Indian ethnic resurgence' in the US (Nagel, 1996: 135).

FROM LOCAL COMMUNITIES TO NATIONAL POLITICAL ORGANIZATIONS

Mobilization against the White Paper led to its eventual demise and, more importantly, a policy vacuum on Aboriginal issues in Canada. The federal government responded to events by establishing a core funding program in 1971 to provide Aboriginals and other interest groups the resources needed to promote their causes at a

Figure 5.1   Canadian Aboriginal Protest, 1951–2000

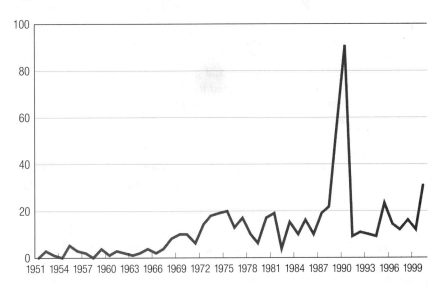

Source: Adapted from Ramos (2006).

federal level (Fleras and Elliott, 1992: 44). In addition, during this period Ottawa officially changed its policy from attempting to terminate Aboriginal rights to supporting Aboriginal organizations. Temporary funding granted to status Indians through the NIB was extended indefinitely and also offered to others. In fact, the Inuit Tapirisat of Canada (since renamed Inuit Tapiriit Kanatami [ITK]) and the Native Council of Canada (NCC—today the Congress of Aboriginal Peoples)[6] were founded during this period. Because of the shift in political opportunities and resource availability, a new form of mobilization appeared, moving attention from local organizing to national-level politics.

This shift also incurred obstacles, as the federal government began to set a number of restrictions and guidelines for organizational funding. It did not fund every Aboriginal organization, but instead prioritized those organizations claiming to represent *all* Aboriginal peoples and those that were urban-based. Evidence of this can be seen in the Secretary of State's policy of supporting only one organization per province during the 1970s (*Globe and Mail*, 18 July 1972; Canadian Press, 1972). The federal government was willing to fund organizations, but on its terms.

As resources to mobilize nationally increased, newly emerging organizations moved away from local communities to exploit political opportunities stemming from the defeat of the White Paper. Ottawa was in search of a viable policy on Aboriginal issues that, at the same time, would not incur social unrest. The Liberal government was open to consultation on such matters and, as a result, organizations during the 1970s began spending less energy on local concerns, focusing instead on government policies. In shifting their efforts, battles were increasingly fought in the courts, through lobbying, and in the media. This led to a move away from building ties with bystander publics in specific communities to an interaction with judicial and bureaucratic institutions.

The change in tactics came with the rise of a young Aboriginal elite who had been educated in the dominant school system because of forced residential schooling. They were also familiar with judicial and governmental institutions. Many of these leaders, however, were cut off from their local communities, and concern over their ability to represent their people without influence of the federal government quickly emerged. As Taiaiake Alfred notes, 'The co-optation of our [Aboriginal] political leadership is a subtle, insidious, undeniable fact, and it has resulted in a collective loss of ability to confront the daily injustices, both petty and profound, of Native life' (Alfred, 1999: 73). In addition, some writers have expressed concern that federal funding increases Aboriginal dependency (Guillemin, 1978; Gagné, 1994), while other scholars worry that such funding has not and will not resolve outstanding issues (Flanagan, 2000).

Nevertheless, the new Aboriginal elite found that past treaties were powerful tools. They could be used to force the federal government to negotiate with Aboriginal people and possibly remedy a wide range of social problems. Evidence of this can be seen in 1970 when the NIB, Canadian Métis Society, and Indian-Eskimo Association[7] released a 300-page report warning that Aboriginals could bog down the courts with trials looking into treaty rights (Platiel, 1970). This was not merely a threat, and indeed a number of grievances were filed with courts across the country, leading to a number of significant Supreme Court decisions during the 1970s that set legal precedents to support Aboriginal struggles. The 1973 *Calder* decision, for example, provided impetus for the federal government to negotiate new treaties. In fact, Canada settled its first 'modern' land claim with the signing of the James Bay and Northern Quebec Agreement in 1975 (www.ainc-inac.gc.ca/pr/info/info14_e.html). Thus, the 1970s saw an opening of the institutional political sphere for Aboriginal organizations; as funding became increasingly available the courts provided a target for redress of past wrongs, and the government turned to the settlement of land claims.

Yet, at the same time the 1970s were also characterized by an unprecedented number of radical protests. In part, this was the result of a series of highly publicized and innovative actions by the AIM in the US that spilled into Canada. In 1972, the AIM occupied the Bureau of Indian Affairs in Washington (Cornell, 1988: 190), and in 1973 and again in 1975 it violently took siege of Wounded Knee on the Pine Ridge Reservation in South Dakota (Josephy et al., 1999: 48–9; Nagel, 1996: 171). These events sparked the 'Red Power' movement in the US and led to a number of protests across the country as well as in Canada.

The most notable Canadian incident of radical action during the 1970s resulted in a riot outside the Parliament in 1974 (Canadian Press, 1974). A similar incident occurred in Kenora, Ontario, when a group of activists claiming ties to the AIM became engaged in an occupation of a municipal park, which later became a stand-off with authorities (Wilkes, 2006: 517). However, the AIM was repressed in the United States after the shooting deaths of two FBI agents in the second siege of

Wounded Knee, and this was linked with its rapid demobilization. It also coincided with a move away from radical protest in Canada for fear of repression and loss of political opportunities. The Canadian government continued to fund and negotiate with national-level political organizations and their leaders.

Divergence among traditional and elected leaders and between local and national interests, urban and rural, and radical and mainstream groups within the Aboriginal movement, as well as the differing legal statuses of Aboriginal peoples, defined the post-White Paper period and remained the case into the 1980s and into our current era. This was exacerbated when young Aboriginal elites pursued recognition of rights. Existing legislation guaranteed only the rights of status Indians and, in some regards, the Inuit, and the federal government did not recognize the rights of non-status Indians, Aboriginal women, and Métis.[8] Tensions resulting from different statuses led to mobilization around different interests instead of common ones, and grievances around rights divided communities rather than bridging them. For status Indians, legal rights were seen as tools to gain self-determination, but for non-status groups they provided a path to formal recognition. The two objectives were at odds, and over time they proved to be obstacles to coalition- and community-building.

THE CONSTITUTION ACT, 1982

By the 1980s differences among Aboriginal interests became further entrenched through the federal government's decision to patriate the Canadian Constitution, which proved to be an immense political opportunity. In the negotiations leading to it, Aboriginal organizations saw an opening for extending and recognizing their rights. Like the White Paper in 1969, the decision to patriate was one that would affect *all* Aboriginals despite their differences. It was an opportunity that created a shared narrative space to negotiate a national-level movement and provided a common target against which to frame grievances. Status Indians and Inuit saw patriation as an opportunity to obtain self-government; non-status Indians saw it as a means to be legally recognized and access benefits; Aboriginal women saw it as a means of achieving legal recognition and equality with Aboriginal men; and the Métis saw patriation as a means of gaining recognition as a First Nation.

In the early stages of the patriation process, the NIB organized a delegation of 347 Aboriginal leaders to petition the British Parliament and Queen to gain the right to sit as a full participant at constitutional discussions (Webster, 1979). Although this was not the first time Canadian Aboriginal peoples sought to use international institutions to pressure for the negotiation of their rights, it was an unprecedented sign of unity.[9] The delegation gained much attention and sparked a short wave of actions against the Canadian government. The mobilization was widespread with protests by Aboriginal peoples across the country. A highlight of these actions was the 1980 'Constitution Express', a train that ran from the west coast to the capital in Ottawa, picking up Aboriginal supporters along the way (Canadian Press, 1980). It created a symbol of Aboriginal unity, organization, and action.

The Constitution provided a rare opportunity to involve bystanders in Aboriginal and non-Aboriginal communities as well as to generate ties among Aboriginal groups and organization. Like the White Paper, it was a critical event that affected all Aboriginal peoples simultaneously. They would either *all* lose their rights or they could use patriation as an opportunity to gain benefits, and possibly even self-determination. But, unlike the White Paper, the Constitution also affected *all* Canadians. As Clément Chartier, president of Métis National Council (MNC) and former president of the Métis Nation—Saskatchewan and organizer for the NCC, recalled, 'only eight provinces supported patriation. In order to justify patriating the Constitution [Prime Minister] Trudeau needed the support of the public and it was very important that they had the support of the Aboriginal people' (quoted in Ramos, 2004: 107–8). In the general public there was increasing support for Aboriginal rights, so that by 1990 a survey conducted by the *Globe and Mail* found that the majority of Canadians supported aboriginal issues, with 78 per cent of English Canadians and 69per cent of French Canadians believing that constitutional amendments should address Aboriginal concerns (*Globe and Mail*, 9 July 1990). As a result, the constitutional process was a critical event for Aboriginal mobilization to raise consciousness of grievances to bystander publics. In other words, the process led to extension of their collective action frames and to the potential alignment of much of the dominant population to their concerns. Yet, despite signs of incorporating a broader community of actors, legal language surrounding the Constitution also limited its potential to generate ties among different actors. Unity created through actions like the 'Constitution Express' was thus quick to dissipate.

By the early 1980s the federal government began showing signs of offering the NIB (representing status Indians) a seat as a full participant at the constitutional discussions. Other national organizations, particularly those representing other groups, worried it would gain the *only* seat open to Aboriginals, fanning tensions among divergent interests. The three main national organizations—NIB, NCC, and ITK—had different views on what should be incorporated in the Constitution. By April of 1981, differences had become apparent. The NCC, mostly representing urban non-status Indians, began lobbying independently of other organizations (Canadian Press. 1981). The coalition among national Aboriginal groups was weak and eventually broke apart. In 1983, the Métis formed their own organization, the MNC. They worried their demands could not be represented if lumped together with non-status urban Indians of the NCC. Another source of tension came from the Native Women's Association of Canada, which feared recognition of Aboriginal rights would exclude them. They also had concerns that reaffirmation of the Indian Act and negotiation by male-dominated organizations would fail to recognize the injustices they faced. During the same period, in 1982, the NIB also changed its name to the Assembly of First Nations (AFN).

Despite these differences and tensions among national organizations, the major Aboriginal groups were incorporated into the Constitution Act, 1982 in section 35. However, the success of gaining recognition was marred by further division among Aboriginal organizations. The definition of 'Aboriginal' adopted was rather vague and did not concretely set out what rights Aboriginals were entitled to. It also did not clarify whether the recognition of Aboriginals would include equal recognition of men and women, which the previous Indian Act did not. In order to resolve these problems as well as other outstanding issues, the federal government hosted several additional constitutional conferences between 1983 and 1987. Aboriginals were invited to a number of these and their mobilization during the 1980s moved further into the institutional realm and away from individual communities.

The decade closed with government cuts to Aboriginal education and organizations, as well as the failure to gain more specific recognition in post-constitutional conferences. At the final conference, in 1987, the Meech Lake Accord was negotiated, to be ratified by 1990. The Accord was to amend the Constitution to better incorporate Quebec but also dealt with broader issues such as Senate reform, immigration, and Supreme Court appointments. Despite the Accord's grand vision, it led to opposition from the women's movement, trade unions, anti-poverty groups, and, not least, Aboriginal groups and leaders. All felt their rights were ignored.

'INDIAN SUMMER' OF 1990

As Figure 5.1 shows, the year the Meech Lake Accord was to be ratified (1990) saw the greatest level of Aboriginal protests since World War II. As in 1969, with the announcement of the White Paper, and the early 1980s, with the patriation process, this was a period of intense political mobilization on the part of Aboriginal peoples. The 'Indian summer' was caused by series of events that sparked widespread Aboriginal protest and led to the generation of a number of new organizations.

The first notable event occurred when status Indians from Manitoba used the ratification process of the Meech Lake Accord as a means to threaten and eventually prevent its adoption. Elijah Harper, an Oji-Cree chief and an NDP member of the provincial legislature, under the advice of the Assembly of Manitoba Chiefs, used the process as a stage to raise consciousness about Aboriginal grievances. By withholding his vote 'on the grounds that procedural rules were not being followed' (Dickason, 2002: 402), he effectively killed the Accord since each province had to ratify it before 23 June 1990 or the agreement would collapse.

Harper's battle gained significant media coverage and brought Aboriginal issues back to the spotlight of Canadian politics. Like the patriation of the Constitution, it brought non-Aboriginal bystanders into the negotiation of grievances. Because Harper's fight was based within the country's legal structures, was grounded in the discourse of the greater Canadian society, appealed to common sense, and was against an agreement many Canadians also did not accept, his plight resonated within the dominant society, incorporating them as supportive bystanders. It aligned Aboriginal interests to the dominant population's master frame.

Aboriginal people saw Harper's stand as a tremendous achievement, signalling their ability to resist unequal relations. They celebrated the failure of the Meech Lake Accord across the country and Harper's action bridged differences among Aboriginals, building a broader imagined community. It drew bystanders into organizations, led to contentious action, and brought communities together. Aboriginal novelist Lee Maracle describes the significance of his actions in her novel *Sundogs*, where the main protagonist tells readers:

If Elijah upset Canada, he upset me a great deal more. His message was profoundly simple; we are worth fighting for, we are worth caring for, we are worthy.... [As Elijah Harper said on the nightly news,] 'When Native people struggle for their rights, they do not do so at someone else's expense, because our rights, the denial of them, is intimately bound to the mistreatment of the aged, the handicapped, women, and the abuse and neglect of children and poor and working people. Our whole philosophy, our way of being, precludes the mistreatment of anyone. Canada has not only erased us as a people, but it has cut its own people off from learning from us, and Canadians have much to learn from us.' That is how I hear your words Elijah Harper from Red Sucker Creek. Those words upset me. I have lived twenty years on this earth making faces at my mother's sense of justice and I live in terror of my sister's womanly consciousness and you stand there Elijah and affirm everything I know is dangerous to think, feel, or believe. (Maracle, 1992: 77)

In essence, Harper's action was a critical event that transcended divisions among Aboriginal peoples and the rest of Canada. He was a charismatic figure who actively managed the political opportunity presented by the ratification process. This in turn led to frame extension and alignment of interests. His message was simple: Aboriginal people were left out and it was time they were included. Across the country his voice and image echoed on national television. He stood in the Manitoba legislature, feather in hand, grinding years of constitutional negotiation to a halt. He delivered cogent arguments that were inclusive, triggering a critical event. He aligned Aboriginal issues to broader interests and raised a consciousness that became even more pronounced later that summer.

Less than a month after the Meech Lake Accord's defeat, Mohawks in Kanesatake, Quebec, faced off against provincial police in a violent standoff dubbed the 'Oka crisis'. The Sûreté du Québec (SQ) attempted to break a roadblock outside the town of Oka, erected by Mohawks from Kanesatake to prevent expansion of a golf course on land they claimed was a traditional burial ground. When the SQ moved in with force, Mohawk warriors defended the roadblock, exchanging gunfire that left one SQ officer dead and resulted in a 78-day armed standoff. Mohawk warriors, from the neighbouring community of Kahnawake, in support, blocked roads going into their reserve and the Mercier Bridge, a major link between the suburbs of Montreal and the city. The standoff escalated over the summer to the point where the Canadian army was brought in to quell the protest.

Like Harper's actions, the Mohawk action gained increasing media coverage, which again raised the profile of Aboriginal issues. It opened the public sphere to their grievances and created a shared collective action frame. Because the standoffs happened soon after Harper's victory, it gave the appearance of a powerful and well-connected Aboriginal movement. Likewise, because the events in Kanesatake and Kahnawake took place within the suburbs of Montreal and were violent in nature, they brought Aboriginal issues to the attention of national media and a wide array of bystander publics. These actions were another critical event that Canadians watched unfold on their televisions and, like Harper's feather in hand, the standoffs produced many sound bites and images sparking intense mobilization.

The period was branded the 'Indian summer' because Aboriginals in communities across the country protested in support of the Mohawks in Kanesatake and Kahnawake. To give just a few examples, members of the Six Nations Reserve in southern Ontario erected blockades on highways and across Canadian National rail lines, threatening to maintain them until the Canadian army pulled out of Oka; likewise, 50 aboriginals on the Bruce Peninsula in southwestern Ontario set up a roadblock to their community to put pressure on the federal government to act; Aboriginals at the Tyendinaga Reserve near Belleville in eastern Ontario blocked a bridge to Prince Edward County in support; and Ojibwa from the Saugeen and Cape Croker reserves set up road blocks as well (*Globe and Mail*, 6 Sept. 1990). Even non-Aboriginals and the international community showed support for resolving the conflict; for instance, the Paris-based International Human Rights Federation sent observers to monitor the conflict (Poirier, 1990).

The standoff ended in the fall of that year and the federal government responded by announcing a Royal Commission on Aboriginal Peoples a year later. It was given the mandate of investigating the evolution of the relationship among Canada's Aboriginal peoples, the Canadian government, and society as a whole (Indian and Northern Affairs Canada, 1996). It was one of the largest commissions conducted in Canada and lasted several years, offering unprecedented visibility for national Aboriginal organizations and their leaders. This led to seats at the negotiating table of the Charlottetown Accord, which was another attempt to resolve outstanding constitutional issues. Aboriginals were largely successful in that negotiation process, but like earlier constitutional meeting, fissures emerged between national organizations representing different status groups. The Charlottetown Accord was put to a national referendum in 1992 and defeated by a majority of Canadians leading to a period of lower profile for national organizations.

The rest of the 1990s and now the current period have reflected both increasing institutional action, by Aboriginal elites and the national organizations, and the rise of more radical tactics by non-formally organized actors in local communities. On the one hand, the 'Indian summer' created another policy vacuum in Aboriginal–Canadian relations and led to more opportunities for Aboriginals to engage in dominant politics. On the other hand, it also shut out local communities and the voices of those most marginalized. Recent years have yielded much success for Aboriginal peoples, as can be seen in the reaffirmation of Aboriginal rights and traditional knowledge in the Nisga'a settlement of 2000, the 1999 *Marshall* and 2003 *Powley* decisions on Aboriginal fishing rights and Métis hunting rights, the official recognition of 21 June as National Aboriginal Day, and the funding of an Aboriginal Healing Fund. At the same time, however, recent years are also characterized by violent actions, as at Ipperwash, Caledonia, and Gustafsen Lake in Ontario and British Columbia, as well as the Mi'kmaq lobster fishery crisis across Atlantic Canada. Divergent interests among Aboriginals continue to present obstacles to widespread or unified mobilization and shared identity (Lawrence, 2003).

INTERNATIONAL ATTENTION AND NATIONS *WITHIN* NATIONS

While the 1970s were characterized by the intense mobilization of the AIM in the US, the 1980s onward were relatively uneventful in terms of indigenous protest in that country. By contrast, internationally a number of opportunities began to emerge. For example, the Working Group on Indigenous Populations was founded in 1982 at the UN; in 1989, the International Labour Organization issued convention 169 on Indigenous and Tribal Peoples in Independent Countries, opening opportunities for Aboriginals to pursue their grievances in an international forum (Speed and Collier, 2000: 881). The year 1992 was significant because of two events, the first being the Rio Earth Summit, which bridged environmental, human rights, and indigenous movements (Morgan, 2004: 495). Second, the year was marked by large numbers of indigenous peoples protesting against the quincentennial anniversary of 'discovering' the Americas (Brysk and Wise, 1997: 95; Collier and Collier, 2005: 456). In fact, significant protests were observed in many countries, with large rallies in Mexico. Whereas mobilization in the US was less apparent during these years, it gained momentum in Mexico and the rest of Latin America throughout the 1990s.

International opportunities increased further in 1993, when the UN declared it the international year of the world's indigenous people, followed by the announcement of the international decade (1995–2004) of the world's indigenous people (www.unhchr.ch/html/menu6/2/fs9.htm). These actions provided an international forum for indigenous activists to meet, share information, create networks, and pressure national governments to address their issues. It allowed Aboriginal peoples an opportunity to question the 'citizenship regimes' of countries and pursue status as nations *within* nations, aiming for self-determination within existing nation-states rather than outright independence. This can be seen in the lobbying of the international community and the United Nations by the James Bay Cree during this period (Niezen, 2000; Jenson and Papillon, 2000). Their actions did not lead to increased sovereignty but did raise their profile in the national consciousness. Elsewhere, indigenous peoples were also using transnational institutions to raise awareness for their grievances. For instance, the Zapatistas announced their rebellion against the Mexican state the day the North American Free Trade Agreement (NAFTA) was to take effect in January 1994 (Brysk and Wise, 1997: 76–7; Morris, 2001: 241; Tarrow, 2005: 113). This event is analyzed in more detail in Chapter 9. With regard to indigenous mobilization, these actions comprised a critical event that gained much international attention and have been heralded by many as successful, inclusive, and transnational by incorporating both indigenous and non-indigenous bystanders to support their struggles (della Porta et al., 2006; Keck and Sikkink, 1998: 115–16; Khasnabish, 2004; Tarrow, 2005). Two years later, the San Andres Accord, an agreement on 'indigenous rights and culture' with the Mexican government, was successfully negotiated (Collier and Collier, 2005: 456); in 1998 the state of Oaxaca in Mexico passed an indigenous rights bill (Morris, 2001: 242), and in 2001 the Mexican government did the same. However, these achievements are far from uncontested (Khasnabish, 2004: 274). The Zapatistas continue to struggle for their rights and increased recognition. Like Aboriginal contention in Canada, their successes are tied to critical events and the ability to bridge differences among communities, which together draw bystanders into supporting their struggles.

CONCLUSION

A constant obstacle for Aboriginal mobilization, in Canada and globally, is the multiplicity of indigenous peoples and their divergent interests. By tracing Canadian Aboriginal contentious action and organizing from the post-World War II period to the present, this chapter has demonstrated that critical events like the White Paper, patriation of the Constitution, and the 'Indian summer' raise consciousness and generate support from bystander publics. Such moments engage many communities simultaneously, drawing them into the negotiation of the event, increasing mobilization, and extending Aboriginal collective action frames.

However, the ability to manage critical events successfully is dictated by access to resources, the creation of shared collective identities, and political opportunities. During the 1950s and 1960s many political opportunities emerged, but Canada's Aboriginal peoples lacked the resources and solidarity to engage them. By the time the White Paper was announced in 1969, creating a critical event, status Indians mobilized and garnered some support, but lacked resources and a shared identity to fully engage it. However, the event signalled a transition in Aboriginal–Canadian relations. During the 1970s, resources and organizations emerged, as did a young Aboriginal elite who took advantage of new opportunities. Thus, when the patriation process was announced, Canada's Aboriginal peoples were able successfully to engage it as a second critical event. Yet, increasing institutionalization of mobilization moved contention away from local communities. Recognition of different Aboriginal statuses and various community and regional concerns also inhibited the creation of a unified identity, and these factors led to demobilization. As the 1980s ended, however, another opportunity emerged with the Meech Lake Accord, and mobilization against it by status Indians led to another critical event, which was compounded by the Oka crisis in Quebec that became the focal point for the 'Indian summer' of 1990.

Overall, Canadian Aboriginals have had success in their mobilization, shifting the discourse away from assimilation, prior to the White Paper, to self-government and nations *within* nations, after the 'Indian summer'. However, their struggles are far from resolved and, increasingly, many non-Aboriginals believe Aboriginal status grants privileges that they are uncomfortable supporting. As Jeffrey Simpson notes, a paradoxical situation exists: 'At a high level of abstraction, Canadians tell pollsters of their sympathy for aboriginals. That begins to wane as the issues become more concrete . . . . As the years go on, fewer and fewer non-aboriginals feel guilty about past wrongs' (Simpson, 1999). Recent polling illustrates this further, with 24 per cent of Canadians feeling that the Constitution has gone 'too far' in recognizing Aboriginals, and 42 per cent saying it has gone 'far enough' (Association for Canadian Studies, 2007). As a result, like before, the Aboriginal peoples of Canada still find it necessary to bridge their concerns to bystander communities and negotiate commonalities among divergent interests. Like all social movements seeking change, they need to extend their claims in an inclusive manner that yields support from bystanders committed to social justice.

Discussion Questions

1. What roles do bystanders play in social movement action?
2. Which collective action frames lend themselves to the alignment of social movements issues with dominant interests?
3. How did resources, political opportunities, and collective identities influence the successful engagement of critical events by Aboriginals?

Suggested Readings

Brysk, Alison, and Carol Wise. 1997. 'Liberalization and Ethnic Conflict in Latin America', *Studies in Comparative International Development* 32, 2: 76–104. This article provides an overview of indigenous mobilization across Latin America.

Nagel, Joane. 1995. 'American Indian Ethnic Renewal: Politics and the Resurgence of Identity', *American Sociological Review* 60, 6: 947–65. This is a key article on Red Power and its impact on Native American ethnic identity.

Wilkes, Rima. 2004. 'A Systematic Approach to Studying Indigenous Politics: Band-Level Mobilization in Canada, 1981–2000', *Social Science Journal* 41: 447–57. This article presents an important analysis of Canadian Aboriginal mobilization.

Chapter 6

The Women's Movement

The 'second wave' of the women's movement that emerged in many countries during the protest cycle of the 1960s mobilized large numbers of activists and created many social changes. By the late 1970s, however, feminism was already being declared 'dead' by some observers, and young women were soon being described by journalists and commentators as the 'post-feminist' generation (Hawkesworth, 2004). Scholars and movement sympathizers also began to assess the fate of the mass women's movement as feminist activism became less visible (e.g., Epstein, 2001; Reger, 2005; Staggenborg and Taylor, 2005). Although many organizations and activities of the women's movement declined after the early 1970s, there is evidence of continued growth: the formation of new types of movement organizations; the rise of feminism within institutions and increased support for feminism by organizations outside the movement; feminist participation and influence in other social movements; the development of feminist culture and collective identity; the creation of new collective action campaigns; and the expansion of the international women's movement. Perceptions of the women's movement depend in part on our conception of a social movement; if we understand social movements only as publicly visible contentious politics, we miss much of this ongoing feminist activity.

This chapter examines how the women's movement has grown and survived since the late 1960s and early 1970s, particularly in North America. We begin by looking at the origins of the contemporary movement in the protest cycle of the 1960s and then consider some areas of feminist activity that originated with the second wave and that remain highly important today, notably reproductive rights and violence against women. Other forms of ongoing feminist activity, including what has been called the 'third wave' of the women's movement and the global women's movement, are also examined. This survey, while by no means comprehensive, provides a basis for a final discussion in the chapter of the important theoretical factors involved in understanding how the women's movement has endured over time and why it continues to be an important social movement, despite some decline and much opposition to movement goals.

Origins of the Second Wave

Women's movements emerged in many Western countries in the nineteenth century as women became involved in various social reforms, including temperance and abolition movements. Women gained valuable political experience through their work in such movements, and they also came to feel sharply the limits of their political influence as women. Consequently, many women became participants in the 'first wave' of the women's movement, which advocated women's suffrage, education, property and custody rights, and other reforms. Although strongest in the West, incipient women's movements emerged in countries around the world and, by the 1920s, women had won the vote in many countries (see Chafetz and Dworkin, 1986). After suffrage was won, women's movements typically became less visible, though various groups survived the decline of the movement's first wave. In the United States, the National Women's Party maintained the feminist movement between the suffrage victory in 1920 and the 1960s (Rupp and Taylor, 1987). In Canada, suffragists also continued less visible activities after enfranchisement, and traditional women's associations gradually developed feminist positions (Black, 1993). In 1960, Canadian women founded Voice of Women, a peace organization that became one of the organizational bases for the new feminist movement of the 1960s. In the US, a women's peace organization called Women's Strike for Peace was founded in 1961, and many of its activists also became receptive to the message of the women's movement later in the 1960s (Swerdlow, 1993).

Although women's movements never disappeared after the first wave, they did not become highly visible again until a 'second wave' of the women's movement emerged, primarily in a number of Western countries in the 1960s. Large-scale socio-economic and political changes, organizational factors, and related changes in women's consciousness were all critical to this revitalization of the women's movement. Increases in women's labour-force participation and higher education, a decline in the birth rate, and increased divorce rates in many Western countries created new interests and grievances among women. Employment discrimination, for instance, became a major issue for the new women's movement. As Jo Freeman (1975: 15–17) argues, middle-class women with professional aspirations, in particular, felt an increased sense of *relative deprivation*; although the ideological justifications for male dominance were eroding, women felt deprived when they compared themselves to their male peers. At the same time that women felt these grievances, they also found *organizational vehicles* through which to organize a variety of different types of feminist groups. These included liberal women's organizations, some of which had their origins in the first wave, radical feminist groups connected to the New Left, and feminist groups arising out of various nationalist and ethnic movements (see Rebick, 2005; Roth, 2004; Springer, 2005).

The US women's movement, by far the best-researched national case, provides a good example of the importance of political opportunity and pre-existing organizational structures, and of the influence of the civil rights movement and the New Left. In *Inviting Women's Rebellion*, Ann Costain (1992) argues that electoral realignments made political parties and government officials receptive to women as a constituency even before the women's movement organized to lobby for change. Shakeups of electoral coalitions, caused in part by the civil rights movement and the desertion of southern Democrats from their party, resulted in efforts by the Democratic and Republican parties to court new voters in order to forge an electoral majority. While urban black voters became increasingly important, women also represented a large block of votes. Consequently, Presidents Eisenhower and Kennedy, a Republican and a Democrat, respectively, made reference in their speeches to sex discrimination without prompting from the women's movement, and in the early 1960s more bills dealing with women's concerns began to be introduced into Congress. In 1961, President Kennedy established the President's Commission on the Status of Women, which spawned state-level commissions on the status of women. When the 1964 Civil Rights Act was passed, Title VII prohibited discrimination on the basis of 'sex' as well as race, ethnicity, and religion.[1]

Political opportunities combined with organizational and ideological bases to support the rise of the contemporary women's movement. Two distinct branches emerged in the US, including an 'older' or 'women's rights' branch founded largely by professional women concerned about employment issues and a 'younger' or 'women's liberation' branch made up of students and other young women concerned about a wide range of issues including women's health and sexuality (Carden, 1974; Freeman, 1975; Hole and Levine, 1971). The older branch, formed earlier and including somewhat older women, spawned organizations such as the National Organization for Women (NOW). These groups were organized in a traditionally formal manner—with elected officers, bylaws, boards of directors, and parliamentary procedure—based on the experiences of their founders in conventional voluntary associations and political parties. The state commissions on the status of women were an important mobilizing structure for the older branch, as many of its activists met one another and discussed their grievances through the state commissions. In contrast, the younger branch created informal organizations based on ideas about participatory democracy from the civil rights movement and the New Left. These earlier movements provided an organizational base and communications network for younger feminists. A number of independent feminist groups formed, including small consciousness-raising groups, which allowed women to discuss their personal experiences in political terms. Experiences of sexism in other movements, and changes in consciousness resulting from their work in the earlier movements, attracted many young women to these groups (see Evans, 1979; Freeman, 1975). Although many of the women who became active in such groups were white and middle class, working-class women and women of colour also organized their own feminist movements through separate community networks, including black nationalist and Chicano movement networks (Roth, 2004).

In Canada, political opportunities and mobilizing structures were also important to the emergence of the new feminist movement. Women already active in organizations such as Voice of Women pushed the government to create a Royal Commission on the Status of Women. Although few women's issues were on the public agenda before women's groups pushed for them, political opportunities were present because the Liberal government was a minority one, with the left-of-centre New Democratic Party (NDP) holding the balance of power, when it agreed to the Royal Commission in 1967 (Bégin, 1992). The activist Liberal government was eager to integrate women's concerns and quite receptive to women's groups that brought together women from Quebec and the rest of Canada (Vickers et al., 1993: 16). Like the US Commission, cross-country hearings for the Royal Commission provided a communications network that helped to organize the new women's movement. And like their counterparts in the US, students and other young women who first became politically active in the Canadian student movement and in leftist politics often found themselves in subordinate positions in these movements. They began to organize independent feminist organizations, beginning with the Toronto Women's Liberation Movement in 1967. Black women in Toronto active in African liberation movements also organized through these movements, and in Quebec the francophone feminist movement used networks of the labour movement and the Quebec independence movement (Rebick, 2005: 3–13).

In other countries as well, radical branches of the new feminist movement built on the organizational structures and ideologies provided by movements that came earlier in the protest cycle of the 1960s, while liberal feminists often had connections to pre-sixties women's organizations and peace movements. Women commonly encountered sexism in the New Left, and they initially attempted to challenge organizations such as the German SDS and the American SDS (Fraser, 1988: 304) before forming their own organizations. In France, young women involved in the May 1968 protests discussed the contradictions between the New Left rhetoric of equality and their experiences as women in the movement, and formed a new women's liberation group, the Mouvement de Libération des Femmes (Duchen, 1994). Owing to the women's movement, which survived the 1960s, New Left ideals and organizational forms also endured, influencing other social movements from the 1970s to the present.

MOBILIZING ISSUES OF THE SECOND WAVE

The modern feminist movement that emerged out of the protest cycle of the 1960s was a new and creative force for change facing a world of gender relations that was very different from that of today. Women lacked access to many educational and occupational opportunities; they had difficulty obtaining birth-control information, much less safe and legal abortions; problems such as rape and wife-battering were not widely acknowledged; and a great deal of sexism existed in everyday life. These grievances provided the early movement with many unifying issues and stimulated the formation of numerous organizations that engaged in a wide range of activities. Feminist goals were not only political and legal, but broadly cultural in that the movement was fundamentally redefining gender relations and challenging cultural attitudes and values as well as seeking to change laws and gain economic opportunities and political power for women. The idea that 'the personal is political' was a central collective action frame for the second-wave movement, which raised issues related to sexuality, domestic violence, and gender roles in the family that had previously been considered outside the political sphere (Evans, 2003: 3). This insight, as we will see, would continue to influence third-wave feminists and the international women's movement after the heyday of the second wave.

The women's movement made great progress in a number of areas, and its successes contributed to a decline in grievances among women and a feeling among many young women today that feminism is no longer so necessary. Because the goals of the women's movement were so far-reaching, however, and because the movement was targeting many different 'structures of authority' (Snow, 2004), the women's movement of the 1960s never really died, but instead spread into many different cultural and institutional structures and arenas. Feminists have been active on numerous issues, such as employment and pay equity, child care, abortion, lesbian rights, the rights of disabled women, and, particularly in Canada, the rights of Aboriginal women. Although the women's movement has changed since the highly visible years of the second wave, a feminist collective identity continues to be shared and developed by new cohorts of feminists, and important ideas and issues developed by second-wave feminists continue to stimulate activity in a variety of arenas. Two of the most important and enduring issues for feminists involve women's health and reproductive rights and violence against women.

Women's Health and Reproductive Rights

Before the second wave of the women's movement, very little information was available to women regarding sexuality, contraception, childbirth, and abortion. Consequently, women who became active in the new feminist movement began educating themselves about their bodies and publishing research about such issues as contraception so that women could take some control of their sexual and reproductive lives. For example, the *Birth Control Handbook* was first published by McGill University students in 1968 and was later revised for the Montreal Health Press, a feminist press. This publication was one of the first sources of information on birth control available in a format that encouraged women to make their own choices about sexuality and birth control, and it was distributed across North America. The *Handbook*, which was also translated to French, was enormously successful and in 1970–1 sold close to two million copies, allowing its publishers to help finance the initiation of a women's liberation group in Montreal (Cherniak and Feingold, 1972: 110). Another important publication was *Our Bodies, Our Selves*, written by a group of women who began discussing sexuality in a women's liberation group in Boston called Bread and Roses. Calling themselves the Boston Women's Health Book Collective, the women decided to gather information about women's health, which they distributed as a pamphlet in 1969. The work was later expanded into a book, which provides information to women in a form that demystifies medical expertise and includes personal accounts by women that focus on sexual self-determination (Evans, 2003: 48). The book was originally published independently, but the collective later signed with a mainstream publisher to distribute it much more widely. *Our Bodies, Our Selves* has been revised and updated over the years, translated into a number of languages, and used in many schools and health clinics, diffusing a feminist perspective on women's health and sexuality to a broad audience.

These and other efforts were part of a larger women's health movement that involved efforts to give women control over their bodies. Feminists critiqued traditional models of health-care delivery, in which doctors simply told their patients what was best for them, in favour of a new model in which women were actively involved in making decisions about their own health care. Feminists developed many women's health centres and services that attempted to deliver health care in a manner that gave women more control over experiences such as childbirth and abortion. For example, the women's movement inspired a trend towards home births and alternative birthing centres and the use of midwives in childbirth. Abortion became a major issue for the women's movement of the 1960s, and numerous countries eventually reformed their abortion laws in response to pressures by feminists and other abortion-law reformers (Francome, 1984).

In Canada, the first nationwide action of the new women's movement was the 1970 Abortion Caravan (see Brodie et al., 1992; Rebick, 2005: 35–46). Before 1969, abortion was illegal in Canada, but in 1969 Parliament passed a law allowing abortions in accredited hospitals, with approval from a therapeutic abortion committee of four doctors, for health reasons. Feminists wanted much broader access to abortion, with the woman making the choice, not doctors. Seventeen members of the Vancouver Women's Caucus, one of the earliest Canadian women's liberation groups, decided to travel to Ottawa to protest the 1969 abortion law. Their Abortion Caravan traversed the country, stopping for rallies along the way and garnering a great deal of media attention. As planned, the Caravan arrived in Ottawa in time for Mother's Day, to much excitement, followed by a march of about 300 supporters on Parliament Hill and the delivery of a coffin to the Prime Minister's residence to symbolize women who had died of illegal abortions. About 30 women chained themselves to their chairs in the galleries of the House of Commons, using a tactic that had been used by British suffragists a century before (Rebick, 2005: 36). The campaign generated a huge amount of media publicity and helped to stimulate the Canadian women's movement, as new groups formed to participate in the Caravan (Jenson, 1992: 44).

In both Canada and the United States, feminists were involved in providing referrals to women for both legal and illegal abortions. In Montreal, students who produced the *Birth Control Handbook* became heavily involved in abortion counselling, as did the Front de Libération des femmes, which took over the counselling to reach French-speaking women (Cherniak and Feingold, 1972). In Chicago, a group of women connected to the Chicago Women's Liberation Union formed an abortion collective known as 'Jane' in 1969 (see Kaplan, 1995). They first developed a list of referrals to doctors who would do abortions and who were considered 'safe' and then worked with an abortionist who turned out not to be a doctor. However, he taught the women how to perform abortions themselves and the collective ended up providing abortions to hundreds of women, including poor women who couldn't afford to travel to states such as New York, where abortion was legalized in 1970. Jane developed a supportive and non-judgmental health service that, like other feminist health projects, was sensitive to women's needs and tried to empower its clients to make informed decisions about their sexuality and reproduction. Jane became famous in feminist circles, particularly after seven of the women were arrested in 1972 and feminists organized in support of them.

Feminists in North America and Western Europe supported many abortion-related demonstrations and service projects, in addition to lobbying for legalization of abortion along with other abortion reformers. Because of their visibility and successes, abortion rights activists also provoked a powerful countermovement opposed to changes in the abortion laws.[2] Anti-abortion movements typically include a variety of constituents, including liberal Catholics as well as more conservative fundamentalist Christians. However, some anti-abortionists are part of a larger anti-feminist movement opposed to various changes in gender relations championed by the women's movement. This anti-feminist movement is in turn part of a larger conservative movement opposed to gay and lesbian rights as well as feminist goals, both of which are seen as threatening the 'traditional family'. In the United States, opponents of feminism battled successfully against an Equal Rights Amendment (ERA) to the US Constitution, which was defeated in 1982 when the deadline for ratification expired (see Mansbridge, 1986). Many opponents of the ERA also became active in the anti-abortion movement in the US. In Canada, some conservative women were shocked when the Charter of Rights and Freedoms was passed in 1982 with an equal rights provision, and they founded REAL Women (Realistic, Equal, Active, for Life) in an effort to counter feminist goals, including abortion rights (Erwin, 1993).

Although anti-feminist activity has been detrimental to the achievement of some feminist goals, including unfettered access to abortion, the opposition has also served to keep feminists mobilized. Abortion, in particular, has continued to serve as a mobilizing issue for feminists as new generations of women defend what many now consider a basic women's right. In both the United States and Canada, numerous challenges to abortion rights have generated much feminist protest along with anti-abortion activity (Meyer and Staggenborg, 1998). In the United States, there have been numerous efforts to pass anti-abortion bills in Congress as well as many Supreme Court rulings on issues related to abortion and battles over Court appointments. In Canada, where the political parties exert greater control over individual members, the issue has generally been kept out of national politics, but local conflicts have occurred over abortion clinics as well as conflicts in the courts. For example, in two high-profile cases in Canada in 1989, the former boyfriends of Barbara Dodd in Ontario and Chantal Daigle in Quebec attempted to block their abortions, resulting in temporary injunctions and court rulings that ultimately upheld abortion rights (Morton, 1992). Abortion remains an important issue for feminists, which arouses a great deal of passion among both movement and countermovement activists.

Violence against Women

Violence against women is another issue of continuing importance that was addressed by the second wave of the women's movement. In North America and in Western Europe, the women's movement played a key role in bringing issues of rape and domestic violence to public attention and in changing public views, as well as the practices of police departments and courts. Before the second wave of the women's movement, rape victims were often considered somehow responsible for the crime owing to provocative dress or behaviour, and rape trials were often humiliating experiences for the victims. Consequently, rape was not seen as a common occurrence because so few women reported it. Domestic violence, similarly, was not considered a serious and widespread crime until feminists changed public perceptions of the problem in the 1970s (Tierney, 1982; Walker, 1990). Feminist writings, such as Susan Brownmiller's influential book, *Against Our Will: Men, Women, and Rape* (1975), helped to spread a radical feminist analysis of rape and other violence against women as means by which women were kept 'in their place' (Rebick, 2005: 69).

In the early 1970s, feminists in countries such as Britain, Canada, and the US began creating rape crisis lines and battered women's shelters or 'transition houses'. They also publicized the high incidence of violence against women and challenged police and hospital practices. In New York in 1971, for example, the Radical Feminists held a 'speak-out' at which women spoke publicly of their rape experiences in an effort to turn feelings of shame among rape victims into anger and action. Feminists also questioned police and hospital treatment of rape victims and legal requirements such as the need for the woman to prove that she resisted the rape in order for her report to be credible (Rosen, 2000: 182). In the late 1970s, feminists in cities across North America began holding annual 'Take Back the Night' marches to publicize violence against women. In addition to creating new services and helping to change public discourse about rape and domestic violence, feminists helped to change laws, such as rape laws in the US and Canada that failed to recognize rape within marriage and that permitted defence attorneys to question rape victims about their sexual histories (Rebick, 2005: 70).

Issues of violence against women, like reproductive rights, continued to mobilize women after the 1970s. Pornography, which first became a feminist issue in the 1970s, was the focus of much activism in the 1980s connected to concerns about violence against women. A group called Women Against Violence Against Women formed in Vancouver in 1982 and soon became active in a number of North American cities as feminists in Canada and the US became concerned about the expanding pornography industry. Canadian feminists made the film *Not a Love Story*, which was released by the National Film Board in 1981 and shown all over North America. Although the issue of pornography created division among feminists, with some organizing against the censorship that they thought resulted from campaigns against pornography, feminists did create a new consciousness about pornography as a form of violence against women. Activists battling against pornography also worked on raising consciousness about sexual harassment. For example, law professor Catharine MacKinnon, a well-known feminist active on the issue of pornography in North America, publicized the problem with her 1979 book, *The Sexual Harassment of Working Women*. Once feminists succeeded in drawing public attention to the issue, they were able to convince government agencies and workplaces in countries such as Canada and the US to implement sexual harassment policies.

Thus, the women's movement brought a number of issues to public attention and created new ways of looking at behaviours that were previously socially acceptable or not addressed publicly. Issues such as reproductive rights and violence against women would continue to be important for third-wave feminists and for the growing international women's movement.

Feminist Survival and the Emergence of the Third Wave

After the decline in the larger protest cycle in the early 1970s, the women's movement became somewhat less visible, and some observers felt that the movement was becoming more involved in internally focused cultural activities rather than in externally targeted political actions (e.g., Echols, 1989). Cultural feminist groups and events did proliferate in the 1970s and 1980s, but, as we have seen, the movement remained very active on issues such as abortion and pornography. In the 1980s, feminists in a number of countries faced conservative political regimes—exemplified by the governments of Margaret Thatcher in Britain, Ronald Reagan in the US, and Brian Mulroney in Canada. As 'new conservatives advanced a pro-achievement, pro-individualist position that ceded little room to competing traditions of collective action, social protest, and progressive political engagement', feminists and other progressive activists were put on the defensive (Bashevkin, 1998: 14). Faced with anti-feminist countermovements and governments hostile to many feminist goals, women's movements often had to defend existing gains, such as abortion rights, and to fight cutbacks in funding for women's groups and services. Despite the lack of political opportunities for pushing feminist goals, however, feminists took advantage of opportunities to mobilize support and to push for new advantages wherever possible. In the United States, after the defeat of the Equal Rights Amendment in 1982, many feminists became convinced that they had to become more involved in electoral politics—replacing legislators whom they could not convince—and new organizations were founded to support these activities. For example, Emily's List was founded in 1985 as a political action committee devoted to the election of feminist candidates and became highly effective in raising money and influencing election outcomes. In Canada, feminists took advantage of the Charter of Rights and Freedoms to litigate for women's rights and continued to push their positions in national debates over issues such as free trade (ibid., 239–40).

While feminists continued to fight in the political sphere despite conservative times, changes in the political climate affected the collective identities of new generations of activists recruited to the movement. An enduring feminist collective identity helps to maintain the movement, but also continues to evolve as new generations of women join and change the women's movement. In a study of feminist generations in Columbus, Ohio, Nancy Whittier (1995) found that different cohorts of feminists shared somewhat distinct collective identities based on their experiences and the political context when they joined the movement. Women who joined the movement during the protest cycle of the 1960s were influenced by the New Left and the sense that revolutionary changes were possible, and radical feminist identities reflected the fervour of the era. As American feminists experienced the defeat of the ERA and feminists worldwide saw the spread of neo-liberal policies, new cohorts became less optimistic about institutional change. Thus, the collective identity of feminists who joined the movement in the conservative climate of the 1980s shifted, and there was 'an increasing focus on personal growth and transformation' through means such as self-help groups and feminist spirituality (Whittier, 1995: 196). The collective identity of the movement continued to shift in the 1990s, creating something of a 'generation gap' between second- and third-wave feminists, but also sustaining the movement.

Beginning in the mid-1990s, a number of anthologies were published by young women in the US and Canada who declared themselves different types of feminists from second-wave feminists (e.g., Walker, 1995; Findlen, 2001 [1995]; Heywood and

Drake, 1997; Baumgardner and Richards, 2000; Mitchell et al., 2001). Some of the authors claimed to be part of a third wave of activism that was already underway, while others called for a third wave (Reger, 2005: xvii). This new 'wave' of feminist activity, which began in the 1980s, was not so much a visible new burst of movement activity (as the second wave had been) as an assertion of feminist identity among young women. Feminism had not died out in the 1980s—it was relevant and important to many women—but young feminists were declaring their generational and ideological differences from the second wave (Henry, 2004). North American women born after the early 1960s took many gains of the women's movement for granted and felt less need for a collective orientation to feminism. Self-declared third-wavers did not reject feminism, but they wanted to recast feminism on their own terms.

For some third-wavers, those terms were more individualized and personal than collective and overtly political. Arguing for an inclusive type of feminism, a number of feminist writers in the 1990s rejected what they saw as the dogmatic approach of the second wave and argued that women could define feminism for themselves (Henry, 2005). Whereas second-wavers declared that 'sisterhood is powerful', third-wavers challenged the idea that women have similar interests, focusing instead on diversity and the need to include women of colour, transgendered people, poor women, and others in the feminist movement. Third-wavers also argued that their brand of feminism is distinguished from second-wave feminism by its orientation to sexuality, which emphasizes 'women's pleasure and power over their victimization' (Henry, 2004: 22). But despite such claims, there are clearly important continuities between the second and third waves. Many second-wave feminists, including women of colour, have also worked for a diverse movement (Henry, 2005: 89) and for a positive approach to women's sexuality (Gilmore, 2005). And issues such as abortion, rape, and lesbian rights, which were central to the second wave, remain critical to young feminists of the third wave.

Although there is much continuity between the second and third waves of the women's movement, the third wave has generated new organizations and activities, including many cultural activities that have a political intent. For example, a group of art activists calling themselves the Guerrilla Girls organized in 1985 to protest an exhibition by New York's Museum of Modern Art that included only a small number of female artists. They donned gorilla masks and took on the names of dead women artists, making posters and using humour 'to convey information, provoke discussion and to show that feminists can be funny' (www.guerrillagirls.com). Since 1985, the Guerrilla Girls have written books, engaged in street theatre, and developed various projects dealing with art, popular culture, and discrimination. Another example of third-wave activism is the Riot Grrrls, a network of young women in the alternative rock music scene that started in Olympia, Washington, in 1991 and quickly spread across North America through band tours, zines (self-published journals), word of mouth, and the Internet. In 1992 there was a Riot Grrrl Convention in Washington, DC, with workshops on a number of topics including sexuality, rape, racism, and domestic violence (Evans, 2003: 216).

The Vagina Monologues, which started as a one-woman play by Eve Ensler, is another cultural and political activity that has engaged the energies of young feminists (see Reger and Story, 2005). The play consists of a series of monologues based on interviews with hundreds of women, celebrating women's sexuality and dealing with issues such as rape, body image, menstruation, and the genocide of Natives in North America. In 1997, Ensler created V-Day, a non-profit organization with the goal of stopping violence against women by acting as 'a catalyst that promotes creative events to increase awareness, raise money and revitalize the spirit of existing anti-violence organizations' (www.vday.org). In 1999, V-Day began the College Initiative to encourage colleges and universities to perform the *Monologues* as a benefit for local organizations fighting violence against women. Since then, feminist students at hundreds of colleges and universities in North America and around the world have performed the *Monologues*, as have hundreds of community groups. In addition to performing the *Monologues*, V-Day groups have held workshops, shown films, and carried out various campaigns opposing violence against women and building networks in Latin America, Africa, the Middle East, and Asia as well as in Europe and North America.

To express their ideas and spread feminist views, third-wave feminists have published books, developed websites, and created zines, which often build on the notion of the personal as political (see grrrlzines.net). In this regard, third-wavers are similar to second-wave feminists. Both have recognized that women's movement activities often are unreported in the mass media and that, when the mass media do cover movement issues and activities, often women are portrayed in stereotypical ways and movement issues lack serious coverage (Goddu, 1999). Second-wave feminists responded to this problem through various means, such as the development early in the movement of an informal rule of speaking only to female reporters and the use of feminist newsletters to spread word of the movement (Freeman, 1975; Tuchman, 1978). Third-wave feminists have avoided reliance on mass media by organizing through the Internet and developing internal movement publications such as zines. Thus, young feminists have continued to engage in innovative collective action, and many issues of concern, including violence against women and abortion rights, provide clear connections between the second and third waves of the women's movement. In Canada, for example, the event of 6 December 1989, known as the Montreal Massacre—when 14 female engineering students at the École Polytechnique at the University of Montreal were murdered by a misogynist gunman who then took his own life—has served as a focal point for annual commemorations that have drawn together second- and third-wave feminists to remember the tragic event and to protest violence against women. Many young feminists are also active in other social movements, including the environmental, gay and lesbian rights, anti-racist, and global justice movements, bringing a feminist perspective to those movements. And young feminists have joined with more seasoned activists in expanding the global women's movement.

THE GLOBAL WOMEN'S MOVEMENT

Although the international women's movement dates back to the nineteenth century (see Rupp, 1997), in recent decades the global women's movement has expanded significantly. Not all women's groups within the international women's movement are feminist, but they are becoming increasingly so. Ferree and Mueller (2004: 577) distinguish between *women's movements*, which they define as 'mobilizations based on appeals to women as a *constituency* and thus an organizational strategy' and *feminism*, which has 'the *goal* of challenging and changing women's subordination to men'. They note that many women's movements start out concerned about issues such as peace or social justice and later become explicitly feminist, while some feminist movements later expand their goals to include other issues such as racism and colonialism. Both dynamics are important to the expanding global women's movement.

The expansion of the global women's movement can be traced to the creation of an organizational infrastructure that aided the formation of transnational women's networks (Antrobus, 2004; Keck and Sikkink, 1998; Moghadam, 2005; Rupp, 1997). Owing to the efforts of first-wave feminists involved in transnational women's organizations such as the Women's International League for Peace and Freedom early in the twentieth century, the United Nations established offices to deal with women's issues early in its history. In response to women's groups, the UN declared 1975 International Women's Year, and worldwide conferences were held under UN sponsorship as a result. In 1975, the first official UN women's conference was held in Mexico City, using the themes of equality, development, and peace. Although this first conference focused on issues such as literacy, education, and health rather than violence against women, sexuality, and sexual orientation, these more controversial issues 'were to appear in subsequent meetings as women found the confidence and power to advance them' (Antrobus, 2004: 42). Most importantly, the 1975 conference resulted in a call to the UN General Assembly to declare 1975–85 the Decade for Women, resulting in a mid-year conference in Copenhagen in 1980 and an end-of-the-decade conference in Nairobi in 1985. On the recommendation of the Nairobi conference, a fourth UN World Conference on Women was held in Beijing in 1995. With resources from the UN, activists met to follow up on the plans for action formulated at the conferences and to plan for subsequent conferences, in the process creating a strong global network of activists. Most significantly, this network included activists from the global South as well as the North, and leaders emerged from developing countries as well as from the developed world. Feminist leadership also came from UN personnel and government delegations, and the UN conferences provided an opportunity for women to interact with government officials and to develop resolutions and challenge governments (ibid., 61).

With each conference, and with the expansion of international women's networks, more and more issues were added to the movement agenda. Feminism was increasingly recognized as relevant to women around the world, rather than only to privileged women from the West, and the feminist movement was broadening its concerns in response to the increased participation of women from developing countries. Although there were important divisions among women from the North and the South, there were also efforts to overcome the divisions. As Keck and Sikkink argue, one of the concerns that first helped to create unity was 'violence against women', a category used to include a wide range of issues such as rape and domestic battery, female genital mutilation, female sexual slavery, dowry death in India, and torture and rape of political prisoners in Latin America. Bringing together these various issues 'implied rethinking the boundaries between public and private' and considering activities carried on in households as well as public and state violations of women's rights (Keck and Sikkink, 1998: 173). The issue of violence against women resonated with many women from around the world, and it underlined the continued relevance of the focus on the personal as political by the second wave of the women's movement. The international women's movement successfully used opportunities such as the UN Conference on Human Rights in 1993 to campaign for recognition of women's rights as human rights and to place the issue of violence against women on the human rights agenda. These efforts resulted in concrete achievements, such as adoption in 1993 of the Declaration on the Elimination of Violence Against Women by the UN General Assembly as well as the strengthening of regional women's human rights networks (Antrobus, 2004: 91–4).

International women's networks have also been active on issues of sexual and reproductive rights, but the issues are complicated and sometimes divisive. Women's groups have opposed forced family planning methods and they have argued against blaming poor women's fertility, rather than economic inequality, for environmental and economic problems in the global South. At the same time, women's groups have argued in favour of safe, accessible women's health programs for all women. A network of feminists in developing countries known as DAWN (Development Alternatives with Women for a New Era), formed in 1984, has argued that women's health should be addressed in the context of socio-economic, cultural, and political conditions (see ibid.; Mayo, 2005). Feminists have clashed with the Vatican and Islamic fundamentalists over abortion and contraception, and an ongoing countermovement, fuelled by the spread of religious fundamentalism, opposes many efforts of the international women's health movement.

Along with issues of violence against women and reproductive rights, the global women's movement has focused on economic issues in a way that emphasizes connections between the personal and the political. Feminists have critiqued policies associated with neo-liberalism, the economic policy championed by countries such as the United States and Britain that became prominent in the 1980s. Neo-liberal economic strategies rely on trade and free-market mechanisms, rather than investment in social services and education, to promote economic growth. Developing countries seeking loans and international aid were forced to scale back government services and focus on debt reduction in order to receive assistance from the International Monetary Fund (IMF), the World Bank, and, later, the World Trade Organization (WTO), which was formed in 1995. Women in both developed and developing countries were affected by neo-liberal economic policies, and the international women's movement was spurred by their concerns. Feminists in global women's networks developed analyses of how women's unpaid labour was required to compensate for cutbacks in government services and how these economic policies affected the everyday lives of poor women. DAWN, in particular, has drawn on the skills of academic feminists to conduct research, prepare policy papers, and conduct workshops at international conferences (see Mayo, 2005: 139–52). Whereas second-wave feminists had conceived of the 'personal as political' primarily in terms of individual experiences, international feminists were expanding this insight to connect macro-level economic policies to women's every-day lives (Antrobus, 2004: 45).

MAINTENANCE AND GROWTH OF THE WOMEN'S MOVEMENT

As the above description of ongoing activities shows, feminism is far from dead; the women's movement has maintained itself into the twenty-first century and even expanded in some areas. Factors identified by theories of social movements help explain the origins and ongoing activities of the women's movement. The grievances emphasized by collective behaviour theorists combined with the pre-existing orga-nizational structures, resources, and political opportunities emphasized by resource mobilization and political process theorists to fuel the modern movement. Once important gains were achieved, it was natural for the movement to lose some of its urgency and visibility, but feminist issues—and, in some cases, specific events—have continued to attract new generations of women. New commitments to an evolving collective identity, emphasized by new social movement theory, along with ongoing mobilizing structures and political opportunities have kept the movement alive. Internationally, grievances created by neo-liberal policies and mobilizing structures and resources provided by the UN and other international organizations have expanded the global women's movement. Enduring issues, and collective action frames such as 'the personal is political', have proved relevant to broad constituen-cies of women. Opposition to the movement from anti-feminist countermovements and governments made it difficult for the movement to achieve some of its goals, but also mobilized feminists to defend against threats to women's rights.

While existing theories of social movements help to explain the maintenance and growth of the women's movement, the trajectory of the movement suggests a need to go beyond theories of social movements that focus primarily on the public face of movements in interaction with the state (Staggenborg and Taylor, 2005). Although contentious politics are critical to social movements, so are the submerged networks emphasized by new social movement theorists. To explain the mainte-nance and development of a movement such as the women's movement, we need to look for social movement activity in a variety of venues rather than only in publicly visible protests targeted at states. And, although it is convenient to talk about 'waves' of the women's movement and 'cycles of protest' generally, we need to recognize that many social movements continue even when periods of heightened protest subside and the activities of particular movements become less visible. In the case of the women's movement, ideologically structured action (Zald, 2000) and collective chal-lenges to authority (Snow, 2004) have continued to maintain the movement. More-over, the movement is still capable of large-scale collective action campaigns even though it does not continually engage in contentious politics.

Much ideologically structured action in support of feminism occurs within institutions. Indeed, scholars have shown that movement activity within institutions occurs at various stages of movement development, aiding the emergence, mainte-nance, and growth of movements. Before the public emergence of the second wave of the women's movement in North America, women working within government agencies, civil liberties organizations, foundations, churches, unions, and traditional women's organizations such as the YWCA helped to push for women's rights and spread feminist ideas to members of their organizations and the larger public (Adamson et al., 1988; Hartmann, 1998). Once the contemporary women's movement was underway in the late 1960s and early 1970s, feminists created footholds within established institutions. In a study of feminism within the US military and the American Catholic Church, Mary Katzenstein (1998: 19) found that 'feminists have created organizational habitats (formal groups and informal networks) within which feminists (mostly women) share stories, develop strategies, and find mutual support.' In universities, feminists have established organizational habitats such as Women's Studies departments and research centres, which continue to develop feminist discourse and disseminate movement ideas to new generations of students. Often, activists inside institutions work with outsiders to promote changes, and organizational habitats may serve as mobilizing structures for the larger movement. In the international women's movement, feminists within the United Nations and national governments have worked with feminists in networks such as DAWN (Mayo, 2005). Thus, feminist activism within institutions has helped the women's movement to maintain itself and to develop in new arenas.

Feminist activism within other social movements is another means by which the movement has survived and spread. As some second-wave organizations declined and women's movement activity became less intense in the 1970s and 1980s, many feminists put their energies into peace, anti-nuclear power, environmental, gay and lesbian, disability rights, anti-racism, and ethnic and community movements, to name a few (Epstein, 1991; Meyer and Whittier, 1994). Through their participation in other social movements, feminists helped to keep alive the participatory democratic tradition championed by movements of the 1960s, and they helped to maintain and spread a feminist collective identity. For example, R.W. Connell (1990) found that feminist pressures in the Australian environmental movement led men in the movement to re-examine their ideas about masculinity and to engage in collective projects. Feminist participants, including young women, have influenced a wide variety of movements, including the recent global justice movement.

Feminists have also been heavily involved in cultural and service activities, which are other means by which a movement remains alive. For example, feminists continue to be active in battered women's shelters, rape crisis lines, women's centres, feminist book stores, spirituality groups, theatrical performances, women's music festivals, writers' groups, and presses. During times when there are few active campaigns, such activities maintain feminist networks and collective identity. Third-wave feminists have participated in a wide range of cultural and political activities around issues such as sexual harassment, sexuality, body image, eating disorders, violence, racism, and sexism in popular culture (see Reger, 2005). Third-wave feminists have been particularly concerned to connect issues of sexism with interlocking oppressions of race, class, and sexuality in cultural and political projects.

In addition to ongoing cultural and service activities, the women's movement also maintains explicitly political organizations and campaigns. The European Women's Lobby, an umbrella organization of some 4,000 women's associations in the European Union, co-ordinates lobbying efforts and campaigns among European and international feminist organizations (www.womenlobby.org). In the United States, the National Organization for Women, founded in 1966, continues to maintain many active chapters and a large national membership (see Barakso, 2004). NOW and other US feminist organizations have successfully organized large-scale collective actions from time to time, including the March for Women's Lives in 2004, which brought over a million women to Washington, DC, in one of the largest women's marches in US history. In Canada, the National Action Committee on the Status of Women (NAC) was founded in 1972 as a national lobby and umbrella organization for many local groups (Vickers et al., 1993). Along with other feminist projects, NAC suffered greatly from cutbacks in government funding beginning in the 1980s and continuing in the 1990s (see Bashevkin, 1998). NAC also went through a period of internal conflict in the 1990s as it attempted to implement affirmative action measures in order to become more inclusive of women of colour. Although the organization elected women of colour to its presidency and executive in this period, the new leaders felt unsupported within NAC and the organization received a great deal of negative media publicity, questioning among other things its ability to speak for all Canadian women (see Rebick, 2005: 236–44). Despite this turmoil, a Young Feminist caucus formed within the organization in 1996 and young women, many of whom were also active in anti-racist, labour, environmental, gay and lesbian, and social justice movements, continued to be attracted to NAC (Cummings, 2001: 312). In Quebec, the Fédération des femmes du Québec (FFQ), founded as a feminist umbrella organization in 1966, continues to expand and change. The FFQ was instrumental in organizing the World March of Women in 2000 and 2005, and has played a leadership role in the international network of women's groups involved in this effort. These national and international campaigns build on grassroots feminist action and help to stimulate local involvement in the women's movement (Staggenborg and Taylor, 2005).

CONCLUSION

Despite the decline of the cycle of protest of the 1960s, the women's movement remains a vital social movement. This chapter points to some important reasons for the continued survival and growth of the movement. The second wave of the women's movement organized around critical issues, including reproductive rights and violence against women, which remain relevant to women around the world. Along with these grievances and collective action frames, pre-existing organizational structures and political opportunities helped to mobilize the movement, and ongoing mobilizing structures, new opportunities and frames, and an evolving feminist identity have maintained the movement. While issues such as abortion have generated much conflict, countermovement activity has also maintained feminist abortion rights activities. Issues of violence against women have united women's movements around the world. An extensive international women's movement has developed, and feminism is increasingly viewed as important to women in developing as well as developed countries. Feminist frames, such as the idea that 'the personal is political', have been adapted to new issues, linking macro-level economic policies, for example, to women's everyday lives. The women's movement has targeted many different systems of authority, and the movement has become insti-tutionalized in many different arenas. Internationally, feminists have worked within the United Nations, national governments, and many organizations and agencies to advance movement goals. Feminists have also worked through a variety of other social movements, spreading feminist ideas and creating coalitions. The women's movement continues to spawn many cultural activities and collective action cam-paigns, attracting new generations of women to the movement.

Discussion Questions

1. How and why might women's movements turn into feminist movements?
2. To what extent has the women's movement declined since the years of the 'second wave'? What explains the endurance or decline of the movement?
3. What are the challenges involved in continued expansion and development of the global women's movement?

Suggested Readings

Ferree, Myra Marx, and Carol McClurg Mueller. 2004. 'Feminism and the Women's Movement: A Global Perspective', in D.A. Snow, S.A. Soule, and H. Kriesi, eds, *The Blackwell Companion to Social Movements*. Oxford: Blackwell, 576–607. This essay provides a historical and transnational perspective on the women's movement.

Rebick, Judy. 2005. *Ten Thousand Roses: The Making of a Feminist Revolution*. Toronto: Penguin Canada. Rebick documents the history of Canadian feminism using exten-sive interviews with activists.

Staggenborg, Suzanne, and Verta Taylor. 2005. 'Whatever Happened to the Women's Movement?', *Mobilization* 10, 1: 37–52. This article analyzes the transformation of the women's movement, arguing that the movement survives in various cultural and political forms.

Chapter 7

The Gay and Lesbian Movement

Since the emergence of a 'gay liberation' movement out of the social movements of the 1960s, movements to improve the lives of gay men, lesbians, bisexuals, and trans-gendered persons[1] have made enormous strides in many countries, particularly in the Western world (Adam, 1995). Gay and lesbian activists have battled against discrimination in areas such as employment and housing. They have also fought for recognition of same-sex relationships, including rights to partner benefits, custody and adoption of children, and marriage or civil unions. Activists have responded to violence against gays and lesbians, and they have battled against the deep-rooted stigma attached to homosexuality. Gays and lesbians have also confronted the AIDS epidemic, targeting both medical practices and governments. In all of these battles, the gay and lesbian movement has met with harsh opposition from an anti-gay countermovement.

Focusing primarily on North America, but also making some comparisons to other countries and regions, this chapter examines some of these struggles to normalize same-sex relationships and to achieve equal rights for gays and lesbians. We begin with a discussion of the origins of the contemporary gay and lesbian rights movement in the context of the 1960s protest cycle and then examine important battles and results of the movement. I attempt to explain how these struggles and their outcomes are influenced by political and cultural opportunities as well as by movement organization and strategy.

Origins of the Gay and Lesbian Movement

The contemporary gay and lesbian movement mobilized in the late 1960s and, like the modern women's movement, survived the decline of other sixties movements. World War II provided opportunities for many gay men and lesbians to meet one another in the armed services, in the war industries, and in the growing gay subcultures of cities, where greater freedom to socialize in places such as bars existed during wartime (D'Emilio, 1983; Kennedy and Davis, 1993). Networks formed during the war helped to support urban gay subcultures after the war, and gays and lesbians formed some organizations in Western Europe and North America before the 1960s, including the Mattachine Society in Los Angeles in 1951. McCarthyism and the Cold War created a repressive political climate in North America and Western Europe, with the result that early 'homophile' organizations took a cautious, assimilationist approach (Adam, 1995: 69). However, public consciousness about homosexuality began to shift with publications such as the Kinsey studies on sexual behaviour, which reported in the late 1940s and early 1950s that homosexual acts were fairly common. In Britain in 1954, the government initiated a Committee on Homosexual Offences and Prostitution, which recommended the decriminalization of consensual homosexual acts between men who were at least 21 years of age (Engel, 2001: 71). In the 1960s, support for the civil rights of homosexuals broadened, as organizations such as the American Civil Liberties Union 'accepted the principle of a basic right to private consensual sex' (ibid., 37). The political opportunities and organizational bases for a gay and lesbian rights movement expanded before the 1960s in a number of countries, and homophile groups such as the Vancouver Association for Social Knowledge, organized in 1964, appeared in Canada and elsewhere (Adam, 1995).

The modern gay rights movement is often dated from the Stonewall Rebellion of 1969, when gay patrons at the Stonewall Inn in New York City rioted in response to a police raid on the bar. McAdam (1995) views the gay rights movement as a 'spinoff' movement that came late in the protest cycle of the 1960s. He suggests that, at least in the United States, there were no obvious political opportunities that affected the emergence of the gay rights movement; after Richard Nixon was elected President in 1968, the political climate became hostile for progressive social movements. In a comparison of the gay and lesbian movement in the US and Britain, however, Engel (2001) shows how features of political institutions in the two countries, which are more stable elements of the political opportunity structure,[2] did affect the emergence and outcomes of the movement in each country. In particular, the separation of powers in the US system of government provides multiple points of access but also multiple veto points for social movements, while the British parliamentary system allows a receptive ruling party to take action and an unsympathetic government to avoid action despite public opinion and interest group lobbying. In Canada, interestingly, the 1982 Charter of Rights and Freedoms created new opportunities for the gay rights movement, but the movement took off in the early 1970s, growing out of the counterculture of the 1960s and using legal strategies to raise consciousness even before the political opportunity associated with the Charter came along (Smith, 1999). Once the Charter opened up greater legal opportunities, the movement was able to make important strides, putting Canada far ahead of the US and many other countries in establishing gay and lesbian rights.

Regardless of political opportunities, the protest cycle of the 1960s clearly had an important impact on the development of a gay liberation movement. Many activists who became involved in the gay liberation movement were first active in other social movements, including the civil rights movement and New Left. They were radicalized by these experiences and ready to apply the new collective action frames and tactics to gay liberation (Adam, 1995; Warner, 2002). The militancy of other movements of the 1960s helped to overcome the previously cautious approach of gay groups and led to new rhetoric and tactics, such as the emphasis on gay pride and the use of 'sip-ins' to demonstrate the right of gays to go to bars without harassment by police (Adam, 1995: 74–8). Before the Stonewall Rebellion occurred, other incidents of street violence had followed police raids on gay bars, but these earlier incidents occurred before an extensive protest environment had developed (Duberman, 1993). By the time of the Stonewall raid, a movement subculture was present, ready to support the protestors and to inspire the formation of gay liberation fronts across North America and Western Europe.

Collective action frames from the 1960s emphasizing 'rights' and 'liberation' were important to the spread of gay and lesbian movements. Although these frames represented different perspectives, which sometimes created divisions between activists advocating the radical idea of liberation and those employing the more mainstream idea of rights, the ideas coexisted and liberationists often used civil rights frames strategically. As Tom Warner (2002: 70) explains, 'civil rights were simple to understand' and the movement used civil rights battles as a way of attracting gays and lesbians to the movement and fighting homophobia even if, for liberationists, these struggles were never an end in themselves. In Canada, provincial human rights frameworks created opportunities for gay and lesbian rights activists to use the strategy of advocating for inclusion of protections on the basis of sexual orientation in the human rights laws. In her study *Lesbian and Gay Rights in Canada* (1999) Miriam Smith shows that, influenced by the American civil rights movement, the Canadian movement used the language of equality in a broad way to develop political consciousness, rather than as a narrow set of legal goals. In addition to talking about gay 'rights', the Canadian movement also began to use litigation as a tactic in the 1970s 'despite the fact that the chances of success were dismal and that the financial and organizational resources of gay liberation groups were meager' (Smith, 1999: 42). Litigation had been used successfully by the civil rights movement in the US, but in Canada, prior to the adoption of the Charter of Rights and Freedoms in 1982 and the coming into effect of its equality rights guarantee (section 15) in 1985, there was little opportunity for movements to use the courts, which did not play a large role in interpreting laws. However, use of litigation by the Canadian movement before the Charter was strategic; it was a way of generating public discussion of homosexuality using the rights frame. At a time when many gays and lesbians were still in the closet, the tactics were important in creating consciousness among gays and lesbians and laying the groundwork for a movement that would later experience great success in changing Canadian laws related to gay and lesbian rights.

GAY AND LESBIAN LIBERATION

The gay liberation movement spawned by the New Left raised issues of gender and sexuality, and connected the struggle for gay liberation to other social movements. From 1969 to about 1972, a number of gay liberation groups formed in North America, Western Europe, Australia, and New Zealand. Like the women's liberation movement, gay liberationists formed consciousness-raising groups, which produced 'immense anger, joy, pride, and a boiling over of new ideas' (Adam, 1995: 83). Gay liberationists did not conceive of themselves as a minority group seeking civil rights; rather, they were challenging conventional notions of sexuality. In the liberationist analysis, homosexuality was seen as 'a natural and normal alternative sexuality that must be liberated from oppression imposed by the church, state, and medical institutions, rigid gender-role socialization, and the supremacy of the nuclear family'

(Warner, 2002: 64). Many of the early groups called themselves gay liberation fronts in solidarity with revolutionary movements of the 1960s, such as the Vietnamese National Liberation Front, and they saw the gay liberation struggle as part of a larger movement against numerous forms of oppression. To tackle oppression on many fronts, gay liberationists felt they had to be militant and highly visible, 'coming out' in many arenas.

Activists engaged in a variety of confrontational tactics aimed at challenging authorities and educating the public. In the United States, the 1969 Stonewall Rebellion was a critical event that inspired a great deal of movement activity. In the year following Stonewall, gay liberation groups picketed a wide variety of institutions associated with the oppression of gay people, such as the *Village Voice* for refusing to print the word 'gay', airlines for their discriminatory employment practices, and Macy's department store for its entrapment of gay men by police in its washrooms (Adam, 1995: 85). Activists staged a number of demonstrations at the sites of professional meetings to protest against the medical definition of homosexuality as a social pathology, and in 1973, as a result of gay protests, the American Psychiatric Association voted to change its official diagnostic manual so that homosexuality was no longer classified as a psychiatric disorder (Kutchins and Kirk, 1997).

In other countries, such as Canada and Great Britain, the Stonewall Rebellion was not such an immediate event, but it was highly symbolic and resulted in much publicity and widely disseminated movement literature, stimulating the growth of gay liberation fronts (Warner, 2002: 66). Gay liberation activists around the world were influenced by the movements of the 1960s, but protests in particular countries took on unique characteristics and organizations formed in response to local and national events. In Britain, gay liberationists tended to be 'far more concerned with personal liberation and cultural development' than with political goals because consensual homosexual relations had been legalized in England and Wales in 1967 (Engel, 2001: 85). For a short time, British activists promoted a unique gender-bending 'radical drag' that included fashions such as the mixing of dresses and beards (Adam, 1995: 90; Engel, 2001: 85). In Canada, the first gay liberation group formed in Montreal in 1970 in reaction to police raids and the closing of gay bars, which took place in the context of the War Measures Act invoked by the Trudeau government in response to the kidnapping of a Quebec cabinet minister and a British diplomat by the FLQ. Gay liberation groups were also founded in Vancouver and Toronto, and a national gay liberation journal, *The Body Politic*, began publishing in Toronto in 1971 (Warner, 2002: 66–9). In Mexico City, a Frente de Liberación Homosexual was organized in 1971 in response to the firing of several gay employees at a Sears store, and in Argentina a Frente de Liberación Homosexual formed in 1973 in response to political changes after the end of a dictatorship (Adam, 1995: 95–6).

Gay liberationists engaged in a range of militant and visible actions aimed at challenging the mainstream culture and constructing a positive collective identity for gays and lesbians. Movement frames and strategies were affected by ideological positions and network connections to the New Left, and gay liberation organizations helped activists to connect issues of sexuality to larger political goals. Participants were attracted to gay liberation organizations because they provided one of the few spaces at the time where gay men and lesbians could come out of the closet and openly express their sexuality and because they offered a vision of social change relevant to the times (Lent, 2003: 44). As an activist in the Gay Liberation Front (GLF) in London explained:

> The GLF made us aware of our sexuality as a political issue. So I could then see the links to other struggles. I wouldn't put it in the same terms today but then the idea was that gay lib would operate as part of social and structural revolution which was the wave of the future. In 1970 we really believed that the whole world was going to crash down and that revolution was on the cards. We wanted sexual revolution to be part of that. (Quoted ibid., 38–9)

Early gay liberation organizations tended to be very short-lived, however, as they often lacked sustaining organizational structures. They were also torn apart by internal conflicts, such as ideological debates and conflicts over sexism. Because gay liberation groups tended to be preoccupied with issues affecting gay men, lesbians in the early 1970s began withdrawing from gay liberation groups and forming autonomous organizations in many countries (Adam, 1995: 99). Whereas gay men enjoyed many of the privileges of other men, lesbians suffered from the discrimination that affected all women, and they were drawn in large numbers to the women's movement. Lesbian feminists created many alternative institutions, such as women's bookstores, presses, music festivals, and theatres that became part of 'cultural feminism' after the early years of the women's liberation movement (Echols, 1989).

The gay liberation movement did not end with the decline of its early organizations, but it did change its strategies. Gay liberationists had wanted to overcome set categories of gender and sexuality, but the goal of liberating sexuality conflicted with the need to create a lesbian and gay identity for political purposes (Smith, 1999: 45). Ironically, liberationists ended up helping to create gay communities and a gay identity (Epstein, 1999: 42). While lesbians created women's communities, gay male culture in major cities came to be organized around gay services, restaurants, bars, bathhouses, and other community organizations and businesses. Armstrong (2002) argues that gay activism in San Francisco underwent an important transformation with the decline of the New Left; the movement became focused on gay pride and identity, but in a way that promoted the acceptance of sexual and political diversity, including the pursuit of equal rights as one way of expressing gay identity and protecting individual differences. In San Francisco and other cities, the number of gay and lesbian cultural and political organizations expanded dramatically in the 1970s, creating a strong basis for the ongoing movement. Gay liberationists remained involved in spreading gay culture in the major cities of North America and Western Europe and continued their involvement in new political organizations founded after the early 1970s. Successor organizations to the GLF groups abandoned their attempts to link gay rights to a larger revolutionary movement, however, and focused on activism surrounding specific gay issues, particularly civil rights, as a strategy for building a movement and providing opportunities for visible collective actions such as demonstrations (Warner, 2002: 68–70).

STRUGGLES FOR EQUAL RIGHTS

Gay and lesbian activists have made great gains in liberal democracies by presenting themselves as a quasi-ethnic group and framing their demands in terms of civil rights. Gay rights activists built national organizations, such as the National Gay and Lesbian Task Force (NGLTF) in the United States and Equality for Gays and Lesbians Everywhere (EGALE) in Canada, as well as local and regional groups, to engage in legislative, judicial, and electoral campaigns. They also pressured businesses, churches, professional associations, and other organizations to adopt non-discriminatory policies. And, as gay and lesbian movement culture and political campaigns became increasingly visible, an anti-gay countermovement mobilized in response.

Beginning in the 1970s, gay and lesbian activists waged campaigns to outlaw discrimination in areas such as housing, employment, and government services through local and state or provincial legislation, ballot initiatives, referendums, and attempts to add sexual orientation to municipal, state or provincial, and national human rights charters. Gay and lesbian rights groups also filed lawsuits to support individuals against discrimination and to attempt to overturn legislation, such as sodomy laws in the United States, which permitted police harassment and arrests of sexual minorities. In Canada, Quebec became the first province to add sexual orientation to its human rights code in 1977, after the election of the Parti Québécois (PQ) in 1976 and in the wake of public outrage at a massive police raid of a gay bar in Montreal (Warner, 2002: 148–9). However, other provinces and territories did not follow suit until the 1980s and 1990s, in part because of backlash against gay and lesbian rights campaigns.

An important source of opposition came from the United States in the late 1970s, where the anti-gay countermovement employed the conservative master frame of protection of the 'traditional family'. In 1977, an anti-gay rights organization called Save Our Children spearheaded a successful campaign in Dade County, Florida, to repeal a new civil rights ordinance that prohibited discrimination on the basis of sexual orientation. The anti-gay rights campaign was headed by former Miss America and evangelist singer Anita Bryant, who went on a speaking tour in the United States and Canada following the countermovement victory in Dade County and helped to defeat gay rights ordinances in several other US cities, including St Paul, Minnesota, Wichita, Kansas, and Eugene, Oregon (Adam, 1995). Bryant was invited to Canada by Ken Campbell, a Christian minister from Milton, Ontario, who campaigned with Bryant against human rights legislation for gays and lesbians on the grounds that homosexuals recruited children and undermined families (Warner, 2002: 136). Around the same time, criminal charges were laid against *The Body Politic* for its publication of an article about intergenerational sex between men and boys, and the murder of a shoeshine boy in Toronto in 1977 was depicted by the press as the act of 'depraved' homosexuals. Police raids against gay bars also intensified in Canada during this period, as they did in other countries, such as Australia, creating a climate of anti-gay repression (Adam, 1995: 124–7).

The rise of a countermovement often helps to increase movement mobilization, and the gay and lesbian rights movement rallied in response to the threats. In Canada, the Anita Bryant crusade 'provided unprecedented opportunity' for gays and lesbians to organize a Coalition to Stop Anita Bryant, to gain a huge amount of media exposure, and to galvanize gay and lesbian communities in cities across the country where Bryant spoke (Warner, 2002: 136–7). Anita Bryant was at the time the national spokesperson for Florida orange growers, and gay and lesbian activists in North America launched a boycott of Florida oranges to protest her role as a crusader against gay rights. In response to the controversy, Bryant was dismissed from her job with the orange growers, while gay and lesbian groups flourished as they battled the countermovement. In California, where Harvey Milk was elected as the first openly gay city supervisor in San Francisco in 1977, the movement organized to defeat an anti-gay rights initiative sponsored by state senator John Briggs, known as the Briggs Initiative, which would have outlawed the employment of gay and lesbian teachers and prohibited positive discussion of homosexuality in the schools. The campaign featured public debates between Harvey Milk and John Briggs and resulted in a strong show of support for gays and lesbians by unions and ethnic group leaders. When Harvey Milk, along with San Francisco Mayor George Moscone, was murdered in 1978 and his killer was convicted only of manslaughter, the movement responded with rage, rather than retreating in the face of repression as gays and lesbians had done in earlier periods (Adam, 1995: 114).

Since the 1970s, gay and lesbian rights groups have made great strides in achieving anti-discrimination measures, although they have also continued to provoke opposition. In the United States, a study of gay and anti-gay rights efforts between 1974 and 1994 found that gay rights advocates were more successful overall than their opponents and increasingly so over time (Werum and Winders, 2001). Most battles were fought at the state and local levels, rather than the federal level, and gay rights supporters were particularly successful in passing local ordinances prohibiting discrimination and in using the state legislatures and courts to secure rights. Anti-gay activists were most successful with ballot initiatives and referendums, which allowed them to arouse public fears about gay rights.

Movement strategies have varied, depending on the state of the opposition as well as the state of the movement. In a study comparing campaigns for gay and lesbian rights ordinances in several locations in the United States, Mary Bernstein (1997) found that activists made different choices as to whether to celebrate or suppress their differences from the majority, depending on the structure of movement organizations, their access to the polity, and the nature of the opposition. In New York City in 1971, gay activists attempted to add 'sexual orientation' to the city's human rights ordinance using theatrical tactics borrowed from the repertoire of the sixties, such as infiltrations of meetings in order to 'zap' or bombard public officials with questions about police raids and discriminatory policies. Activists in Eugene and Portland, Oregon, also waged campaigns for anti-discrimination laws in the 1970s, but they chose very different strategies, discouraging mass participation in favour of private meetings with elected officials.

Bernstein argues that these sharply different strategies can be explained by the needs of New York activists to build participatory organizations, their lack of a strong infrastructure, and their lack of access to political authorities. Whereas New York activists were trying to build a movement, Oregon activists had more resources and business connections to elected officials. In Vermont in the 1980s, activists also enjoyed positive relations with government officials, and they engaged in strategies aimed at educating public officials about the need for policy change. In places where opponents became more organized, however, strategies shifted. After a virulent countermovement formed in Oregon, and hate crimes against gays and lesbians increased dramatically in the late 1980s and early 1990s, the movement became divided. Some activists focused on abstract principles of equality, stressing the similarity of gays and lesbians to other citizens, while groups such as Queer Nation and Bigot Busters became more militant in confronting the dominant society and stressing an alternative collective identity (Bernstein, 1997: 555).

As gay and lesbian movements became more widespread and activists became more confident, they responded boldly to opposition. In 1991, for example, the Cracker Barrel restaurant chain issued a policy against the employment of 'homosexuals' and then fired a number of gay and lesbian employees in locales in the US that lacked gay rights ordinances prohibiting discrimination (Raeburn, 2004: 43). In response, movement activists quickly held demonstrations and sit-ins at Cracker Barrel restaurants and called for a boycott of the chain. Consequently, shareholders rebelled against the discriminatory policy, the national media gave extensive coverage to the story, and the company eventually rescinded the policy. The incident helped to publicize gay and lesbian employee grievances and resulted in a great deal of moral outrage, which helped to further mobilize the movement (ibid., 45). Thus, opposition can actually help a movement by arousing emotions and stimulating strategic responses.

At the federal level in the United States, lesbian and gay rights advocates have had a more difficult time, both in the courts and in Congress (see Engel, 2001; Rayside, 1998; Rimmerman, 2002). During the conservative Reagan era of the 1980s and the one-term George H.W. Bush administration of the late eighties and early nineties, there was little national opportunity for progress, and the Christian right continued to thrive. After the election of President Bill Clinton in 1992, the friendlier Democratic administration provided more political opportunity to the movement, but issues such as the proposed end of the military ban on gays and lesbians also helped the right to mobilize strong opposition. Consequently, the movement failed to win a full lifting of the military ban on homosexuals—instead, a 'don't ask, don't tell' policy won the day in the American military—and passage of the Employment Discrimination Act in 1996 was blocked in Congress, while a federal Defense of Marriage Act that prohibited same-sex marriages was passed in the same year. Following the lead of the American civil rights movement, gay rights activists tried to use the courts to establish civil rights, but progress was slow. Although many American states quietly dropped laws prohibiting sodomy, a challenge to Georgia's sodomy law by a man who was arrested for having consensual sex with another man in his own home failed when the US Supreme Court in the 1986 *Bowers v. Hardwick* case refused to grant protection to sexual minorities (Pierceson, 2005: 23). It was not until 2003 that the Supreme Court in *Lawrence v. Texas* finally overturned 14 remaining state sodomy laws in a case that provided strong impetus to the anti-gay rights movement.

In Canada, sodomy as an indictable offence was dropped from the Criminal Code in 1969, influenced no doubt by the British precedent (ibid., 172), as part of a package of family law reforms. After introducing the amendments to the Criminal Code in December 1967, then Justice Minister Pierre Trudeau famously remarked to the media that 'there's no place for the state in the bedrooms of the nation.' Although this comment attracted much attention, there was little public conflict over the change as support for decriminalizing homosexual acts among consenting adults already existed in Canada (Warner, 2002: 44–5). In the 1970s, the gay and lesbian movement continued to generate further support for gay and lesbian rights. Even though there was little opportunity in Canada to make progress on gay and lesbian rights through the courts prior to adoption of the Charter of Rights and Freedoms, Canadian activists used litigation in the 1970s to create public awareness and to raise consciousness and create a political identity among Canadian gays and lesbians (Smith, 1999). At the same time, the movement took advantage of other opportunities for change, such as the creation of provincial and federal human rights commissions, which activists lobbied for inclusion of sexual orientation as a prohibited ground of discrimination in human rights codes. After the equality rights provisions of the Charter of Rights and Freedoms came into effect in 1985, the role of the courts in Canada expanded greatly and movements had new opportunities to use litigation to bring about legal change. Between 1986 and 1999, despite opposition from anti-gay rights forces, the movement succeeded in getting the federal government, all provinces, and one territory to amend their human rights laws to prohibit discrimination on the grounds of sexual orientation (Warner, 2002: 197).

Outside of North America, gay and lesbian activists also struggled for and won changes in human rights laws and other civil liberties measures. In 1984, the European Parliament adopted a comprehensive position on the civil rights of gays and lesbians, and a number of European countries, including France, Denmark, Sweden, Norway, and the Netherlands, passed anti-discrimination and anti-hate crime legislation in the 1980s and early 1990s. In New Zealand, a national human rights law was passed in 1993, despite an intensive anti-gay campaign by religious conservatives when male homosexual relations were decriminalized in the mid-1980s (Adam, 1995: 132–3). In countries other than advanced capitalist ones, in regions such as Latin America, Asia, and Africa, gay and lesbian groups have organized, but they often face a great deal of state repression and societal condemnation (Adam, 1995: 165–76). International organizations, such as the International Lesbian and Gay Association, have formed to assist in the promotion of human rights worldwide.

AIDS ACTIVISM AND QUEER POLITICS

The AIDS crisis that began in the early 1980s profoundly affected the gay and lesbian movement in both negative and positive ways. Most obviously, AIDS led to the deaths of many gay activists and leaders. The spread of the disease also prompted increased opposition from the right in countries such as the United States, Canada, and Britain. On both sides of the Atlantic, gays were attacked for engaging in unnatural and dangerous behaviour that resulted in the 'gay plague'. In the US, conservative politicians and religious leaders spoke about AIDS as 'the cost of violating traditional values' and as 'an awful retribution' (Engel, 2001: 50). In 1987, Congress passed the Helms Amendment to the AIDS appropriation bill, which prohibited the use of federal money for any educational materials that 'promote or encourage, directly or indirectly, homosexual activities' (Rimmerman, 2002: 94). In Britain, the Conservative government introduced Clause 28 to the 1988 Local Government Bill, which did not restrict spending as the Helms Amendment did, but sought to prevent local authorities from intentionally 'promoting homosexuality' or teaching in schools 'the acceptability of homosexuality as a pretended family relationship'. The threat of Clause 28 in Britain had a similar effect to the Stonewall Rebellion, resulting in an unprecedented new wave of protest that included several marches in London and Manchester of 10,000–30,000 protestors (Engel, 2001: 92–3).

   In North America and Europe, the AIDS epidemic and opposition from the political right sparked renewed mobilization and new strategies in the gay and lesbian movement. Owing to the crisis, increased numbers of gay people came out of the closet and gay visibility in the mass media increased dramatically. The AIDS movement spawned a large number of service organizations to assist people with AIDS, creating new forms of gay community. Many lesbians who had been disillusioned by the earlier gay movement were appalled by right-wing opposition and evidence of homophobia as well as government inaction, and they returned to work with gay men (Engel, 2001: 48–9). AIDS movements developed both national lobbies to influence government policies and new grassroots organizations that engaged in a new round of direct-action tactics. The AIDS Coalition to Unleash Power (ACT UP) was organized in New York in 1987 and soon spread to cities across the United States, Canada, Europe, and Australia. Returning to the street theatre employed by counter-cultural movements of the sixties and the gay liberation groups of the early seventies, ACT UP and similar groups engaged in tactics intended to raise public consciousness about AIDS and to challenge the stigma attached to homosexuality (Gamson, 1989). They staged 'die-ins' where activists drew police-style chalk outlines around one another's bodies, likening AIDS deaths to murders and shifting responsibility away from the victims of AIDS. The pink triangle, which was the emblem used by the Nazis to mark homosexuals, was reclaimed by AIDS activists and used along with the slogan 'silence = death' as an indictment of homophobia and indifference to gay deaths.

   ACT UP converted feelings of grief into anger, resulting in a period of militancy that helped to create a new 'queer' identity (Gould, 2002). By the mid-1990s, the AIDS movement had made progress, and some of the anger that fuelled ACT UP subsided. ACT UP chapters were often short-lived and in some cities, including Vancouver, ACT UP was never particularly strong compared to local groups such as AIDS Vancouver (Brown, 1997). Nevertheless, grassroots AIDS activism by ACT UP and other radical groups helped to renew liberationist challenges. Queer Nation was founded in New York in 1990 by ACT UP activists and others who wanted to go beyond the AIDS issue and address concerns such as homophobia and gay bashing. Bisexual and transgender politics, which had often been left out of gay and lesbian movements, became part of the queer agenda, as activists challenged the idea of a fixed sexual identity and the assimilationist approach of trying to 'fit in' to mainstream society (Epstein, 1999: 61).

Queer Nation groups formed in a number of cities in the US and Canada, and they engaged in tactics intended to raise consciousness about homophobia and heterosexism. For example, same-sex couples held 'kiss-ins' in places like shopping malls and straight bars. Like ACT UP, Queer Nation groups tended to be short-lived, but they left a legacy of activism and consciousness in gay communities. Queer Nation Toronto, for example, was founded in 1990 and lasted for about two years, attracting some 200 activists. The group put up posters in downtown Toronto with messages like 'Queers are Here, Get Used to It' and held demonstrations against the religious right, anti-abortionists, and the war in Iraq as well as gay bashings. Queer Nation tried to be inclusive of all sexual orientations and to work in coalition with anti-racists, feminists, peace activists, and others. However, groups such as Queer Nation Toronto found themselves lacking the processes and strategies needed to resolve differences and effect change, and they often succumbed to internal conflict over problems such as how to deal with racism and sexism as they attempted to create inclusive organizations (Warner, 2002: 259–60). Queer activism nevertheless helped to expand the boundaries of gay and lesbian organizing, pushing for greater inclusion of bisexual and transgendered people and raising more awareness of racial and cultural diversity in gay communities. The movement also reclaimed and popularized the use of the term 'queer' and helped to launch the academic field of 'queer theory' (ibid., 262).

RELATIONSHIP RECOGNITION AND SAME-SEX MARRIAGE

As part of campaigns to secure equal rights, gay men and lesbians began pressuring governments, unions, and employers to provide benefits to same-sex partners and recognize same-sex relationships. Issues of relationship recognition became increasingly important in the 1980s and 1990s, and same-sex marriage became legal in a handful of countries after the turn of the century. European countries led the way in same-sex partnership recognition, with Denmark becoming the first country to allow the registration of partnerships in 1989. Since then, a number of other countries have allowed same-sex registered partnerships or civil unions, including Norway, Sweden, France, Germany, and Britain. The Netherlands became the first country to allow same-sex marriage in 2001, followed by Belgium in 2003, Canada and Spain in 2005, and South Africa in 2006.

In Canada, the enactment of section 15 of the Charter of Rights and Freedoms in 1985 provided a major political opportunity for lesbian and gay rights advocates, who participated extensively in the public hearings on equality rights. Although only a few of the numerous briefs submitted by gay and lesbian groups to the parliamentary subcommittee on equality rights concerned relationship recognition issues such as regulations for pensions, income tax, insurance, and wills, these issues became a focus of much of the Charter litigation of the late 1980s and 1990s (Smith, 1999: 80–2). Gay and lesbian activists also organized within unions, particularly the Canadian Union of Public Employees (CUPE), to get same-sex benefits included in collective bargaining. At the instigation of gay and lesbian activists, unions such as CUPE also launched lawsuits to secure same-sex benefits, using the political opportunities created by the Charter (ibid., 121).

Although the Vancouver Gay and Lesbian Community Centre argued in its brief on section 15 that equality rights entailed a right to same-sex marriage, this was a bold claim in the mid-1980s (ibid., 82). Other activists involved in litigation based on Charter rights were initially cautious to avoid the 'M-word'. A court case challenging Ontario's Family Support Act turned into a landmark Supreme Court ruling in 1999, but the lawyer who argued the case, Martha McCarthy, maintained at the time that it had nothing to do with marriage (Graff, 1999: 23). The Canadian federal government stalled for years, but after the Supreme Court declared the Ontario law unconstitutional because its definition of a spouse excluded men and women in same-sex relationships, the Liberal government finally introduced legislation to extend to gays and lesbians the legal rights and obligations applied to common-law heterosexual unions. At the same time, the Liberals argued that the legislation would not affect the legal definition of 'marriage' as being between a man and a woman, and in 1999 the House of Commons voted overwhelmingly in favour of a motion to uphold the definition of marriage as a union between a man and a woman. However, other court rulings followed and several provinces, beginning with Ontario in 2003, legalized same-sex marriage. In 2004, the Supreme Court of Canada cleared the way for federal legislation on same-sex marriage, and in 2005 the federal government followed the lead of the courts and passed a bill allowing same-sex marriage throughout the country.

Although there was controversy over this momentous change in Canada, same-sex marriage was the culmination of years of equality-seeking by gay and lesbian activists that resulted in laws against discrimination and protections for same-sex relations and parenting rights (Smith, 2005: 225). In the United States, in contrast, laws still permit discrimination against gays and lesbians in many states, and same-sex marriage remains highly controversial. Several US states have legalized same-sex civil unions, beginning with Vermont in 2000 after a court ruling, and the state of Massachusetts began permitting same-sex marriages following a Supreme Court of Massachusetts ruling in 2004. However, many other states have passed laws banning same-sex marriage. In an analysis of which states were most likely to ban gay marriage, Sarah Soule finds that both citizen ideology and interest group activity had an influence and, surprisingly, that states were more likely to ban gay marriage if they had previously passed some type of gay-friendly legislation. These findings suggest important interactions between movement and countermovement; movement groups play a key role in making gains, but these victories provoke countermovement retaliation. Thus, Soule finds that 'same-sex marriage bans represent a backlash against policy gains made by gays and lesbians' (Soule, 2004: 472).

In a comparison of the US and Canada, Miriam Smith argues that differences in political institutions in the two countries are also important. In Canadian federalism, criminal law is controlled by the federal government, and sodomy was legalized as part of law reforms in 1969. In the US, battles against criminal laws prohibiting sodomy had to be fought in various states until the 2003 Supreme Court ruling struck down remaining sodomy laws. While conflict over the legality of homosexuality in the US helped to reinforce religious and moral opposition to gay rights, in Canada the debate over same-sex marriage was framed in terms of human rights.

Moreover, the Canadian parliamentary system made it easier for the Liberal Party to push forward the change despite opposition, whereas in the United States the division of powers makes it easier for opponents to resist change (Smith, 2005: 226).

Despite much opposition to same-sex marriage and other gay and lesbian rights measures in the US, marriage became an important goal for the movement owing to new developments in gay and lesbian communities. As a result of the AIDS epidemic, many gay couples were suddenly faced with issues such as control over medical decisions, needs for health insurance, and funeral arrangements, resulting in a greater need for relationship recognition (Chauncey, 2004: 96). Around the same time, a lesbian 'baby boom' was taking place in many major cities, as lesbians began to live openly and to have children, creating another impetus for legal protections for gay and lesbian families (ibid., 105). In addition to these practical concerns, 'the freedom to marry, including the right to choose one's partner in marriage, has come to be regarded as a fundamental civil right and a powerful symbol of full equality and citizenship' (ibid., 165; see also Hull, 2006).

Besides campaigns for same-sex marriage, battles for partnership recognition have also been waged in the private sector, as lesbian and gay employee networks have lobbied employers to provide same-sex benefits. Raeburn (2004) finds a dramatic increase in the provision of same-sex benefits by major corporations in the United States in the 1990s in response to pressures from gay, lesbian, and bisexual employees. Employees who joined together in networks to pressure employers to provide same-sex benefits were often active in the larger gay and lesbian rights movement, and they received a great deal of support from the movement, including extensive research on employer practices posted on websites and national conferences on workplace organizing that allowed activists to exchange information and mobilize support (ibid., 85). Once some corporations began to adopt benefits, others were motivated to do so in order to compete for top employees.

INFLUENCES ON MOVEMENT STRATEGIES AND OUTCOMES

Gay and lesbian movements have clearly made important gains, and they also continue to face strong obstacles. Movement strategies have played an important role in changing political and cultural climates and creating new opportunities for gay and lesbian rights. The strategies employed by activists are in turn influenced by political and cultural opportunities, as well as by the organization and resources of the movement, and they have varied across time and place. Frequently, gay and lesbian activists have focused on achieving equality through means such as anti-discrimination legislation, emphasizing similarities between themselves and other citizens. However, even when pursuing seemingly 'assimilationist' strategies such as litigation to achieve equal rights, activists were often at the same time trying to build a movement and a collective identity (Smith, 1998). Movements can 'deploy' identity for different strategic purposes (Bernstein, 1997). In some instances, activists aim to empower constituents with a sense of collective identity and to create a shared community before they can engage in more instrumental action. In other instances, the goal is to transform the values, categories, and practices of mainstream culture rather than to win specific policy changes, and activists may focus on developing community and collective identity among gays and lesbians by emphasizing their uniqueness and differences from the mainstream culture.

Extreme repression of a movement, such as occurred during the McCarthy era, can lead to cautious tactics and difficulty in mobilizing support, but with the development of supportive cultural and political organizations and a positive collective identity, movements can defend themselves against opponents (Adam, 1995: 115). By the end of the 1970s, when an anti-gay countermovement emerged, the gay and lesbian movement had created this type of infrastructure and identity in North American cities (Armstrong, 2002). Although the countermovement has created obstacles for the gay and lesbian movement, such as opposition to same-sex marriage in the US, it has also stimulated movement organization and strategies. Threats, as well as opportunities, have helped to mobilize the movement and to shape its frames and tactics.

Cross-national comparisons point to the importance of political and cultural opportunities in accounting for variations in movement strategies and outcomes. Despite many similarities between the United States and Canada, differences in the political institutions of the two countries help to account for the much greater success of the gay and lesbian movement in achieving human rights and relationship recognition in Canada (Pierceson, 2005; Smith, 2005). Before the adoption of the Charter of Rights and Freedoms, there was little opportunity for Canadian activists to engage in the type of rights-seeking litigation used by movements in the US, notably the civil rights movement. Nevertheless, Canadian activists used court cases in the pre-Charter era to raise public consciousness and to create collective identity, and then took advantage of the new political opportunity presented by the Charter to use litigation more instrumentally (Smith, 1999). Supportive rulings by the courts then helped to spread an 'equal rights' frame, which further influenced public opinion in Canada in favour of gay rights (Matthews, 2005). The parliamentary system and party discipline in Canada made it possible for sympathetic elites to pass gay-friendly legislation, despite remaining opposition to policies such as same-sex marriage. In the United States, some court rulings have been favourable to the movement, but the separation of powers in the American federalist system has provided more opportunities for opponents to block non-discriminatory reforms.

In a comparison of the British and American gay and lesbian movements, Engel finds that variations in strategies and outcomes are related to both political institutions and cultural differences in the two countries. In Britain, interest groups tend to focus on the executive because there is no judicial review and the Prime Minister, in a majority government, can exert party discipline and control legislation in Britain's parliamentary system. Consequently, under sympathetic governments, British gay and lesbian activists have achieved much greater national-level success in reforming laws related to sexual orientation than have American activists. In the US, however, activists have enjoyed greater success in mobilizing, in part because the American federalist system, with its separation of powers, provides more targets for movements and interest groups. At the same time that American federalism creates more points of access for the movement, however, it also has more veto points and more possibilities of conflict with the anti-gay countermovement in different venues and at different levels of government. These differences in political institutions have structured the tactics of the movements in the two countries (Engel, 2001: 120). The cohesion and centralization of the British parliamentary system has encouraged focused campaigns and a targeting of resources at the executive when the ruling party is sympathetic. Alternatively, when the party in power is not so sympathetic, the European Court of Human Rights now offers a political opportunity for the movement as an alternative venue to the British Parliament as this pan-European forum has established precedents sympathetic to gays and lesbians (ibid., 115). In the US, lack of party discipline and decentralization have encouraged more grass-roots activism and a wider range of strategies, including many direct-action tactics as well as institutional strategies.

Cultural factors are also critical to movement strategies, and cultural outcomes, as well as political ones, are an important consequence of social movements. The political culture in the US encouraged the gay and lesbian movement to frame issues in terms of 'rights' and to present itself as a quasi-ethnic group. In contrast, the British political culture encouraged a framing of the issue in terms of conscience and the acceptability of private behaviour, although membership in the European Union has resulted in more acceptance of a human rights frame (ibid., 135–7). In the United States, the greater religiosity of the population compared to that of Britain has created greater institutionalized homophobia and more need for the movement to counter the frames of the Christian right (ibid., 147–50). In Canada, where there is less influence from religious conservatives, a culture of political liberalism made the courts receptive to the equal rights claims of the gay and lesbian rights movement (Pierceson, 2005). Thus, movements make different strategic framing decisions and experience different outcomes, depending on the cultural contexts in which they operate.

Just as movements are influenced by larger cultural contexts, they also help to change the dominant culture. One of the accomplishments of the gay and lesbian movement is the creation of new forms of culture and discourse regarding sexual orientation. In addition to targeting the state, gay and lesbian activists have greatly expanded the cultural spaces available to them, such as social clubs, bars, churches, commercial services, and mass media (Engel, 2001: 126). This expanded cultural 'field' of gay-friendly organizations (Armstrong, 2002) helps to maintain the movement and to spread the acceptance and inclusion of gay culture within the larger society. As the nature of gay and lesbian organizations changes, so do the strategies of the movement. Whereas early gay liberation groups shared the values and networks of the New Left and operated in a culture in which gay sexuality was strongly repressed, by the late 1980s and 1990s, gay men and lesbians could come out to an extensive cultural and commercial arena and the movement became more open to a variety of gay lifestyles (Lent, 2003: 45–6).

CONCLUSION

The gay and lesbian movement has created a great deal of cultural and political change since the birth of gay liberation in the late 1960s. This chapter illustrates the role of a number of factors emphasized by social movement theorists in shaping the strategies and outcomes of the movement. The movements of the 1960s created a climate of social and political change that inspired gay liberation groups, which built on the networks and ideology of the New Left. Developing in the counterculture of the 1960s, the early movement began to create its own internal culture and collective identity. As the cycle of protest of the 1960s declined, gay and lesbian culture continued to expand and many groups began to pursue civil rights strategies. By the late 1970s, an anti-gay countermovement had organized in response, but this development served to further mobilize the movement, as did homophobia and threats in the wake of the AIDS epidemic. Cultural and political opportunities, including political institutions and cultural values, have resulted in varying degrees of support for gay and lesbian rights in different countries. But with major social changes such as the spread of same-sex marriage, it is clear that the movement has had a profound cultural impact.

Discussion Questions

1. How did public opinion on homosexuality change, and what role did changes in public opinion play in advancing gay and lesbian rights?
2. What have 'liberationist' and 'equal rights' strategies each contributed to the movement and its successes?
3. How do we explain differences in movement outcomes in comparing countries such as the United States, Britain, and Canada?

Suggested Readings

Bernstein, Mary. 1997. 'Celebration and Suppression: The Strategic Uses of Identity by the Lesbian and Gay Movement', *American Journal of Sociology* 103, 3: 531–65. Based on empirical research on gay and lesbian movements in several American cities, this article provides an analysis of factors affecting movement strategy.

Engel, Stephen M. 2001. *The Unfinished Revolution: Social Movement Theory and the Gay and Lesbian Movement*. Cambridge: Cambridge University Press. This comparative study of gay and lesbian movements in the US and Britain employs political process theory and usefully expands the approach with its analysis of cultural factors.

Smith, Miriam. 1999. *Lesbian and Gay Rights in Canada*. Toronto: University of Toronto Press. This is an important study of national gay and lesbian rights activism in Canada, both pre- and post-Charter of Rights and Freedoms.

Chapter 8

The Environmental Movement

Environmental problems are extremely complex, long-term, and critical to the future of our planet and its species. The environmental movement, which originated in a number of countries in the nineteenth century, is faced with the difficulties of maintaining effective campaigns of action over many decades. Maintaining a vital environmental movement involves keeping activists involved, influencing public opinion and holding public attention, creating lasting organizations, and devising collective action campaigns that have a real impact on environmental problems. The stakes are extremely high: beyond long-standing problems of pollution and habitat destruction, global warming is now causing the oceans to warm and the glaciers to melt at an alarming rate, with consequences such as increased hurricanes, floods, a potentially catastrophic rise in sea levels, droughts, and accelerated loss of species. Environmentalists face enormous challenges in tackling the causes of such devastation, and, despite the urgency of the issues, difficulties in motivating individuals, industries, and governments to participate in bringing about the radical changes necessary.

In this chapter, we examine some of the problems involved in sustaining an influential environmental movement, concentrating on the movement in North America. We begin with a discussion of the origins of the contemporary movement in the 1960s and then turn to questions of individual and public interest in the environment: the extent to which environmentalism is backed by public opinion; how active participants are recruited from among those members of the public who believe in the goals of the movement; and how participation is maintained. Next, we examine some debates on the direction of the environmental movement and consider a selection of organizations and campaigns: Greenpeace and such media-focused efforts as anti-whaling campaigns; green lobbies and consumer-based boycotts; and anti-logging and anti-roads direct-action campaigns.

Origins of the Environmental Movement

The environmental movement did not originate in the 1960s, but the protest cycle gave impetus to new types of environmental organizations and activities. Conservation movements emerged in a number of countries in the nineteenth century to promote national parks, wilderness preservation, resource management, and the exploration of nature (Lowe and Goyder, 1983: 15–17). In the United States, organizations such as the Sierra Club, the National Audubon Society, and the Izaak

Walton League formed in the late nineteenth and early twentieth centuries. In Europe, Australia, and North America, campaigns were initiated to connect environmental concerns such as sewage disposal and clean air and water with public health (Rootes, 2004: 612). Canada's first conservation organization, the Canadian Nature Foundation, was founded in the 1930s (Paehlke, 1997: 254). Women active in Progressive Era organizations in North America supported the conservation movement by lobbying for clean air and water, pure food, and public parks, and, in the early 1960s, activists in the women's peace movement raised environmental issues in connection with their concerns about atmospheric testing of nuclear weapons (Rome, 2003: 534–6). Voice of Women in Canada and Women's Strike for Peace in the US created public awareness of the environmental effects of the nuclear arms race by organizing events and collecting children's baby teeth to dramatize the issue of high levels of strontium 90, a by-product of radiation, in milk (Swerdlow, 1993; Rebick, 2005). With the publication of such landmark works as Rachel Carson's *Silent Spring* (1962), which focused attention on pollution from pesticides, the concerns of the environmental movement broadened. In the US, many women became part of a network that championed Carson's work and led campaigns for conservation (Rome, 2003: 536–7). Established conservation organizations such as the Sierra Club enlarged their agendas and expanded their organizations.

The cycle of protest of the 1960s led to a major new wave of environmentalism, providing activists, tactics, and energy for a number of new environmental organizations founded in the late 1960s and early 1970s, such as Friends of the Earth and Greenpeace. Many New Left activists, like women's peace activists, became concerned with the issue of nuclear arms in the 1950s and early 1960s, which helped make them receptive to environmental issues. The counterculture of the 1960s created and supported 'back to the land' rural communes and natural food restaurants as well as street theatre on environmental issues. For example, activists in New York held a 'soot-in' at the Consolidated Edison building, at which they sprayed black mist and passed out darkened flowers (ibid., 544). By the late 1960s, activists in political groups such as SDS were increasingly connecting the degradation of the environment to capitalism and the Vietnam War (ibid., 544–7). Student anti-war activists formed eco-action groups on a number of North American campuses. An activist at Berkeley in 1969 started 'Earth Read-Out', a radical report on environmental issues that appeared in many underground newspapers. Anti-Vietnam War activists accused the US government of 'ecocide' for use of chemical defoliants and bombs that devastated the landscape of Vietnam (ibid., 546).

Environmental activists who came out of the protest movements of the 1960s adopted many of the direct-action tactics used by the civil rights, anti-war, and women's movements. In the United States, massive demonstrations were held on the first Earth Day in 1970, which was envisioned as a nationwide 'teach-in' modelled on the teach-ins held by anti-Vietnam War activists, and campus activists made connections between military activity and chemical pollution (Sale, 1993: 24). The influence of sixties tactics continued in later decades, with huge celebrations of the twentieth anniversary of Earth Day in 1990 in the US, Canada, and many other countries. 'Redwood Summer', influenced by the 1964 'Freedom Summer', was also organized in 1990 to protest logging in the old-growth forests of northern California (Devall, 1992: 59). Canadian environmentalists also used tactics from the 1960s, such as sit-ins, to protest logging in British Columbia in the 1990s.

Greenpeace, which was founded in Canada in 1971 and quickly became an international organization, is perhaps the environmental organization best known for its use of media-oriented direct-action tactics. The founders of Greenpeace were Canadian and American peace activists and journalists from the protest movements of the 1960s. The political context of the student New Left and anti-Vietnam War protest was critical to Greenpeace's first action in 1971, when activists sailed an old fishing boat from Vancouver to the site of a planned US nuclear test on the island of Amchitka in the Aleutian Islands. Because the US test, which would occur underground, could create tidal waves on Canada's west coast, the Greenpeace organizers called themselves the 'Don't Make a Wave Committee' in reference to the tidal wave threat. Although the Greenpeace campaign was framed to appeal to mainstream Canadian nationalism, it was also calculated to build on previous peace movement and student protests against US military tests (Dale, 1996: 16). Exploiting both Canadian patriotism and anti-US sentiment created by the Vietnam War, Greenpeace took off during a period of expanded activism generated by the movements of the 1960s.

In addition to inspiring direct action by Greenpeace and other environmental organizations, students and other activists in the movements of the sixties also supported other forms of environmentalism. In West Germany, activists from the student movement became involved in environmental issues and founded the Green Party in 1979, which became the most successful environmental party in Western Europe. The German Green Party attempted to be a different type of political party, incorporating ideas about participatory democracy into its structure and rotating its members of parliament (McKenzie, 2002: 58). Thus, the cycle of protest of the 1960s helped to spawn an enduring environmental movement that has influenced the laws and policies of many countries, despite the numerous difficulties the movement encounters in achieving its goals.

PUBLIC SUPPORT FOR ENVIRONMENTALISM

Public interest in the environment and membership in environmental organizations has ebbed and flowed over the years, as has media attention to environmental issues. Anthony Downs (1972) argues that there is an 'issue attention cycle' whereby the public becomes alarmed about a problem and very concerned with its amelioration. Once the public comes to realize the cost of significant progress, however, enthusiasm for solutions to the problem dampens. Eventually, a decline in public interest is followed by a 'post-problem phase' during which the problem may sporadically recapture public interest. In 1972 Downs wrote that the public was already starting to realize the enormity of the social and financial costs involved in cleaning up the environment. Between 1965 and 1970, numerous environmental groups formed in North America and there was a great sense of urgency about environmental issues (McKenzie, 2002: 89). After extensive North American media interest in the environment in the early 1970s, which was stimulated in part by the large Earth Day demonstrations in the US in 1970, media coverage of environmental issues dropped off dramatically by the late 1970s (Steinhart, 1987).

Media attention is one factor that affects public concerns and, although there have been periods of heightened media attention to the environment in North America since the early seventies, the movement has struggled to maintain ongoing, serious coverage of environmental problems. Media coverage of environmental issues tends to focus on dramatic events, such as oil spills and nuclear power accidents. For example, the 1989 *Exxon Valdez* oil spill in Alaska and the confrontation over logging in British Columbia in the 1990s were major stories (Hacket and Gruneau, 2000: 169). As Downs (1972) suggests, coverage also tends to go in cycles. For example, one study shows that coverage of global warming by the *New York Times* and the *Washington Post* increased dramatically in the late 1980s, but declined in the 1990s (McComas and Shanahan, 1999). Systematic, ongoing coverage that does not involve major crises or movement-created drama is generally lacking in the North American media, which have difficulty sustaining interest in idea-based issues, and this has important consequences for public attention to environmental issues.

The extent of public concern about the environment also depends on competition from other concerns, such as economic problems. During periods of economic recession and high unemployment, for example, environmental concerns tend to be less salient than economic ones, meaning that they take on less immediate personal importance for members of the public. New social movement theorists have argued that support for environmental protection is associated with 'post-materialist' values, which focus on quality of life and self-expression, rather than 'materialist' values, which emphasize economic and physical security (Inglehart, 1990, 1995). Some countries, such as the Scandinavian countries and the Netherlands, score high on measures of post-materialism and also have high levels of support for environmentalism. Within countries, individuals with post-materialist values are more likely to support environmentalism and to join environmental groups (Inglehart, 1995: 57). However, environmental concerns are also based on 'essentially materialist concerns with safety and security' (Rootes, 2004: 618). Support for environmentalism is linked to objective problems such as water and air pollution as well as post-materialism, and high levels of support for environmental protection exist in low-income developing countries where these problems are most severe as well as in developed countries that score high on post-materialism (ibid., 58).

Worldwide, public support for environmentalism has risen to strikingly high levels. The 1990–1 World Values Survey found that on average 96 per cent of people in over 40 countries approved of the ecology movement. Ten years later, another World Values Survey in a larger number of countries, together with other global surveys, again found very high levels of environmental concern (Leiserowitz et al., 2005). Moreover, support for environmentalism remains high even when it is seen as costly. For example, 65 per cent of the combined global sample in the 1990–1 World Values Survey said they would agree to a tax increase if the money went towards preventing environmental pollution (Inglehart, 1995: 59). In the 2000–1 World Values Survey, 52 per cent of respondents worldwide agreed that environmental protection should take priority over economic growth and job creation. In

Table 8.1   Percentages of Global Public Calling Environmental Problems
             'Very Serious'

	Percentage
Water pollution	72
Rain forest destruction	70
Natural resource depletion	69
Air pollution	69
Ozone layer	67
Species loss	67
Climate change	56

Source: Data from *2000 Environics International Survey,* adapted from Leiserowitz et al. (2005).

another global survey in 2000, 69 per cent of the sample said that environmental laws and regulations in their countries were not strong enough; however, despite the willingness of substantial numbers of people around the world to pay more for less polluting cars, few support higher gasoline prices (Leiserowitz et al., 2005: 26). Thus, there are high levels of public support for environmentalism, but it is not clear how willing people are to sacrifice lifestyles based on high levels of consumption and conveniences such as automobiles. Table 8.1 provides a picture of global concern regarding particular environmental issues.

On the all-important issue of global warming, it appears that significant numbers of people are waking up to the urgency of the problem, but the environment still competes with other issues for public attention. In the United States, Gallup polls show increasing awareness of global warming, with 58 per cent of Americans believing in 2006 that global warming has already begun, but only 36 per cent worrying 'a great deal' about the problem (Saad, 2006: 20). However, a Zogby post-election survey of voters in November 2006 found that, although the war in Iraq was the main preoccupation of voters, 58 per cent of them wanted their government to make it a priority to combat global warming (Zogby International, 2006). In Canada, a Decima Research survey conducted from 22 December 2006 to 2 January 2007, a period of unseasonably mild weather in the country, found that the environment was the top concern for Canadians and that 74 per cent of them felt that their government was not doing enough to fight climate change and environmental pollution (Decima Research, 2007). For the environmental movement, the challenge is to convert this base of public support into the major changes necessary for limiting the impacts of the global warming crisis and other environmental problems.

PARTICIPATION IN THE ENVIRONMENTAL MOVEMENT

Attitudinal support for the environmental movement does not necessarily translate into environmentally conscious behaviour or support for environmental organizations. Because environmental protections are a public good, and because individual contributions to the reversal of large-scale environmental degradation are not likely to make a dent in the problem, the movement is, not surprisingly, faced with a free rider problem. Many more people believe in environmental goals than actively support the movement, and recent surveys suggest that only 10–13 per cent of the worldwide public supports the movement by donating to environmental organizations, writing letters, and signing petitions (Leiserowitz et al., 2005: 28–9). Table 8.2 shows environmental group membership in selected countries for the years 1981, 1990, and 1999. Global surveys also show clear differences in richer and poorer societies with regard to behaviours such as recycling and selection of 'green' products. For example, one survey found that among respondents from high-income countries 67 per cent reported buying 'green' products and 75 per cent reported recycling compared to only 30 per cent of respondents from low-income countries who reported buying green and 27 per cent who reported recycling. However, such results may reflect the lack of facilities and markets in lower-income countries and it is unlikely that surveys adequately represent the very poor, 'who are most likely to reuse and recycle as part of survival' in low-income countries (ibid., 28). Moreover, residents of wealthier countries engage in high levels of consumption and use large amounts of energy.

Despite gaps between attitudes and behaviour and variations over time and place in levels of support, environmental organizations have attracted members and contributions, even at times when environmental concerns are low in saliency because people are preoccupied with other concerns such as the economy or terrorism. During the 1980s, for example, support for environmentalism among North Americans remained high, but economic issues were far more salient. When Ronald Reagan was elected President in 1980, 'there was no evidence that environmental protection was a salient issue to more than a very small percentage of the general public' (Mitchell, 1984: 54). Nevertheless, threats to environmental progress by the Reagan administration elicited a great deal of financial support for national environmental groups. During the 1980s, a number of large American environmental organizations, such as the Wilderness Society, the Sierra Club, Defenders of Wildlife, and Friends of the Earth, experienced dramatic growth (Mitchell et al., 1992: 15). In Canada, large environmental organizations such as the Canadian Nature Foundation, the David Suzuki Foundation, and the Sierra Club of Canada also expanded or established themselves and helped to place new issues on the political agenda in the 1980s and 1990s (Wilson, 1992, 2001). Worldwide, membership in environmental groups more than doubled in the 1980s and 1990s (Dalton, 2005). In 1990, celebrations of the twentieth anniversary of Earth Day were held in 140 countries, attended by an estimated 200 million people (McKenzie, 2002: 65).

Although such extensive participation in the environmental movement is not always in evidence, many people have attended movement events and joined environmental organizations over the years in part because 'public bads' such as toxic dumps and air and water pollution are powerful motivators (Mitchell, 1979). As collective behaviour theorists argue, environmental degradation creates grievances, which help to motivate collective action—though grievances in themselves are not enough to sustain a social movement. Another reason for ongoing mobilization is that many large environmental organizations, such as the Sierra Club and the World Wildlife Fund, are professionalized organizations with paid staff. As resource

Table 8.2   Environmental Group Membership

Nation	1981	1990	1999
Netherlands	11.4	23.8	45.1
United States	5.1	8.3	15.9
Denmark	5.4	12.5	13.2
Venezuela			11.9
Sweden	6.7	10.6	11.7
Greece			11.0
Belgium	3.1	6.6	10.5
Uganda			9.7
Austria		2.9	9.6
Philippines			8.2
Canada	4.9	7.6	8.1
India			7.0
South Korea	2.7	2.0	6.2
Finland	0.7	5.4	4.8
Mexico	3.2	2.8	4.7
Iceland	4.5	4.8	4.6
Italy	1.7	3.3	3.8
South Africa	3.1		3.8
Ireland	2.7	2.3	3.2
Japan	0.7	1.1	3.2
Chile		1.6	3.1
West Germany	3.3	4.6	2.8
Argentina	1.1	0.2	2.2
France	1.5	2.3	2.1
Spain	2.4	1.4	1.9
Hungary		1.4	1.9
United Kingdom	5.0	5.0	1.5
China		1.0	1.2
Russia		1.7	0.7
Turkey			0.2

Source: Adapted from Dalton (2005), per cent of World Value Survey respondents from selected countries who report being members of environmental groups.

mobilization theorists have suggested, such groups make the free-rider problem less significant because they provide easy, low-risk ways for individuals to participate. For example, many people join environmental organizations by contributing money in response to direct-mail solicitations.

There are also, of course, more active ways to participate in the environmental movement, and social movement theorists have looked at the types of organizational bases and ideological commitments that affect participation beyond financial contributions. Active participation can take numerous forms, including relatively low-cost and low-risk behaviours such as attending legal rallies, writing letters, and signing petitions as well as more costly and riskier activities such as joining illegal blockades, participating in 'tree sits', and setting up protest camps. In predicting who will participate in various types of activities, social movement analysts have explored the role of various types of attributes, such as ideological commitments, and structural variables, such as network connections and organizational affiliations. For example, in a study of relatively low-cost, low-risk participation in the British Columbia Wilderness Preservation Movement, David Tindall (2002) finds that people are most likely to continue to participate if they have numerous network ties within the movement, which provide them with information about movement events and issues and encourage identification with the movement. In contrast to research on high-risk activism (McAdam, 1986), Tindall found that weak, rather than strong, network ties and only minimal ideological support were conducive to low- to moderate-risk activism, such as attending non-violent demonstrations and meetings, signing petitions, or participating in information campaigns.

In a study of several environmental groups in California, Paul Lichterman (1996) looks at how political communities are developed and maintained. He found two types of foundations for community in the environmental groups that he studied: 'communitarian' and 'personalized' commitments. In an anti-toxic waste group located in an African-American community, for example, participation was based on pre-existing racial and religious community ties; members of the group were mostly black, church-going citizens who were already integrated into a larger community. By participating in the environmental group, they were acting as good citizens of their community seeking particular goals, and they willingly allowed community leaders to direct their participation in a traditionally organized group. In contrast, Lichterman found that members of a group associated with the US Green movement, which organized in the 1980s to promote 'green values' through Green electoral parties as well as other means, did not have ties to a pre-existing community; they were acting as individuals with a 'personalized commitment' to values they wanted to put into action. Their participation was not strictly instrumental, and the groups they joined tended to spend a great deal of time discussing ideology and creating structures that allowed for extensive participation and the development of collective identity. Although participants were developing their identities as activists and seeking self-fulfillment, Lichterman argues that this type of 'personalism' was not simply therapeutic and did not detract from public-spirited action. Rather, individuals with personalized orientations were developing long-term commitments to political activism that would help to sustain certain types of participatory groups such as the Greens.

This sort of value orientation to political activism clearly underlies many environmental activities. In addition to community-based local groups and national environmental organizations, the movement includes many grassroots organizations that mobilize individuals motivated by a desire to act on their personal values and activist identities. Such individuals often remain active in various groups for many years, even a lifetime. An example of the type of group supported by such activists is Earth First!, which was founded in the US in 1980 by activists seeking to create an environmental movement based on strong commitments to the value of nature (Brulle, 2000: 198). Earth First! became known in North America for its radical environmental values and use of direct-action tactics by highly committed activists. An Earth First! group launched in the UK in 1991 became heavily involved in the British anti-roads movement and attracted activists looking for personal empowerment and committed to social justice (Wall, 1999). In Canada, Earth First! and other grassroots groups have carried out radical environmental protest in a similar activist tradition, such as the Clayoquot Sound protests against logging in British Columbia in the 1990s.

DEBATES ON THE DIRECTION OF THE ENVIRONMENTAL MOVEMENT

Because contributions to environmental groups vary with changes in political opportunities and other socio-economic shifts, the environmental movement has not enjoyed continuous growth and stability. Environmental movements in different countries have experienced periods of upsurge and decline, depending on local and national as well as international factors (Rootes, 2004). These movements have also had varying amounts of success in influencing public policies, and serious environmental problems such as global warming remain urgent. Consequently, there have been many debates over the organization, strategies, and effectiveness of the environmental movement. One important theme in these debates is the impact of **institutionalization**, which generally refers to the tendency of movement organizations that survive over many years to develop bureaucratic structures, rely on professional staff, and cultivate relations with government officials and other elites. Environmental movements in most developed countries are highly institutionalized based on indicators such as size, income, formalization of organizational structures, number and professionalization of employees, and relations with government and other established actors (ibid., 624). The strategic choices of environmental movements are also a prime subject of debate, involving questions about the importance of direct-action tactics versus institutional ones, the use of media-oriented tactics, efforts to influence and work with corporate elites, and other issues.

In an influential study of the decline of American environmentalism, *Losing Ground*, Mark Dowie reports that between 1990 and 1994 membership in the Sierra Club fell from 630,000 to 500,000; membership in Greenpeace dropped from 2.5 million to 800,000; and the National Wildlife Federation laid off 100 staff (Dowie, 1995: 175). The economic recession of the early 1990s was one factor, but Dowie notes that the crisis for environmental organizations outlasted the economic recession. The election of the Clinton-Gore administration was another factor; because Vice President Al Gore was an environmentalist, many people apparently believed that financial contributions to environmental organizations were less important during this period. Dowie also notes a problem with 'list fatigue' in that mailing lists were being overused by national environmental groups; direct-mail solicitation ceases to work when the same people keep getting the same type of appeals from various groups. In addition, other issues such as AIDS and homelessness were competing with the environment for donors (ibid., 176). But Dowie argues that mainstream environmental groups also had themselves to blame for their decline; they became overly institutionalized and co-opted by government and corporate elites. Nevertheless, he is encouraged by new forms of environmental activism, such as multiracial struggles for environmental justice and grassroots direct-action campaigns.

Studies of environmentalism in other countries have also noted negative effects of institutionalization (see Rootes, 1999). However, not all assessments of the consequences of institutionalization are negative. In a report on the Canadian environmental movement, Jeremy Wilson (2001: 60–1) notes that many of the large national organizations in Canada, such as the Sierra Club and the David Suzuki Foundation, have managed to create opportunities for volunteer participation despite their bureaucratic structures. In addition, these large organizations continue to cover a range of issues, and numerous smaller local and regional organizations also thrive alongside the national groups in Canada. Moreover, Wilson notes that there are distinct advantages to institutionalization, including organizational stability and access to government insiders and other decision-makers. In their analysis of the German environmental movement, Rucht and Roose (1999, 2001) similarly argue that institutionalization helps the movement to gain influence in established politics (e.g., through the Green Party) and that other types of groups also flourish in the decentralized German environmental movement.

Related to concerns about the effects of institutionalization, observers have also debated the effectiveness of movement strategies. In another widely debated critique of mainstream American environmentalism, Shellenberger and Nordhaus, in their essay 'The Death of Environmentalism', claim that the movement has become overly narrow in its strategies and objectives, acting as a 'special interest' that lobbies for limited legislative proposals but fails to supply the vision needed to address the global warming crisis and other major issues. They argue that environmentalists need to frame issues in new ways to create new alliances. For example, an overall vision for creating jobs in new types of energy industries, rather than a focus on isolated technological fixes, could unite environmentalists, workers, and businesses. Instead of looking for the 'short-term policy payoff', environmentalists need to offer 'alternative vision and values' to support long-term strategies such as 'big investments into clean energy, transportation and efficiency' (Shellenberger and Nordhaus, 2004: 25–6). The 'Death of Environmentalism' thesis sparked much debate, including rebuttals to Shellenberger and Nordhaus's contention that the movement is declining and public support is fading (e.g., Dunlap, 2006). Although there is general agreement among environmentalists that pressing problems such as global warming require new strategies, many doubt that a reframing of the issues will lead to solutions to major problems. Brulle and Jenkins (2006: 84) point to the power dynamics and financial costs involved in addressing global warming; beyond changing values, the movement has to figure out how to deal with 'the inevitable economic trade-offs' and 'the strong vested interests and sunk costs in the existing carbon-intensive economy'. Thus, the environmental movement faces huge obstacles in developing effective strategies and tactics.

Environmental activists and organizations have waged a wide variety of campaigns and employed various strategies and tactics aimed at dealing with many different issues and problems. The following discussion of a small number of these campaigns and tactics points to some of the organizational and strategic dilemmas facing the environmental movement. The efforts of Greenpeace, one of the most successful international environmental organizations, to harness the power of the mass media reveal that movement organizations can exert some control over media frames, but at a cost. The use of consumer boycotts shows the promise, but also the complexities, of green consumption. The anti-logging movement in Canada and the anti-roads movement in Great Britain show the potential of direct-action campaigns for influencing public policy and mobilizing activists, but also opponents.

GREENPEACE AND THE MASS MEDIA

Greenpeace was founded in Vancouver in 1971 by Canadian and American activists, including some experienced journalists, who wanted to create an international organization capable of manipulating the increasingly global mass media. Despite its beginnings as 'a rag-tag collection of long-haired, bearded men' (Dale, 1996: 1), Greenpeace became a powerful, multinational movement organization through the use of its trademark strategy of creating dramatic events that generate sympathetic media coverage and large numbers of supporters (see Brown and May, 1991; Weyler, 2004). Initially calling themselves the 'Don't Make a Wave Committee', the group got its start with a campaign to stop a US military nuclear test at Amchitka in the Aleutian Islands (see Hunter, 2004, for a detailed account). Led by media-savvy activists, the campaign exploited anti-US sentiment in Canada by emphasizing the threat of tidal waves on Canada's west coast from the nuclear test. The activists bravely sailed an old fishing boat to the test site, thereby creating a 'David-versus-Goliath spectacle of ordinary people defying a morally bankrupt and intellectually unsound enterprise' (Dale, 1996: 18). The campaign provoked an enormous amount of opposition to the nuclear test among the Canadian public and an equally large amount of media coverage. Although the test proceeded as planned, the US military later announced that it would cease nuclear testing in the North Pacific, allowing Greenpeace to claim victory.

In choosing a strategy of non-violent direct action, Greenpeace leaders were influenced by their political ideology, and they framed the issue in terms of the need for organizations and individuals to stand up to corrupt and unjust governments and corporations (Carmin and Balser, 2002: 379). Through direct action, Greenpeace aimed to create dramatic confrontations that would generate media coverage and direct public attention to environmental issues. The Amchitka campaign proved highly successful in this regard, but in adopting this strategy Greenpeace was already limiting its public presentation of the issues. To win the favour of the media and the mainstream public, the group had chosen to appeal to Canadian patriotism and to avoid more radical and controversial issues such as Canada's participation in the Vietnam War effort through the sale of war materials to the United States (Dale, 1996: 20). Nevertheless, Greenpeace's media-oriented direct-action strategy did allow the group to avoid compromising its ideals in the political arena (Carmin and Balser, 2002: 381).

Greenpeace continued sailing ships to confront opponents, including whaling vessels. The organization's first big breakthrough came in 1975 when its ship confronted a Soviet whaling fleet in San Francisco Bay and a Greenpeace photographer captured Soviet whalers plunging a harpoon into the back of a sperm whale. The close-up of 'blood and gore as the huge creature died' was irresistible to the mass media, and 'allowed Greenpeace to use the image to change the way millions of people thought about whales' (Cassidy, 1992: 169). Greenpeace activists, who took great risks, came across as 'a noble and brave group of crusaders up against a heartless and barbaric band of murderers' (Dale, 1996: 150). Once again, however, the Greenpeace strategy required a certain type of frame, in this case blood and conflict, to attract media coverage. In two later anti-whaling campaigns, efforts at diplomacy and temporary success in stopping the whale hunts were not newsworthy (Cassidy, 1992: 170–1; Dale, 1996: 151).

As a result of all the media attention, Greenpeace became very 'hot' as an organization and grew rapidly. Greenpeace eventually developed into an organization with the kind of professional expertise among its staff that allowed it to engage in all of the 'preparation, training and research' that goes into putting on sophisticated 'media events' (Eyerman and Jamison, 1989: 107). This expansion and professionalization came at a cost, however; as Greenpeace transformed from a small group of activists into a large, respected organization, the group placed 'new emphasis on organizational structure, merchandising, and cash flow' (Cassidy, 1992: 170). Greenpeace did develop an effective media strategy, which involved providing 'emotionally charged images to counter the effects of negative framing by the mass media' (ibid., 171). Whereas many movement organizations are stymied by undesirable media frames, Greenpeace gets around this problem by providing images that send a powerful message regardless of how the mass media frame the story. To hone this strategy, the organization invested enormous resources and acquired the technological expertise to meet the production needs of television (Dale, 1996). Greenpeace learned to create an event, film it, and deliver a video news release designed to allow news editors to select short video clips with great ease. In this way, Greenpeace was able to get air time for important environmental issues. In 1993, for example, Greenpeace created international publicity about Russian dumping of nuclear waste in the Sea of Japan by catching the polluters in the act and beaming back live pictures with sophisticated equipment on board the Greenpeace ship (ibid., 110).

Although Greenpeace has enjoyed great success, its media strategy has some clear limitations. To maintain its media expertise, Greenpeace has had to develop a professionalized organization, making it difficult to encourage initiatives from rank-and-file activists, and some Greenpeace activists have become disenchanted with 'the inflated attention they give to media coverage of their events' (Rucht, 1995: 82). One problem is that many serious environmental problems lack dramatic visuals and are difficult to address with a media-based strategy. Complex and long-term issues cannot easily be framed into the kind of stories with narrative structures that appeal to the mass media, and the content of Greenpeace communications had to be limited to 'easily understood and accepted messages' (Eyerman and Jamison, 1989: 108). Because it is extremely difficult for movements to present issues with any nuance through the mass media, another problem is that new constituents attracted through media presentations may have a different understanding of issues than older activists and leaders. For example, Greenpeace's anti-sealing campaigns in the 1970s used images of baby seals being clubbed, which attracted many animal rights sympathiz-ers to Greenpeace (Dale, 1996: 94). The successful anti-sealing campaigns resulted in a collapse of the seal-pelt markets, which devastated the Inuit economy in Canada. When Greenpeace tried to address these economic problems, arguing for a ban on sealing that exempted indigenous peoples, there was a great deal of conflict and many animal rights activists eventually left Greenpeace to form a new organization.

In conveying its messages to the public through the mass media, Greenpeace is limited by media features, such as the tight formats of television news programs and the need to frame messages in ways that appeal to mass audiences (ibid., 8). Some Greenpeace leaders have recognized the need to branch out in terms of strategies in order to address complicated environmental issues. The organization has offices in both the global North and the South, and staff in regions such as Latin America have helped to develop the organization's thinking about problems that cannot be addressed easily with media-oriented tactics. Consequently, Greenpeace has devel-oped a greater understanding of the relationship between environmental degrada-tion and globalized trade and the need to address disparities between developed and developing countries in solving environmental problems. Nevertheless, Greenpeace is structured to engage in dramatic tactics and remains reliant on media attention to generate support. Following its decline in membership in the early 1990s, Green-peace revived itself using its classic tactics in an anti-nuclear testing campaign against France in 1995—10 years after French agents sunk Greenpeace's *Rainbow Warrior* in New Zealand, provoking international outrage (ibid., 9). After France announced its intent to end the global moratorium on nuclear testing by resuming its test program in the South Pacific, Greenpeace deployed its ship and generated headlines to mobilize world opinion against the French. France went ahead with the test, but agreed to a moratorium on further testing and the campaign 'rocketed Greenpeace back to superstar status' (ibid., 206). Although it is rarely possible for Greenpeace to generate this level of attention, the organization has difficulty depart-ing from the strategies that have brought it so much success.

GREEN LOBBIES AND CONSUMER BOYCOTTS

Like Greenpeace, other large environmental organizations also have problems devis-ing effective strategies and tactics. In the United States and Canada, large national organizations, such as the Sierra Club, the World Wildlife Fund, and the Nature Conservancy, lobby the federal and state or provincial governments. In both coun-tries, there are also a variety of local and regional groups and diverse strategies are employed in the movement. During periods when the national government is hos-tile to movement initiatives, as in the case of the United States during the Rea-gan–Bush years of the 1980s and early 1990s, lobbying strategies tend to be largely futile. Corporate lobbies have countered the efforts of environmentalists by oppos-ing environmental regulations and, in the US, by increasing political donations to congressional candidates (Beder, 2002: 34). In Canada, corporations far outspend environmental lobbies and 'no Canadian environmental group has resources ade-quate enough to cover all of the government officials who play significant roles in the typical policy process' (Wilson, 1992: 116). Moreover, even when environmental policies are passed into law, it is often difficult to get them implemented so as to have a real impact (McCloskey, 1992). Consequently, it has been very difficult for North American environmental organizations to influence public policy and there is a great need for coalition work among environmental groups to pool resources and carry out effective strategies.

Green lobbies have played an important role in putting issues on the public agenda and they do enjoy strong public support. Michael McCloskey, a long-time activist, suggests that mainstream environmental groups can do a better job of tapping into high levels of public support by using their own strengths at gathering information. In particular, national environmental groups can use their research capabilities to provide information about various products and engage in marketplace tactics such as boycotts, letter-writing campaigns, and protests at stockholders' meetings—tactics that could be employed in coalition with grassroots groups. McCloskey gives the example of Alar, a chemical commonly used on apples, which was the subject of a television exposé by the Natural Resources Defense Council in the US in 1989. Although the US Environmental Protection Agency had debated the safety of Alar for years, no action was taken; after the NRDC exposé, however, consumers revolted and refused to buy Alar-treated apples, stores refused to sell them, and growers agreed to stop using Alar (McCloskey, 1992: 86).

This kind of consumer power, in conjunction with the skills of national environmental organizations and the energies of grassroots activists, seems to hold great potential for the environmental movement. Insofar as the strategy of harnessing public concerns relies on the mass media, however, the movement risks oversimplification of issues. This can be seen in the case of a tuna boycott organized by environmental groups in the late 1980s to protect dolphins, which are often caught and killed in tuna-fishing nets because they swim with schools of tuna. Many environmental groups used the image of the dolphin as a very sympathetic sea mammal to get the public to boycott tuna so that they could force the international tuna industry to change its technology to use nets that allow dolphins to escape. In 1990, the major US tuna companies announced that they would buy only 'dolphin-safe' tuna, labelled accordingly. While most environmental organizations were thrilled with this outcome, 'Greenpeace began to consider the social consequences of an international boycott of dolphin-caught tuna' (Dale, 1996: 161). Greenpeace had learned from its earlier boycott of seal pelts that the issues were often more complex than simply saving an attractive animal, and the organization's Latin American bureaus also offered a different perspective on the tuna boycott. They argued that the US companies were acting to protect themselves from foreign competition insofar as the industries of poorer countries did not have the technology to avoid killing dolphins and would be driven out of business by the boycott. Greenpeace wanted to try to address these economic problems and look for a long-range solution to the dolphin-tuna problem, but that position created public relations problems for Greenpeace as well as tensions with other environmental groups, which wanted to declare victory (ibid., 161–3).

As this example shows, there are no easy strategies for dealing with complicated environmental and socio-economic problems. Many national environmental organizations in the US and Canada have been working with industries to promote 'sustainable development' practices to save both energy and money. Critics argue, however, that industries want to define sustainable development on their own terms, and that they assume workers will bear much of the cost of greater efficiency in the form of loss of jobs (Adkin, 1992: 138). And, indeed, many businesses lobbied against ratification of the Kyoto Protocol to the United Nations Convention on Climate Change, warning that many jobs would be lost. Nevertheless, environmentalists have worked hard to form coalitions with labour unions and others and to address socio-economic issues in both developed and developing countries. In Canada, where the Kyoto Protocol was ratified in 2002 with strong public approval, the David Suzuki Foundation collaborated with the Communications, Energy and Paperworkers Union to report on the economic benefits of Kyoto, effectively countering the 'doom-and-gloom job-loss' framing by corporate lobbyists, and labour unions backed ratification together with 'Just Transition' programs to assist displaced workers (Stewart, 2003: 42). The Climate Action Network Canada is strongly committed to 'a just transition for workers, First Nations and other communities affected by a change to a sustainable energy system' (www.climateactionnetwork.ca). Thus, green lobbies are pursuing a variety of strategies as they attempt to tackle global warming and other complex problems.

GRASSROOTS ENVIRONMENTALISM AND DIRECT-ACTION CAMPAIGNS

While many large national environmental organizations have become highly institutionalized, grassroots environmental groups have also mobilized to expand the goals and tactics of the movement. Some of these local groups organized to oppose the siting of environmental hazards in their own neighbourhoods—critics labelled them NIMBYs (not in my back yard)—but many developed into environmental justice groups with expanded understandings of the political and economic underpinnings of environmental problems (Szasz, 1994: 80). In some instances, local environmental disasters served as critical events that helped to mobilize grassroots movements. Movement organizations then successfully framed issues in ways that appealed to local activists and they devised direct-action tactics that allowed for grassroots participation.

In the United States, a toxic waste movement emerged in the late 1970s, based primarily in white working-class and middle-class communities and spurred by the saga of an abandoned chemical waste site and its devastating impact on a neighbourhood community built atop the Love Canal, which had been a dumpsite for a chemical plant in Niagara Falls, New York. In Canada, residents and workers campaigned against chemical pollution in highly industrialized areas such as southwest Ontario (Adkin, 1998). Racial and ethnic communities also mobilized around concerns such as toxic contamination and public health threats (Brulle and Pellow, 2006). The environmental justice movement raised issues of racism and inequality, charging that the working poor and people of colour typically pay the highest price for environmental pollution in that industrial facilities and toxic waste dumps are often placed in poor and minority neighbourhoods (Szasz, 1994: 75). This branch of the movement continued to develop internationally and in 1991 delegates from the US, Canada, and Central America gathered in Washington, DC, for the first People of Colour Environmental Leadership Summit (Dowie, 1995: 151).

Radical environmentalists, who were motivated by ideology and an activist commitment rather than being connected to local communities and ethnic groups, also organized grassroots groups in the 1980s and 1990s. Many of these activists were influenced by the philosophy of 'deep ecology', which emphasizes 'ecocentrism' or human solidarity with nature and the rights of nature as opposed to a human-centred view of the world (Devall, 1992: 52). Organizations inspired by the deep ecology philosophy, including Earth First! and the Rainforest Action Network, became active in North America, Europe, and Australia. Not all radical environmentalists consider themselves deep ecologists, but they advocate direct-action tactics as an alternative to institutionalized environmentalism and as a way to empower activists, and these tactics have attracted many participants. Some groups, such as the US branch of Earth First!, have advocated controversial tactics such as tree-spiking to damage logging equipment, which critics argue can also endanger loggers.

Because of their visibility and apparent threat to the interests of groups such as loggers, miners, and farmers, radical environmental groups helped to provoke countermovement activity. Owing to the successes of grassroots environmental groups in mobilizing new supporters, opponents have mimicked their organizational forms. Some artificial grassroots coalitions, known as 'astroturf' for the synthetic grass product, have been created for corporations by public relations firms to give the appearance of citizen support for anti-environmental positions (Beder, 2002: 32). The Wise Use Movement was created in 1988 when representatives of US and Canadian groups, including interest groups such as the American Mining Congress and corporations such as Exxon and MacMillan Bloedel, came together to create an anti-environmental movement, known as Wise Use in the US and the Share Movement in Canada (ibid., 45). Industry-backed Wise Use groups have highlighted radical activities of environmentalists and attempted to recruit to the countermovement rural dwellers, loggers, and other workers concerned about loss of jobs and land. By adopting the form of a social movement, anti-environmentalists are able to claim a greater legitimacy for opposition to environmental policies than industrial lobbies, and countermovement entrepreneurs can appeal to the fears of local activists by painting environmentalists as 'the enemy' (see Switzer, 1997).

Opposition to social movements, particularly in the form of a countermovement, is often a sign of the movement's success (Meyer and Staggenborg, 1996). The emphasis on direct action helped to reinvigorate the grassroots environmental movement, resulting in some dramatic campaigns in the 1990s. In Canada, radical environmentalists worked in coalition with organizations such as Greenpeace to protect the forests of Clayoquot Sound, British Columbia. In the UK, Earth First! led a militant anti-roads movement, which involved many local communities in the environmental movement.

The Clayoquot Sound Protests
In 1993, after the provincial government of British Columbia announced that it would allow clear-cut logging in much of the old-growth forests of Clayoquot

Sound on the west coast of Vancouver Island, one of the most dramatic direct-action campaigns in the history of the environmental movement was organized in British Columbia. As many as 12,000 protestors blocked access to a logging road and some 800 people were arrested in largely non-violent protests. A local group called Friends of Clayoquot Sound, which had been fighting for preservation of the forests for over a decade, established a peace camp, which became a base for protestors involved in the blockades. The protests drew attention around the world, and numerous environmental organizations, including Greenpeace and the Sierra Club, became involved. A countermovement also mobilized; in the spring of 1994, 20,000 forestry workers and their families lobbied the provincial legislature, and in July of that year thousands of people held a festival designed to celebrate 'timber culture', which they felt was threatened by the protests (*Globe and Mail*, 14 July 1994).

Nevertheless, public opinion was strongly opposed to clear-cutting, and the campaign employed market-based tactics as well as direct action, using the resources of large international organizations as well as local groups. After Greenpeace threatened to boycott their products, two British paper companies cancelled contracts to buy pulp from the Canadian timber company MacMillan Bloedel. The BC government eventually set stricter limits on logging in Clayoquot Sound, and the direct-action protests ended, but the struggle over clear-cutting continued. In a boycott campaign led by the Sierra Club and Greenpeace against Home Depot, the huge home improvement and building supplies retailer based in the US, environmentalists deluged the company with postcards, sent an exhibit on the Great Bear Rainforest (located on the central mainland BC coast) to a shareholder meeting, and erected a Home Depot protest billboard over a clear-cut patch near Vancouver. The campaign resulted in a major victory when Home Depot, which has over 850 stores worldwide and sells 10 per cent of the world's market supply of wood, announced in 1999 that it would phase out sales of wood from endangered forests by 2002 (*New York Times*, 22 Oct. 1999). Boycotts also forced timber companies to agree to more sustainable practices, although conflicts over logging in British Columbia continue. Overall, the movement campaign made important gains by building on favourable public opinion, using the resources of large environmental organizations, and harnessing the energies of grassroots activists with direct-action tactics.

The Anti-Roads Movement

Another dramatic direct-action campaign took place in the UK in the early 1990s, spearheaded by the Earth First! network founded there in 1991. As Derek Wall describes, protests against new roads and anti-car campaigns first occurred in the late 1960s and early 1970s, as local NIMBY activists fighting the loss of their neighbourhoods to motorways joined with environmentalists who framed car use in terms of global environmental destruction (Wall, 1999: 27). Activists in cities such as London and Manchester blocked roads to demand car-free streets and free public transportation with actions such as Reclaim the Streets parties held on busy roads and 'bike-ins' by large numbers of cyclists (ibid., 29). Some anti-car and anti-roads activity continued after the early 1970s, but radical activists in Britain became increasingly involved in anti-nuclear protests and peace campaigns, including the well-known women's peace camp at Greenham Common (ibid., 33). In the 1980s a 'green movement' was emerging in Britain and some anti-roads activity continued. Protest accelerated dramatically in the 1990s after the Conservative government issued a call for increased road construction in its 1989 White Paper, *Roads for Prosperity*, and after the founding of Earth First! (UK) in 1991 (ibid., 37).

During the 1990s, anti-roads campaigns were mounted in a number of locations, involving thousands of activists and resulting in major reductions in the government's plans for road construction. The first major campaign took place in Twyford Down, near the city of Winchester, in protest of construction of the M3 motorway there. Inspired by the Greenham Common peace camp and similar tactics used by the Australian rain forest movement, activists created an anti-roads protest camp at Twyford, which attracted large numbers of activists (ibid., 67). Alliances were created between local activists and radical environmentalists from groups such as Earth First! (UK), and direct-action tactics such as digging and occupying tunnels, sitting in trees, and blockading roads were employed to raise the costs of road construction. Campaigns in other locations used similar tactics and the 'green network' in the UK expanded greatly, spreading strategies and a radical environmentalist collective identity. Reclaim the Streets parties were held in many cities, and the movement built on youth counterculture as well as environmental networks and memberships of large groups such as Friends of the Earth and Greenpeace. The movement faced great obstacles, including countermovement activity in favour of road construction and strong opposition from the government. Despite opposition and an initial lack of political opportunities and extensive resources, however, the movement was able to create divisions within the government (Doherty, 1999: 284). The movement spawned effective alliances between local activists and radical networks and gained a great deal of media attention with its use of innovative direct-action tactics. Activists felt empowered by the protests, and an expanded network of radicalized green activists and a repertoire of direct-action tactics are among the movement's enduring outcomes (Wall, 1999).

CONCLUSION

The modern environmental movement has endured for decades despite ebbs and flows in its organizational strength and activity. The movement's organizational and strategic diversity is one important reason for the continued salience of environmentalism. Large national organizations have created green lobbies in numerous countries. International organizations have spread to many countries and are capable of mounting both national and transnational campaigns. Greenpeace, in particular, is expert at generating media coverage. Local and regional groups, such as Friends of Clayoquot Sound and Earth First!, have demonstrated the potential of non-violent direct action for the environmental movement. Networks of environmental activists and collective identities endure, even when particular organizations and campaigns decline. The movement has provoked significant countermovement activities, but these responses are an indicator of environmentalism's appeal, even though they are harmful to the movement cause.

Strong public support for environmentalism helps the movement to endure, creating financial support for movement organizations and political support for movement positions. Environmental problems are subject to issue attention cycles, but the movement continues to be relevant to the public because critical environmental problems are ongoing and local populations are often affected by environmental devastation. Public support creates the potential for greater use of market-based strategies, but also the risk of developing only strategies that appeal to the mainstream public. Strategies that are difficult to convey through the mass media, and that involve slow and complicated solutions, may be difficult to sell to the public. Organizations that depend on donations from large numbers of people may fail to develop solutions that require lifestyle sacrifices on the part of the public. Moreover, even with public support to combat enormous problems such as global warming, economic interests and financial costs create major barriers. Opposition to the movement from industry and an industry-backed countermovement has often stymied progress. Coalitions with labour unions and other groups are clearly necessary, as are international efforts to address the global scope of environmental problems. Many environmentalists are involved in such efforts, including the global justice movement, which is the subject of the following chapter.

Discussion Questions

1. How can the environmental movement overcome the free rider problem and get citizens to contribute to the movement and its goals, either through individual action such as recycling or through participation in collective action?
2. What are the strengths and weaknesses of Greenpeace's media-based strategy?
3. How might the environmental movement convert public concern about the environment into cultural changes and public policies that address major issues such as global warming?

Suggested Readings

Brulle, Robert J. 2000. *Agency, Democracy, and Nature: The U.S. Environmental Movement from a Critical Theory Perspective*. Cambridge, Mass.: MIT Press. This book analyzes the major forms of environmentalism in the US.

McKenzie, Judith I. 2002. *Environmental Politics in Canada: Managing the Commons into the Twenty-First Century*. Oxford: Oxford University Press. This book describes major trends in Canadian environmentalism.

Rootes, Christopher. 2004. 'Environmental Movements', in D.A. Snow, S.A. Soule, and H. Kriesi, eds, *The Blackwell Companion to Social Movements*. Malden, Mass.: Blackwell, 608–40. This essay provides a comparative perspective, analyzing trends such as the institutionalization of environmental organizations in Western countries.

Chapter 9

The Global Justice Movement

A seemingly new movement burst on the scene with massive demonstrations at the meetings of the World Trade Organization in Seattle in 1999. As many as 50,000 demonstrators, including environmentalists, labour unionists, human rights advocates, students, and feminists, descended on the city, resulting in major disruptions to the week-long WTO meetings, intense clashes with police, and a great deal of media attention. The 'battle in Seattle' and subsequent protests in Washington, DC, Quebec City, Genoa, Italy, and elsewhere were manifestations of a 'movement of movements' to protest the neo-liberal economic policies promoted by the WTO and other global financial institutions. International financial institutions and their policies—and global capitalism more generally—became targets for multiple movements because they were seen as worsening poverty in developing countries, burdening women and families, promoting environmental destruction, and lowering labour standards. Initially, the emerging movement was commonly known as the 'anti-globalization movement' for its opposition to global capitalism, but activists gradually defined their cause as a 'global justice movement' promoting global democracy rather than simply opposing globalization. From the start, the movement faced enormous difficulties in bringing together diverse participants and formulating strategies that would have an impact on global political and economic institutions. After the terrorist attacks on the United States on 11 September 2001 the movement faced even stiffer challenges in mobilizing and strategizing. Nevertheless, the global justice movement remains alive, representing an important attempt to bring together many different movement constituents to develop solutions to world problems.

This chapter begins with a description of the origins of the global justice movement and the various protests that led up to the Seattle demonstrations, including the anti-free trade movement that began in Canada. We then look at some key factors that help to explain how the movement was able to mobilize diverse activists, including framing activities, mobilizing structures, and international opportunities. Finally, the chapter examines some of the strategies and outcomes of the movement.

ORIGINS OF THE GLOBAL JUSTICE MOVEMENT

The Seattle demonstrations captured world attention, in part because they occurred in the US and consequently received a great deal of media coverage, but they were not the first collective actions targeted at international institutions and their neo-liberal trade and monetary policies. The global justice movement grew out of earlier local, national, and international mobilizations involving many of the organizations and activists present in Seattle (Smith, 2001). Neo-liberal economic policies, which were promoted vigorously by the Reagan administration in the US and the Thatcher government in Britain, provided a common target for protests around the world in the 1980s and 1990s. Moreover, cultural changes associated with globalization created threats to national and ethnic identities and local cultures, while new technologies such as the Internet promoted greater awareness of these issues and increased potential for global mobilization (della Porta et al., 2006: 14–15). Thus, global economic policies and cultural threats provided numerous targets for protests: intrusions on national identities and cultures; government cutbacks to social programs; and trade policies, economic projects, and corporations considered exploitive of workers and the environment. At the same time, activists began to see themselves as part of a global movement for social justice and a new type of 'globalization from below' (ibid.).

The emerging movement was highly heterogeneous, incorporating multiple movements and identities but converging around opposition to the institutions of global capitalism and supporting the right of peoples to determine their own futures quite apart from the influence of international financial institutions and transnational corporations. Among the many collective actions targeted at neo-liberalism (described in Starr, 2005: 20–5), 'IMF riots' or 'bread riots' involving general strikes and massive protests took place in some 23 countries in the 1980s. These protests were responses to the structural adjustment programs (SAPs) promoted by the IMF and World Bank, which required developing countries to cut social programs and privatize services and investments in order to pay down their debts while increasing private production and trade. In 1990, the African Council of Churches called for debt relief in response to neo-liberal policies and a debt relief movement known as the Jubilee 2000 campaign mobilized in a number of countries. In Europe, a variety of movements used direct action to take control of buildings, for example, and to protest policies such as welfare cuts and racism in immigration. Greenpeace London initiated an International Day of Action against McDonald's on 16 October 1985, which became an annual protest of McDonald's business practices, environmental damage, and treatment of animals. A movement of European farmers in support of family farming and sustainable farming practices mobilized in the 1980s, and in 1988 some 80,000 demonstrators from across Europe protested against the IMF meetings in Berlin.

Economic adjustment policies have particularly strong impacts on poor, indigenous peoples, and the adjustment process following the 1982 debt crisis provoked a variety of ethnic conflicts in Latin American states such as Bolivia, Mexico, and Peru (Brysk and Wise, 1997). In Colombia, beginning in 1992, indigenous people protested against a drilling project by Occidental Petroleum until the project was finally withdrawn in 2002. In Brazil, a Landless Workers' Movement became very active in large-scale land occupations. In 1992, European and Latin American farmers created an international farmers' organization of small and medium-sized producers. In India, a long-term protest movement opposed a World Bank project, the Sardar Sarovar dam, which the Bank pulled out of in 1993; by 1997, when the Supreme Court of India ordered a halt to the Sardar Sarovar project, the anti-dam movement had spread to other projects. Such struggles 'gained intense international attention in the context of an emerging comprehensive case against corporations' and attracted environmental organizations to the cause (ibid., 24).

In North America, the movement in the 1980s against the Canada–US Free Trade Agreement (FTA) was important in creating transnational networks among activists in Canada, the US, and Mexico. As Jeffrey Ayres (1998) describes, a coalition of 'popular-sector groups' in Canada, including churches, labour unions, farmers, Aboriginals, and women's groups, organized to oppose the free trade agreement with the US. All of these groups were affected by the economic recession of the 1980s and alarmed by the political shift to the right when the Conservatives were elected in 1984. Aroused by these grievances and threats, popular-sector groups took advantage of mobilizing opportunities created by public hearings on free trade and political opportunities in the form of divisions among levels of government and disputes between Canada and the US, which delayed the FTA and allowed opponents time to organize. Although the movement lost the battle over the FTA, Ayres argues that the form of coalition-building used by the Canadian movement diffused to the US and Mexico and, in the battle over the extension of the free trade agreement to Mexico in the North American Free Trade Agreement (NAFTA), co-operative ties created among activists in the three countries helped form the basis for the broader global justice movement.

On 1 January 1994, the day that NAFTA took effect, an army of indigenous people and peasants in the Chiapas region of Mexico calling itself the Zapatista Army of National Liberation took over a number of towns and set up autonomous zones. The Zapatistas were protesting NAFTA and neo-liberal policies of the Mexican government such as elimination of protections on coffee prices and the dismantling of a program that provided communal plots of land to indigenous farmers. Although the Mexican government met the insurrection with military force, the Zapatistas quickly mobilized national and international support, which forced the government to declare a ceasefire. The Zapatistas were able to generate support through their extensive network connections to peasant organizations and other NGOs within Mexico and through connections to other activists in North America created by the anti-NAFTA coalition (Schulz, 1998: 593–4). The Zapatistas also generated international solidarity through use of the Internet to win sympathy for a broad set of demands focusing on justice, democracy, and dignity. In 1996, 3,000 activists from around the world gathered in Chiapas at a meeting hosted by the Zapatistas, which resulted in an intercontinental network of activists opposed to neo-liberal policies and committed to common values such as social justice, environmentalism, and women's rights.

Around the world, local and national movements diffused internationally and supported emerging global justice networks, with a large number of protests occurring in the wake of the founding of the World Trade Organization in 1995 (Starr, 2005: 25–6). In Nigeria, the Ogoni people had been waging a long struggle against exploitation in their homeland, but gained little notice until Ken Saro-Wiwa and other activists formed the Movement for the Survival of the Ogoni People (MOSOP) to fight for political autonomy and against ethnic, economic, and environmental exploitation by the Nigerian government and Royal Dutch/Shell, the major oil company operating in the region (Bob, 2005: 54). In 1995, large demonstrations were organized to protest the execution of Ken Saro-Wiwa and eight other MOSOP activists by the government of Nigeria following a trial on trumped up charges and despite world condemnation. In France, the largest demonstrations since May 1968 took place in December 1995 in the form of massive strikes by workers, students, women's groups, and others in protest of government plans to reform social security and in support of the welfare state; in 1998, some of the same organizations joined together to create the Association for the Taxation of Financial Transaction for the Aid of Citizens, known as ATTAC (Ancelovici, 2002: 432). ATTAC became an 'international movement for democratic control of financial markets and their institutions' with branches in over 30 countries (www.attac.org).

In many cities, local movement activity picked up in the 1990s, involving participants in causes that would feed into the global justice movement. In what Janet Conway (2004) calls the 'activist city' of Toronto, for example, a group created in 1992, called the Metro Network for Social Justice, brought together unions, community-based social service agencies, housing and anti-poverty activists, feminists, and others who connected local problems such as cutbacks in municipal services with larger issues of free trade and neo-liberal economic policies. In London, the anti-roads movement that originally protested motorway construction and the takeover of cities by cars developed a broader anti-corporate critique. Joining with other countercultural groups, anti-roads activists promoted Reclaim the Streets parties in the 1990s as a way of reclaiming public spaces (Klein, 1999: 312–13). Reclaim the Streets also spread internationally, and in May 1998 a global street party was held simultaneously in cities around the world (rts.gn.apc.org). Police reaction to the parties varied greatly, in some cities resulting in riots, but everywhere a great deal of emotion was aroused regarding the power of the movement (Klein, 1999: 320–1). The mobilization of such local movements made a scale shift to the international protests in Seattle and elsewhere possible, and the stability of local organizations provided a place for local activists to return after participating in episodic transnational activism (Tarrow, 2005).

Among the transnational networks of activists formed, Peoples' Global Action (PGA), inspired by the Zapatista vision, was created in 1998. The coalition sponsored the first 'global day of action' in May 1998 to coincide with the meetings of the G8[1] in Birmingham, England, and the WTO in Geneva (Wood, 2005a, 2005b). The second global day of action was called by the PGA to protest the June 1999 meeting of the G8 in Germany and the third global day of action was called to protest the WTO meetings in Seattle in November of that year. Thus, numerous protests organized by various networks of activists occurred around the world before the events in Seattle in 1999. The dramatic protests in Seattle did create new momentum for the movement, and a record number of organizations participated in the protests, both in Seattle and in cities around the world. After the Seattle protests, the PGA and other activist networks continued to organize protests to coincide with the meetings of international financial organizations such as the WTO and to target corporate symbols of global capitalism such as McDonald's and Nike. Although the events of 11 September 2001 slowed the momentum of the movement, particularly in the US and Canada, a massive protest took place in over 150 cities worldwide against the WTO meetings in Qatar as soon as November 2001 (Wood, 2005a: 80). Despite a brief pause in protests in response to the terrorist attacks of 2001, the global justice movement continued to be active worldwide after 9/11, and in fact the ranks of the movement were expanded by anti-war activists around the world after the US invasions of Afghanistan and Iraq (Podobnik, 2005).

MOBILIZING FRAMES, STRUCTURES, AND OPPORTUNITIES

Theories of social movements suggest some key factors that help to explain how and why the global justice movement emerged when it did. Global economic changes and the advocacy of neo-liberal policies created widespread *grievances* and *threats* in both developed and developing countries. Conflicts over the consequences of these policies became widespread in the 1980s and 1990s, and—significantly for the creation of a transnational movement—activists in different locations began linking various socio-economic and political problems to neo-liberal policies. In other words, they were creating a *master frame* that diagnosed specific problems as consequences of neo-liberalism and its practice by international financial institutions (Ayres, 2004, 2005). This 'broadly interpretive, increasingly transnationally-shared diagnostic frame' helped to mobilize a global movement by linking different types of social problems worldwide to the rise of neo-liberalism (Ayres, 2004: 12). Thus, problems such as rising debt loads in developing countries, cuts to social programs and rising unemployment in both developed and developing countries, and instability in the international economy could all be attributed to neo-liberalism. As a result, activists working on a variety of projects were able to adopt a common *collective identity* as global actors opposed to neo-liberalism and seeking social and environmental justice and democracy from below (della Porta et al., 2006).

Not only was it possible to trace many different problems to neo-liberal policies, but political opportunities for transnational protest were expanded by **internationalism**, which Tarrow (2005: 25) defines as the 'structure of relations among states, non-state actors, and international institutions, and the opportunities this produces for actors to engage in collective action at different levels of this system'. Tarrow expands earlier political process theories to analyze how the **international opportunity structure** has changed with the enlarged role of institutions such as the World Bank and the European Union (EU). Although international institutions often represent the interests of global capitalism, they 'also offer an opportunity space within which opponents of global capitalism and other claimants can mobilize' (ibid., 26). In the past few decades, as international governmental institutions and activities such as high-profile international summits have proliferated, so have parallel summits and global movements (Pianta, 2003). International institutions are key targets and arenas for transnational activism and, as in the case of national governments, actors within these institutions may be divided in their sympathies, creating both opportunities and obstacles for protestors.

Tarrow (2005: 32) identifies some of the important political processes involved in transnational contention. In some instances, collective action occurs in a domestic arena, but with global connections the process of **global framing** involves the use of 'international symbols to frame domestic conflicts' and **internalization** is 'a response to foreign or international pressures within domestic politics'. Both of these processes were involved when French farmers blockaded Euro-Disney in 1992 to protest EU agricultural reforms and the 'Americanization' of Europe (ibid., 31; Bush and Simi, 2001). In **diffusion**, forms of contention spread from one site to others, as in the case of Reclaim the Streets parties. In **scale shift**, co-ordination of collective action shifts to a different level, as in the case of a local group like ATTAC becoming international. Two other processes identified by Tarrow occur at the international level. **Externalization** involves 'the vertical projection of domestic claims onto international institutions or foreign actors', as in the case of a Renault plant closure in Belgium that activists brought to the attention of the EU (Tarrow, 2005: 32). **Transnational coalition formation** involves creating a network or coalition among actors from different countries such as Peoples' Global Action or the World Social Forum (WSF). The WSF originated in 2001 through 'upward scale shift' as activists engaged in local struggles created the annual global justice summit as an alternative to the World Economic Forum; since then, there has been a 'downward scale shift' with the proliferation of regional, local, and national forums modelled on the WSF (ibid., 128–34).

Activists at different levels built on a variety of mobilizing structures, including the meetings of international institutions, as they began to create an international global justice movement. To create a movement of movements, they used collective action frames that linked the concerns of different social movements. Gerhards and Rucht analyze these processes of mobilization in two protest campaigns in West Germany, against US President Ronald Reagan's visit to Berlin in 1987 and against the meetings of the IMF and the World Bank in Berlin in 1988, which included an alternative conference critiquing the policies of the international financial institutions. To explain how the campaigns mobilized, Gerhards and Rucht look at what they term the 'micromobilization' and 'mesomobilization' actors that comprised the mobilizing structure for the protest activities. **Micromobilization actors** are the various groups that mobilize individuals to participate in protest, including trade unions and environmental, religious, neighbourhood, student, peace, and women's groups. In the case of the anti-Reagan demonstration, participants were all part of a large network of local Berlin groups whereas in the anti-IMF campaign local groups were joined by national groups, including the Green Party. **Mesomobilization actors**, who work to integrate participating groups, formed co-ordinating groups to organize the micromobilization actors (Gerhards and Rucht, 1992: 558). One of the critical tasks they performed was the creation of collective action frames that allowed individual groups to engage in **frame bridging** to connect their particular concerns to the larger concerns of the campaigns (ibid., 584–6). Thus, in an early example of what would become a unifying anti-neo-liberalism frame, the IMF and World Bank were portrayed as agents of a world economic order that exploits developing countries. This frame helped mobilize numerous groups such as ecological groups, which focused on how projects of the IMF and World Bank led to the destruction of rain forests, and women's groups, which emphasized that women bear the brunt of the burden created by economic policies that increase poverty in developing countries.

To be successful in linking actors from different movements and at different levels together, movements need effective mesomobilization actors and frames that bridge movement concerns and link local, national, and international issues. In the global justice movement, local activists have engaged in global framing to enhance the appeal of local issues, in some instances strengthening their causes by connecting to international organizations and resources. For example, Clifford Bob (2005: ch. 3) shows how the Ogoni, a little-known ethnic group in Nigeria facing a hostile domestic environment, sought international help in their struggle for ethnic autonomy and against degradation of the environment. The Movement for the Survival of the Ogoni People initially failed to convince major international NGOs such as Greenpeace and Amnesty International to take up the Ogoni cause, but MOSOP eventually learned to frame its concerns in ways that were more appealing to international environmental and human rights groups. By focusing on Shell Oil's environmental abuses of the Niger Delta, and aided by widespread concerns generated by deepening state repression, MOSOP convinced international NGOs to lend resources and generate publicity.

International networks of NGOs and coalition organizations such as ATTAC and the PGA have served as mesomobilization actors for the global justice movement, helping to build organizations within countries and to mobilize transnational protests such as global days of action. Networks of co-operating organizations have encouraged not only participation in protests but also active participation within the network organizations, which have stressed participatory forms of internal decision-making (della Porta et al., 2006). These heterogeneous networks of organizations have been able to work together within the global justice movement because participants share a collective identity that is inclusive of diverse groups. In an extensive study of global justice networks in Europe, Donatella della Porta and colleagues show that this identity was constructed by the movement through counter-summits and documents, which stress a number of values and commitments, including global citizenship, diversity, democracy from below, ecopacifism, and opposition to neo-liberalism and global capitalism. This master frame resonates with activists, who share a collective identity based on these ideas (ibid., 82–4).

Although master framing helps to unite a diverse movement, resource inequalities and other North–South differences make it extremely difficult to create and maintain coalitions that include participants from both developed and developing countries. The PGA has attempted to deal with such problems by creating 'a structure and process explicitly aimed at avoiding Northern domination of the coalition' (Wood, 2005b: 99). Thus, participation by those from the developed global North at conferences is sometimes limited; the Conveners Committee, which is the PGA's only central decision-making body, is regionally balanced in its composition; and the overall structure of the coalition is decentralized to allow grassroots participation (ibid., 100–1). While there are ongoing struggles over organizational processes in the

PGA, the coalition has worked to create collective identity among participants through practices such as the drafting of 'living documents' that are revised at each gathering. This process allows participants 'to challenge any perceived consolidation of power' and to 'build trust by reworking the basis of their collaboration in new ways' (ibid., 111). Despite differences, 'movements participating in the PGA increasingly see themselves as part of a connected global struggle against neoliberalism' (ibid., 113).

In addition to creating workable mobilizing structures and unifying collective action frames, the global justice movement has organized with the aid of the mass media and particularly the Internet. The Internet has become a critical strategic tool for global justice activists, which allows them to co-ordinate global protests and to send information around the world quickly and cheaply. Use of the Internet helped to bring together 'a variety of national and regional anti-neoliberal collective action frames' and to develop a critique of neo-liberalism through the use of listservs, e-mail, and websites as well as face-to-face meetings (Ayres, 2004: 19). The Zapatistas built national and international support and inspired global justice activists around the world through mass media coverage and dissemination of their messages on list-servs and websites. For example, their proposal for an international communication and resistance network was posted on a German 'Initiatives Against Neoliberalism' website, which linked the Zapatista proposal with a wide variety of other struggles such as the European March against Unemployment (Schulz, 1998: 603).

The Internet became increasingly important in North American campaigns against free trade and neo-liberalism. In 1998, the Council of Canadians (COC), a public interest group with 100,000 members, was instrumental in defeating the Multilateral Agreement on Investment (MAI) through a campaign that relied heavily on the Internet to disseminate information on the MAI and to communicate with other anti-MAI activists around the world (Ayres, 1999). Whereas earlier campaigns by the COC and its allies against the FTA and NAFTA had relied on costly and time-consuming mailings and cross-country meetings, the anti-MAI campaign could quickly reach a national and global audience with up-to-date information at little cost (ibid., 140). In advance of the Seattle protests in 1999, websites and listservs were used extensively to mobilize participants. For example, the Ad-Hoc Student Coalition for Fair Trade was a virtual umbrella organization that sent out e-mails to groups across Canada, such as the Canadian Federation of Students, which forwarded the e-mails to their own listservs. The Canadian Coalition also co-ordinated with US groups, such as the Boston Center for Campus Organizing, which often sent messages to the Canadian network (*Toronto Star*, 29 Nov. 1999).

Internet use became even more sophisticated in ongoing mobilization against the Free Trade Area of the Americas (FTAA), a proposal to extend free trade throughout the Americas. The campaign, which brought tens of thousands of demonstrators to Quebec City in April 2001, used the Internet to disseminate information about the FTAA, to communicate strategies, and to pressure authorities (Ayres, 2005). Prior to the Quebec City demonstrations, listservs available in English, French, Spanish, and Portuguese, together with a protest website, posted updates on demonstration plans, rider boards for those looking to share rides to Quebec City, information on what to bring and expect, and 'action alerts' from groups such as Public Citizen in the US and the COC in Canada encouraging participation in call-ins, letter-writing campaigns, and e-mail protests directed at the US and Canadian governments (Ayres, 2005: 47). Internet communications helped to bring together activists from different cultures and geographic regions by creating solidarity and a sense of common purpose, spreading tactical innovations and co-ordinating strategies (ibid., 48). Internet communications also aided in the creation of a coalition organization called the Hemispheric Social Alliance (HSA) and in the drafting of an *Alternatives for the Americas* document, which provided movement alternatives to the FTAA (ibid., 48–51).

Della Porta and her colleagues investigated a number of issues related to use of the Internet in the cases of global justice demonstrations at the G8 meetings in Genoa in 2001 and at the European Social Forum in Florence in 2002. They found that the Internet played a major role in the organization of logistics and in the development of documents and ideas via websites and e-mail. Websites available in English, French, German, Italian, Portuguese, and Spanish disseminated a steady stream of information about the events and recruited international volunteers (della Porta et al., 2006: 96–7). Although della Porta et al. found some evidence of a 'digital divide' or inequality with regard to those who have access to the Internet and skills in using it and those who are less privileged (see Rucht, 2005), they also found that movement organizations helped to socialize members in the use of the Internet (della Porta et al., 2006: 98). Beyond using the Internet to co-ordinate protests and as a source of information about the movement, activists used the Internet as a means of protest through activities such as on-line petitions and 'net strikes' in which large numbers of people jam websites at prearranged times (ibid., 105–6). Activists also developed their collective identities via the Internet insofar as they actively participated in on-line forums and mailing lists to discuss issues and ideas as well as form new social ties (ibid., 108–11).

Thus, the Internet provides social movements with an alternative to other mass media in reaching large numbers of potential constituents, and it seems to hold great potential for movement organization and development. Nevertheless, in addition to the digital divide, limitations to its use include a lack of quality control regarding the information posted on the Internet (Rucht, 2005). While the Internet facilitates the mobilization of long-term campaigns, it may also produce relatively weak ideological ties and collective identity (Bennett, 2003). The Internet clearly does not replace face-to-face organizing, and global justice campaigns and projects typically combine use of the Internet and other new technologies with other forms of organizing. Independent media centres (IMCs), for example, have been established in a number of cities around the world since the first IMC was set up in Seattle following the WTO demonstrations in 1999. These IMCs are active centres of local activity that are also part of the international Indymedia network of independent journalists and activists, which maintains a website (www.indymedia.org) and attempts to support the global justice movement by providing alternative, non-corporate coverage of local, national, and international issues and movements (Halleck, 2003; Rucht, 2005).

Although the Internet has been critical to the global justice movement, the conventional mass media remain important. Securing favourable coverage in the established press is always a challenge for social movements, as the mass media often focus on drama and violence rather than on the content of movement demands. Nevertheless, mass media coverage of the global justice movement has aided its spread and some coverage has helped to publicize movement concerns. In the case of the Zapatistas, the dramatic 1 January 1994 guerrilla attacks immediately captured media attention and brought the group to world attention. The movement's articulate and charismatic spokesperson, a masked leader calling himself Subcomandante Marcos, gave many press conferences and interviews and disseminated numerous manifestos and communiqués, resulting in a great deal of international media attention (Bob, 2005: 127–34). The Jubilee 2000 debt campaign, with extensive involvement of churches and other organizations, also received a great deal of media coverage (Pianta, 2003: 252). And, despite generally negative reporting of disruptive public protests, media coverage of movement issues in the 1999 Seattle protests was fairly extensive, owing to factors such as the novelty of the protests, President Clinton's statements of support for some movement demands, and the presence of unions and church organizations that were 'credible media sources' (Bennett, 2003: 162). Moreover, mass media reports continue to attract movement participants. For example, a survey of protestors in Germany against the Iraq War in 2003 found that, among the one or more sources of information they reported, about 55 per cent heard of the demonstrations through newspapers, about 51 per cent heard through radio or television, and only about 11 per cent learned of the protest through the Internet (Rucht, 2005: 82). In a study of Australian anti-capitalist activists, twice as many saw the mainstream mass media as central to recruitment as saw the Internet as a way to expand the movement (Bramble and Minns, 2005).

Movement Strategies and Outcomes

The global justice movement has experienced significant success, but also faces strategic difficulties in achieving its goals. Among the successes, large demonstrations at the meetings of international financial institutions and governmental groups have put new concerns on the public agenda. Activists have articulated a critique of neo-liberal policies, created linkages among struggles around the world, and increased public awareness of the role of international trade and monetary policies in problems such as the exploitation of workers and the environment. The various movements and organizations that comprise the global justice movement have used a combination of political strategies and new cultural forms in their attempts to challenge global capitalism. Nevertheless, the movement faces major challenges in maintaining coalitions, agreeing on solutions to the problems identified, and devising strategies that have a real impact.

The creation of a master frame opposing the neo-liberal policies of state and institutional actors is, as we have seen, an important accomplishment of the movement. In combination with the Internet, counter-summits known as parallel summits or People's Summits, held in response to international meetings such as the

WTO and G8, are an innovative tactic for developing the critique of neo-liberalism and crafting documents such as *Alternatives for the Americas* in response to the FTAA proposal. Through this process, the movement created a master frame with the 'breadth and capacity to absorb and accommodate the variety of movement and region specific frames that had spurred collective action against neoliberal agreements and institutions' (Ayres, 2005: 18). Protests against neo-liberal targets, such as the WTO in Seattle in 1999 and the FTAA negotiations in Quebec City in 2001, involved parallel summits as well as numerous other tactics, such as blockades, teach-ins, street theatre, rallies, and marches. The protests and counter-summits generated numerous discussions, position papers, and proposals for further action.

While movement frames and tactics clearly mobilized the movement, it is less clear how much impact they have had on targets. Part of the difficulty is that it is easier for the movement to articulate a critique of international institutions and policies than it is to propose workable solutions. As Ayres (2005: 20) argues, movement activists have generally agreed on a 'diagnostic frame' that focuses on the shortcomings of neo-liberalism, but they have had a more difficult time agreeing on a 'prognostic frame' that would direct challenges to neo-liberalism and present alternatives. Instead, a variety of different solutions have been proposed, ranging from reform of institutions such as the WTO to a complete dismantling of global capitalism.

The Seattle protests and others that followed did have some impact in terms of a reform agenda aimed at making international institutions and intergovernmental meetings more inclusive and open to public scrutiny. As a result of large-scale protests, some world leaders called for greater openness in the process of trade negotiations and other global decision-making. For example, then US President Bill Clinton met with WTO protestors in Seattle to hear the concerns of farmers and others about world trade liberalization and made a speech saying people were protesting in part because they have never been allowed inside WTO deliberations. Similarly, the Canadian International Trade Minister at the time, Pierre Pettigrew, made a statement during the Seattle protests that it was time to include groups that had been shut out in the past (*National Post*, 30 Nov. 1999). The agendas of various intergovernmental bodies targeted by protestors were also affected. For example, the G8 meeting in Genoa, Italy, in July 2001 included the issues of AIDS and African development on its agenda, and invited addresses by the South African president and the head of the World Health Organization in an attempt to show concern for a broad range of global issues (*Gazette*, 20 July 2001). Public opinion in Europe and North America also showed strong support for movement positions, and leaders of the G8 made some concessions on the issues of AIDS and debt relief in response to public acceptance of movement demands (*Gazette*, 19 July 2001).

Despite some progress in raising issues of accountability and democratic process with regard to international institutions and intergovernmental bodies, however, many activists began to question the value of ongoing demonstrations at international meetings—which some activists derided as 'summit hopping'. Policing of the protests became increasingly effective in curbing demonstrations with escalated use of force, despite the largely non-violent orientation of movement activists (della Porta et al., 2006: ch. 6). After 9/11, a number of meetings were held at remote locations that were inaccessible to protestors, such as the 2002 meeting of the G8 in Kananaskis, Alberta. Although protests and parallel summits continue to be held at the sites of international meetings, simultaneous events are also organized around the world, and activists continue to work on local and national as well as global campaigns. While searching for a long-term global strategy, activists have mounted campaigns against corporate abuses of workers, against environmentally destructive projects, and in support of fair trade policies.

One of the most promising strategies of the global justice movement involves the targeting of corporations that symbolize the abuses of global capitalism. Anti-sweatshop, living wage, and fair trade movements picked up steam in the 1990s as labour unions, students, religious groups, and community organizations attempted to counter the impacts of global capitalism on workers. In the United States since the mid-1990s, living wage campaigns led by unions and community organizations convinced a number of cities and counties to pass 'living wage' legislation requiring private-sector firms with government business to provide wages above the federal minimum wage (Levi et al., 2004). Activists have also pushed for a 'global living wage' that pays workers enough to allow them to live at an adequate local standard of living (Shaw, 1999). In Canada, anti-poverty movements and their allies have focused on raising provincial minimum wages. Activists in countries around the world have also been involved in a fair trade movement, co-ordinated by networks such as the International Federation for Alternative Trade (see www.ifat.org) based in the UK. The movement works to secure fair prices for the goods of economically disadvantaged producers and to promote gender equity, environmental sustainability, and safe working conditions.

The anti-sweatshop movement, backed by unions, churches, students, and other supporters, is active in a number of industrialized countries. The movement encourages consumer boycotts of products produced in sweatshops, pressures corporations to adopt codes of conduct for their suppliers, and attempts to monitor their compliance. University students, co-ordinated by groups such as United Students Against Sweatshops (USAS) in the US and the Ethical Trading Action Group (ETAG) in Canada, became quite active in the 1990s in pressuring their universities to adopt plans that ensured that clothing with university logos is produced in 'no-sweat' conditions (Cravey, 2004; Ross, 2005). Canadian author and activist Naomi Klein provided one source of inspiration for anti-corporate activity among students and others with her book *No Logo* (1999), which analyzes the spread of brands such as Coca-Cola, McDonald's, Nike, and Starbucks and how the production of these products is related to the exploitation of workers and the environment. Because their images are so important to them, corporations are vulnerable to attacks on their brands, leading activists to target well-known corporate brands to call attention to issues of working conditions and trade practices.

Beginning in the early 1990s, activists launched one of the most significant anti-corporate campaigns, against Nike, for sweatshop abuses by its subcontractors in countries such as Indonesia (see Shaw, 1999, for a detailed account). As a major manufacturer of sports shoes and clothing and a company with a very positive image in North America, Nike represented an extremely important and difficult target for anti-sweatshop activists. Activists struggled for a number of years before managing to get some mainstream media coverage of Nike's abuses in publications such as the *New York Times*, aided by the extensive publicity created by revelations that the clothing line of talk-show host Kathie Lee Gifford was produced in Honduran sweatshops. After the anti-Nike campaign received media publicity, and with the media know-how of organizations such as the San Francisco-based human rights organization Global Exchange, the campaign was able to build momentum. The campaign gained international support from unions, religious groups, students, and women's organizations, which played an important role in publicizing abuses to the largely female labour force in sweatshops. The anti-Nike campaign was eventually able to secure some genuinely important concessions from Nike, which suffered some important blows to its image from the campaign, although organizations such as Global Exchange continue to monitor Nike practices (ibid., 93).

Beginning in 2003, unions and other groups called for a boycott of Coca-Cola, accusing the company of international human rights, labour, and environmental abuses (Blanding, 2006). As part of this campaign, a number of unions and universities banned Coke and activists protested at stockholder meetings and sports events where Coke is sold. Although companies such as Nike and Coke responded to protestors with announcements of new workplace standards—and advertising campaigns to refurbish their images—long-term, persistent campaigns are required to produce real and lasting change in corporate practices. Extensive resources are also required to maintain organizations such as the Workers Rights Consortium (WRC), which was created in 2000 to monitor factories. And, despite some efforts to provide 'sweat-free' alternative products, the lack of easily accessible alternatives remains an impediment to widespread consumer boycotts of companies with questionable human rights and environmental records (La Botz, 2002).

Anti-sweatshop and fair trade organizing helped to forge alliances between groups such as unions, environmentalists, students, and community activists. Such alliances are both an important accomplishment of the global justice movement and an ongoing challenge. Although the anti-neo-liberalism frame creates some common ground among the different movements that make up the global justice movement, many ideological and strategic differences exist within the movement. These include differences over whether to reform or abolish international institutions and conflicts over tactics. Violence and the unruly tactics of anarchists at protest events have created internal conflict, particularly after the 2001 terrorist attacks, when some more moderate groups in the movement were anxious to distance themselves from any form of violence. Different elements of the global justice movement also have different types of constituents and varying concerns. Although much was made of the 'blue–green' alliance that seemed to emerge with the Seattle protests, symbolized by the image of 'Teamsters and Turtles' coming together, coalition work between unions and environmentalists was not terribly extensive (Gould et al., 2005). After Seattle, environmental concerns became less central to the movement than social justice and global inequality themes, but to attract a broad constituency the movement needs to develop an inclusive discourse and ideology that includes environmental concerns (Buttel and Gould, 2005).

CONCLUSION

The global justice movement has generated some of the most exciting social movement activity since the decline of the protest cycle of the 1960s. Feminists, environmentalists, labour activists, students, community activists, and others have joined together, in at least temporary coalitions, out of concern about the impacts of neoliberal economic policies and the practices of global capitalism. As a result of movement activities, public consciousness has increased regarding the exploitation of women, workers, and the environment connected to these policies and practices, and international institutions and governmental bodies are subject to greater public scrutiny. Although large-scale demonstrations are necessarily sporadic, the movement has diffused widely to many different venues, using a variety of strategies. New generations of activists, together with veterans of the movements of the 1960s, are continuing to use a repertoire of collective action to promote social change. New mobilizing structures such as Global Exchange, ATTAC, and the PGA, aided by the Internet, have helped to maintain the movement. The extent to which the movement succeeds depends on its ability to develop long-term campaigns with solutions to the problems that global justice activists have identified. As this chapter has shown, an international opportunity structure, together with movement frames, mobilizing structures, and collective action tactics, are central to that process.

Discussion Questions

1. How can collective action framing help to unite a 'movement of movements' such as the global justice movement?
2. What are the central challenges facing transnational coalitions and how might these be resolved?
3. What strategies are likely to be most effective in keeping the global justice movement mobilized and advancing its goals?

Suggested Readings

Ayres, Jeffrey M. 1998. *Defying Conventional Wisdom: Political Movements and Popular Contention against North American Free Trade*. Toronto: University of Toronto Press. This book provides a detailed history and political process analysis of the anti-free trade movement in Canada.

della Porta, Donatella, Massimiliano Andretta, Lorenzo Mosca, and Herbert Reiter. 2006. *Globalization from Below: Transnational Activists and Protest Networks*. Minneapolis: University of Minnesota Press. Based on studies of European protests, this study provides a good analysis of how the global justice movement emerged, how it mobilizes participants, and how it interacts with elite targets.

Tarrow, Sidney. 2005. *The New Transnational Activism*. New York: Cambridge University Press. This is an important assessment of transnational contention, offering many theoretical concepts and propositions.

Conclusion: Social Movements and Social Change

The histories of Aboriginal, women's, gay and lesbian, environmental, and global justice movements provide but a few examples of the importance of social movements and collective action to social change. Social movements have had major impacts on social policies, cultural norms, and public opinion. They often profoundly affect the lives of movement participants and others who are touched by the movement and its outcomes. Social movement theories help to explain the extent to which movements are able to bring about social changes and the obstacles that they face in doing so. In this concluding chapter, I briefly revisit the successes and challenges of the movements discussed in the book in light of some of the theoretical ideas about social movements outlined in earlier chapters. I conclude by noting the ongoing challenges facing social movements as they try to bring about social changes.

LARGE-SCALE CHANGES, GRIEVANCES, AND OPPORTUNITIES

All of the major theories of social movements point to the effects of large-scale socio-economic and political changes on the emergence and outcomes of social movements. Macro-level societal changes often create widespread grievances and political or cultural opportunities. Although grievances and opportunities alone do not mobilize collective action, they can be exploited by movement activists who build on the organizational changes that accompany large-scale social change. In the case of the American civil rights movement, economic changes and the resulting urbanization of southern blacks made it possible to organize a movement through the black churches. International and domestic political conditions, including the Cold War and the breakup of previous electoral alliances, created new political opportunities. Grievances had long existed, but there were now more opportunities for people to share them and new opportunities to be heard. Demographic changes were also important to the New Left student movement of the 1960s, as large numbers of students entered universities. In many ways, these students were privileged members of society who might not be expected to have major grievances, but they were also part of a generation that was alarmed by issues of nuclear arms proliferation, racism, and the Vietnam War. Once the cycle of protest of the 1960s was underway, new movements were inspired to mobilize.

Among the groups spurred by the protest cycle of the 1960s were Native Americans, who responded to political opportunities through organizations such as the

American Indian Movement (Nagel, 1996). In Canada, as Howard Ramos shows in Chapter 5, Aboriginals intensified their protests in response to the political opportunities associated with a number of critical events, including the 1969 White Paper, which provided a common target for Aboriginal groups with varying interests. Increased collective action then led to government responses, creating new political opportunities and available funding, which helped to generate national mobilization. The Constitution Act of 1982 and the 1987 Meech Lake Accord, which was defeated in 1990, provided further opportunities for the mobilization of Aboriginal protest. Internationally, the United Nations created opportunities for worldwide mobilization of indigenous peoples through forums such as the Working Group on Indigenous Populations.

Another movement spurred by the protest cycle of the 1960s, the women's movement, was clearly aided by large-scale transformations such as changes in labour markets and declining birth rates. Women's increased participation in the workforce and in higher education created new interests and grievances, and as women participated in more areas of social and political life, they experienced sexism that fuelled their participation in the women's movement. They also had political opportunities in democratic polities as political parties came to value the women's vote. Women's movements in countries such as Canada and the US made great advances and, in fact, their successes may partly explain the relative decline of the movement in recent years insofar as women have fewer grievances. The maintenance of some second-wave groups and the rise of third-wave feminism show, however, that ongoing issues such as violence against women and reproductive rights continue to involve new generations of women in the feminist movement. Although a countermovement has opposed feminist gains on issues such as abortion, the opposition has also helped to keep the movement mobilized. Moreover, feminists in the North have increasingly joined feminists in the South in an expanded global women's movement.

Before the rise of gay liberation movements, gay men and lesbians met with a great deal of repression and few obvious political opportunities, but cultural changes accompanying the protest cycle of the 1960s created greater public space for sexual minorities. In particular countries, political opportunities did come along with developments such as the adoption of the Charter of Rights and Freedoms in Canada. As in the case of the women's movement, strong opposition to the movement helped to further mobilize it, providing countermovement targets and opportunities for media exposure. Federal systems such as the US and Canada provided political openings at different levels of government in various states and provinces, whereas in more centralized systems, such as the UK, opportunities arose when sympathetic governments were in power. The creation of the European Union also brought political opportunities in Europe, where the movement has enjoyed a great deal of success in winning gay rights. In relatively tolerant countries such as Canada, the gay and lesbian movement might, like the women's movement, be faced with perceptions that the battle has been won. Indeed, while many participants were enjoying the party at the annual Gay Pride Parade in Toronto in 2006, organizers stressed the responsibility of the movement to work for freedoms of gays and lesbians in countries such as Russia and Iran, where they are denied basic rights (*Gazette*, 26 June 2006).

The environmental movement also built on the activism of the protest cycle rather than on clear political openings. Environmental threats have created grievances that helped to stimulate a sense of urgency among the public in the 1960s and 1970s and that continue to arouse activists concerned with issues such as toxic waste, the destruction of forests, and global warming. Public support has helped to create political openings, particularly in countries such as Germany with successful Green Parties. Large environmental organizations, which can boast extensive constituent support, have enjoyed some access to government officials, but they are criticized for being overly institutionalized and subject to co-optation by government and business interests. Large-scale economic structures, with their reliance on carbon-fuelled economic growth, are major impediments to the success of the movement in dealing with major environmental problems.

Expanding internationalism brought political opportunities for a new global justice movement and neo-liberal policies created new grievances around the world. By generating public support and some sympathy among elites, the movement was able to force some changes in the operation of international institutions and win some concessions from corporations. Widespread grievances and threats related to neo-liberal policies helped to mobilize a transnational movement, but the movement faces major obstacles in tackling global capitalism and building more democratic and equitable political and economic structures.

MOVEMENT ORGANIZATION AND STRATEGY

Movements face different types of cultural and political contexts and varying opportunities. However, all opportunities must be perceived and movements have to interpret threats and grievances to mobilize people for collective action. Movements also have to use and develop mobilizing structures to bring potential constituents together and to remain mobilized over time. The agency of movement leaders and other activists is essential for effective organizing, framing, and strategizing. The protest cycle of the 1960s popularized a repertoire of strategies that appear over and over in subsequent social movements. For example, movements continue to use mass demonstrations and street theatre, various types of teach-ins, and sit-ins (with creative variations such as 'kiss-ins' by gay activists, 'tree-sits' by environmentalists, and 'die-ins' first by anti-nuclear war and later by AIDS activists). Activists from the sixties generation have continued to join with new generations of activists, most recently in the global justice movement. Some long-standing organizational structures have been maintained and new movement organizations have formed. Collective action frames, such as the civil rights master frame, have been adapted by various movements, and new frames, such as the master frame opposing neo-liberalism, have been developed. The successes of movements depend on their ability to innovate strategies and frame grievances as well as to take advantage of political and cultural opportunities.

In the case of Aboriginal protest, activist groups such as the AIM in the United States built on the frames and tactics of the 1960s as they called for 'Red Power' and demanded justice by occupying spaces. Although some critical events were created by government actions, these events did not automatically mobilize a nationwide protest; the frames and tactics used by activists in response to such events were essential to the spread of the movement. Aboriginal activists used both institutional tactics, such as lawsuits, and radical protest tactics to build new organizations and create national and international movements.

The women's movement successfully transformed problems such as rape and domestic violence, which were once seen as private concerns, into political issues, framing 'the personal as political'. The movement targeted numerous types of authorities and issues and developed within many institutions, such as universities and churches. Although many women's movement organizations have declined, some have remained active and new organizations have formed. Third-wave feminists have developed new cultural projects and used new media for spreading movement ideas, including zines and websites. Globally, the women's movement has organized through UN mobilizing structures and developed international women's rights networks. Despite the difficulties involved in creating international coalitions, the movement has developed frames that unite feminists around problems such as poverty and violence against women.

The gay and lesbian rights movement adapted to the decline of the sixties protest cycle by building community structures and a collective identity that helped to maintain the movement. Although the movement has had difficulty pursuing some of the liberationist goals of its early years, gay rights activists made great gains in using a civil rights frame and quasi-ethnic group identity to pursue legal rights. New forms of activism, such as Queer Nation, helped to expand the movement to include more bisexual and transgendered people. With victories such as the right to marriage or civil unions in a number of countries, the movement has had an important cultural influence. Finding strategies to tackle repression in many countries around the world remains a major challenge for the movement.

The environmental movement has used a range of organizational forms and strategies to pursue its goals, including large, formalized organizations capable of lobbying governments and decentralized, radical groups able to engage in risky direct-action tactics. The formalized organizations have helped to maintain the movement over many years, and the radical groups have prodded the movement to innovate strategically. Grassroots environmentalists have invigorated the movement with anti-logging blockades, protest camps, and bike-ins to reclaim city streets from cars. Public support for environmentalism is strong, and consumer boycotts have at times been used effectively, but the movement also faces obstacles in changing consumer lifestyles and addressing complicated issues through the mass media. The environmental movement also faces countermovement opposition to lifestyle changes and corporate opposition to the major structural changes needed to address global warming and other major issues. Environmentalists have formed alliances with unions and indigenous peoples, and have worked to promote new understandings of sustainable development, such as the Just Transition approach, in searching for solutions to environmental problems.

The global justice movement created a unifying collective action frame that connects various types of problems and inequities to global capitalism and neo-liberal economic policies. The movement has made excellent use of the Internet to organize activists around the world. Although it is difficult to sustain global alliances, the movement has created some durable coalitions and other mobilizing structures, such as independent media centres. The movement has developed some innovative strategies, such as parallel summits, anti-sweatshop boycotts, and fair trade initiatives. Public awareness of issues associated with global economic policies has increased as a result of movement initiatives, but the movement must struggle to maintain its momentum and to come up with workable solutions to the large-scale problems identified. The movement also faces the challenge of keeping many local activists connected during lulls in global campaigns.

CONCLUSION

Social movements have helped to bring about many political and cultural transformations, but they also face numerous challenges in effecting change. Movements typically confront powerful adversaries and long-standing structural arrangements, and they rely on cultural and political openings to afford the possibility of success. In democratic polities, the mobilization of public support helps movements to influence government officials and other elites. The mass media are critical in reaching masses of supporters, but movements have to use dramatic tactics and attractive packages to convey their messages through the mass media. Coalitions of different types of constituents strengthen movements, but they are difficult to form and maintain. Movements need leadership and vision to create the collective action frames, organizational vehicles, and strategies and tactics needed for ongoing and effective campaigns. Despite the many obstacles to effective social movements, however, the movements discussed in this book provide examples of how significant change can be achieved through collective action.

Notes

CHAPTER 5

1. I would like to thank Paul Armstrong for his assistance with this chapter. Any deficiencies that remain are solely my own.

2. Over time, four categories of Aboriginal peoples emerged in Canada: (1) *status Indians* or those who are registered Indians and descendants of 'Indians' at the time of signing the Indian Act; (2) *non-status Indians* who identify themselves as Aboriginal but who are not legally recognized; 3) the Métis, who are descendants of the historic *Métis* nation of Alberta, Saskatchewan, Manitoba, and northern Ontario, with roots in mixed communities of French and Scottish fur traders and First Nations; and (4) the *Inuit*, who are recognized as having the same rights as status Indians but are ethnically and nationally different (Asch, 1993: 3–5). With the exception of non-status Indians, each of these Aboriginal peoples is recognized in section 35 of the Constitution Act, 1982. It is also worth noting that international and American discourse often refers to Aboriginals as indigenous (or indigenous peoples) (Wilkes, 2006).

3. Interestingly, the NIB was not incorporated in the *Canada Gazette* until 1970. It also later changed its name to the Assembly of First Nations, which currently represents the interests of status Indians in Canada.

4. After World War II, the United Nations adopted and proclaimed universal human rights, the International Labour Organization (ILO) was charged with resolving the 'Indian problem', and by 1960 the UN issued the Declaration on the Granting of Independence to Colonial Countries and Peoples (Niezen, 2000: 126–7; Morgan, 2004: 486). Each of these had direct implications for indigenous mobilization.

5. Dickason (2002:375–6) notes that anthropologist Harry B. Hawthorn was appointed by the federal government in 1963 to study and report on the social, educational, and economic conditions of Canada's Aboriginal peoples. His report appeared in 1966, listing 151 recommendations, one of which emphasized Canadian Indians were Canadian citizens plus had additional Aboriginal rights.

6. The Native Council of Canada set out to build a broad movement organization representing all Aboriginals, including status and non-status Indians, as well as Métis. However, it now predominantly represents only non-status Indians.

7. The organization was also referred to as the Indian and Eskimo Association in a number of documents.

8. A number of different Aboriginals were not recognized by the Indian Act or, worse yet, were excluded from their Aboriginal status because of it. For instance, those who voted prior to 1960, those who declared themselves (and their descendants) as non-Indians, those who were voluntarily enfranchised, and those who lost their Indian status were all denied Aboriginal status by the Act (Asch, 1993: 3). In particular, Aboriginal women are the best-known example of the latter. They, and their children, would lose their status by

marrying anyone who was not a status Indian. This remained the case until the federal government was forced to amend its policies due to the efforts of Jeanette Corbière Lavell, who filed a case with the Supreme Court, and Sandra Lovelace, who lobbied the United Nations, as well as the Native Women's Association of Canada, which worked to entrench equal rights among Aboriginal men and women in the Constitution Act, 1982. In 1985, the federal government amended the Indian Act with Bill C-31 to address its historic discrimination (Congress of Aboriginal Peoples: www.abo-peoples.org/programs/C-31/c-31-1.html; Eberts, 2005).

9. In the 1920s (Levi General) Deskaheh of the Six Nations lobbied to obtain a hearing at the League of Nations over a dispute on self-government in Canada (Niezen, 2000: 123). Since then, many others have also targeted extra-national institutions to pursue their grievances.

CHAPTER 6

1. The congressman who chaired the House Rules Committee apparently proposed adding 'sex' as a way of making the legislation seem ridiculous, but female legislators backed the amendment as a serious goal (Rosen, 2000: 70–4). Because the legislation was designed to deal with racial discrimination, with sex an afterthought, the Equal Employment Opportunity Commission (EEOC), which was set up to enforce Title VII, failed to take sex discrimination seriously. This became a major grievance for politically active women and spurred creation of the National Organization for Women in 1966.

2. In Canada, these opposing views were epitomized over the course of more than two decades by Dr Henry Morgentaler, a leading abortionist and abortion rights advocate, and Joe Borowski, a former NDP cabinet minister in Manitoba and anti-abortion activist, both of whom fought legal cases up to the Supreme Court of Canada and both of whom spent time in jail for their beliefs (see Morton, 1992).

CHAPTER 7

1. Like a number of other scholars (e.g., Adam, 1995; Armstrong, 2002; Engel, 2001; Raeburn, 2004; Rayside, 1998; Smith, 1999), I use 'gay and lesbian movement' to refer to efforts to advance the rights of sexual minorities, even though it would be more accurate to talk of *movements* (Epstein, 1999), which may include gay, lesbian, bisexual, and transgendered activists. Although the term 'queer' provides a convenient label to include bisexuals and transgendered persons as well as gay men and lesbians, it also tends to refer to a more specific brand of action that departs from the gay and lesbian identity-based activism that became dominant in the 1970s and remains important (cf. Armstrong, 2002: xix; Engel, 2001: xii–xiii).

2. Gamson and Meyer (1996) distinguish between 'volatile' aspects of political opportunity, such as shifting political alliances, and 'stable' aspects, such as judicial and legislative capacity and independence.

CHAPTER 9

1. The Group of Eight, known as the G8, is an annual gathering of the heads of eight major industrialized democracies—Canada, France, Germany, Italy, Japan, Russia, the UK, and the US. The group began as the G6 in 1975, becoming the G7 with the addition of Canada in 1976 and the G8 with the addition of Russia in 1997.

Glossary

adherents Those who believe in a cause and want to see movement goals achieved.

beneficiary constituents Aggrieved persons or groups that stand to benefit from the successes of a movement.

bureaucratization (formalization) Characteristic of movement organizations with established procedures for decision-making, a developed division of labour, explicit criteria for membership, and rules governing subunits such as standing committees or chapters.

bystander public A public that defines issues from a bystander's perspective, but may become involved in a conflict.

campaigns Public interactions among movement actors, their targets, the public, and other relevant actors.

centralization Characteristic of movement organizations in which there is a single centre of decision-making power.

charivari A traditional form of collective action directed towards individuals who had transgressed community norms.

collective action frames Interpretations of issues and events that inspire and legitimate collective action.

collective behaviour theory A theoretical approach to social movements that focuses on the grievances or strains that are seen as leading to collective behaviours outside of established institutions and politics.

collective campaign An 'aggregate of collective events or activities that appear to be oriented toward some relatively specific goal or good, and that occur within some proximity in space and time' (Marwell and Oliver, 1984: 12).

collective good A public good, which cannot be withheld from any members of a group or population, regardless of whether or not they work to achieve it.

collective identity A sense of shared experiences and values connecting individuals to movements and making them feel capable of effecting change through collective action.

conscience constituents Persons or groups who contribute to movements but do not personally benefit from their achievements.

constituents Supporters who contribute resources to a movement.

contentious politics Episodic, public interactions of claim-makers and their targets, typically government authorities, based on claims related to the interests of social movement actors or other claim-makers; includes both *contained contention* by established political actors and *transgressive contention*, which involves at least some 'newly self-identified political actors' and/or 'innovative collective action' by at least some parties (McAdam et al., 2001: 7–8).

countermovement A 'set of opinions and beliefs in a population opposed to a social movement' (McCarthy and Zald, 1977: 1217–18).

critical events   Events that focus the attention of movement supporters, members of the public, and authorities on particular issues, creating threats and opportunities that influence movement mobilization and outcomes.

cultural opportunity structure   Elements of cultural environments, such as ideologies, that facilitate and constrain collective action.

cycle of contention (protest cycle)   A period of heightened conflict when a number of social movements are mobilized and engaged in collective action.

diffusion   The spread of forms of contention from one site to others.

discourse analysis   Textual analysis of language and meanings in rhetoric and documents.

discursive opportunity structure   Factors, such as cultural context and mass media norms, which shape movement discourse.

externalization   '[T]he vertical projection of domestic claims onto international institutions or foreign actors' (Tarrow, 2005: 32).

frame bridging   Extension of collective action frames to connect together the concerns of different groups or movements.

free rider problem   The problem of getting individuals to participate in social movements or other collective action when they will reap the benefits of the collective action regardless of their personal participation or contributions.

global framing   The use of international symbols in the framing of domestic issues.

ideologically structured action   Activities inspired by or promoting movement ideology that take place in everyday life and within organizations and institutions.

institutionalization   The tendency of movement organizations that survive over many years to develop bureaucratic structures, rely on professional staff, and cultivate relations with government officials and other elites.

internalization   A 'response to foreign or international pressures within domestic politics' (Tarrow, 2005: 32).

internationalism   The 'structure of relations among states, non-state actors, and international institutions, and the opportunities this produces for actors to engage in collective action at different levels of this system' (Tarrow, 2005: 25).

international opportunity structure   The international space created by international institutions.

mass society theory   A theory of collective behaviour as a response to social isolation occurring in societies lacking in the secondary groups needed to bind people together and keep them attached to the mainstream society.

master frames   Generic types of frames available for use by a number of different social movements.

material incentives   Selective incentives that involve tangible rewards such as money.

mesomobilization actors   Co-ordinating groups that integrate participating groups into a movement or campaign.

micromobilization actors   The various groups that mobilize individuals to participate in protest.

mobilization   The process whereby a group that shares grievances or interests gains collective control over tangible and intangible resources.

mobilizing structures   The formal and informal networks, groups, and organizational vehicles that movements use to recruit participants and organize action campaigns.

movement entrepreneurs   Social movement leaders who take the initiative to mobilize people with similar preferences into a movement or movement organization.

multi-organizational field   The total set of organizations with which movement organizations might interact, including those that might either oppose or support the movement.

new social movement theory   A theoretical approach focusing on the new types of social movements emerging in 'post-industrial' or 'advanced capitalist' society, thought to differ in structure, type of constituents, and ideology from older movements.

political opportunity structure (political opportunities)   Features of the political environment that influence movement emergence and success, including the extent of openness in the polity, shifts in political alignments, divisions among elites, the availability of influential allies, and repression or facilitation by the state.

political process theory   A theoretical approach focusing on the interactions of social movement actors with the state and the role of political opportunities in the mobilization and outcomes of social movements.

professionalized movements   Movements that have paid leaders who work full-time for movement organizations and that often attract conscience constituents rather than beneficiaries and rely on financial contributions rather than activism from large numbers of participants.

purposive incentives   Selective incentives that come from the sense of satisfaction at having contributed to the attainment of a worthwhile cause.

rational choice theory   A theoretical approach that focuses on the costs and benefits of collective action for individuals.

recruitment   The process of getting individuals to commit resources, such as time, money, and skills, to a movement.

relative deprivation theory   A theory that collective behaviour is most likely when conditions start to improve and expectations rise, but the rate of improvement does not match expectations and people feel deprived relative to others.

repertoire of collective action   The limited set of protest forms familiar during a given time.

resource mobilization theory   A theoretical approach focusing on the resources, organization, and opportunities needed for social movement mobilization and collective action.

resources   The tangible and intangible assets available to social movement organizations and other actors.

scale shift   The shifting of co-ordination of collective action to a different level.

selective incentives   Benefits available exclusively to those who participate in collective action.

social movement   Alternatively defined as 'collective challenges, based on common purposes and social solidarities, in sustained interaction with elites, opponents, and authorities' (Tarrow, 1998: 4) or 'a set of opinions and beliefs in a population which represents preferences for changing some elements of the social structure and/or reward distribution of a society' (McCarthy and Zald, 1977: 1217–18).

social movement community   Networks of political movement organizations, individuals, cultural groups, alternative institutions, and institutional supporters in a social movement.

social movement industry   The collection of social movement organizations within a movement.

social movement organization (SMO)   A 'complex, or formal, organization which identifies its goals with the preferences of a social movement or a countermovement and attempts to implement those goals' (McCarthy and Zald, 1977: 1218).

social movement sector   All of the social movement industries in a society.

solidary incentives   Selective incentives that come from associating with a group.

spinoff movement   A movement that comes late in a protest cycle, modelled on earlier movements.

symbolic interactionism   A social-psychological theory that focuses on the ways in which actors construct meanings through social interaction.

transnational coalition formation   The creation of a network or coalition among actors from different countries.

References

Adam, Barry D. 1995. *The Rise of a Gay and Lesbian Movement*, rev. edn. New York: Twayne.

Adamson, Nancy, Linda McPhail, and Margaret Briskin. 1988. *Feminist Organizing for Change: The Contemporary Women's Movement in Canada*. Toronto: Oxford University Press.

Adkin, Laurie E. 1992. 'Counter-Hegemony and Environmental Politics in Canada', in William K. Carroll, ed., *Organizing Dissent*. Toronto: Garamond Press, 135–56.

———. 1998. *Politics of Sustainable Development: Citizens, Unions and the Corporations*. Montreal: Black Rose Books.

Alfred, Taiaiake. 1999. *Peace, Power, Righteousness: An Indigenous Manifesto*. Toronto: Oxford University Press.

Almeida, Paul. 2003. 'Opportunity Organizations and Threat-Induced Contention: Protest Waves in Authoritarian Settings', *American Journal of Sociology* 109, 2: 345–400.

Ancelovici, Marcos. 2002. 'Organizing against Globalization: The Case of ATTAC in France', *Politics & Society* 30, 3: 427–63.

Anderson, Benedict. 1991. *Imagined Communities: Reflections on the Origin and Spread of Nationalism*, rev. edn. New York: Verso.

Andrews, Kenneth T. 2004. *Freedom Is a Constant Struggle*. Chicago: University of Chicago Press.

Antrobus, Peggy. 2004. *The Global Women's Movement: Origins, Issues and Strategies*. London: Zed Books.

Armstrong, Elizabeth A. 2002. *Forging Gay Identities: Organizing Sexuality in San Francisco, 1950–1994*. Chicago: University of Chicago Press.

Asch, Michael. 1993. *Home and Native Land: Aboriginal Rights and the Canadian Constitution*. Vancouver: University of British Columbia Press.

Assembly of First Nations. *Assembly of First Nations: The Story*. At: <www.afn.ca/article. asp?id=59>.

Association for Canadian Studies. 2007. 'You Be the Judge—How Canadians View Court Decisions and How Far Has the Charter Gone in Protecting Selected Groups', poll on Charter of Rights and Freedoms commissioned from Leger Marketing, 1 Feb.

Ayres, Jeffrey M. 1998. *Defying Conventional Wisdom: Political Movements and Popular Contention against North American Free Trade*. Toronto: University of Toronto Press.

———. 1999. 'From the Streets to the Internet: The Cyber-Diffusion of Contention', *Annals, Academy of Political and Social Sciences* 566: 132–43.

———. 2004. 'Framing Collective Action against Neoliberalism: The Case of the "Anti-Globalization" Movement', *Journal of World-Systems Research* 10, 1: 11–34.

———. 2005. 'From "Anti-Globalization" to the Global Justice Movement: Framing Collective Action against Neoliberalism', in Podobnik and Reifer (2005: 9–27).

Barakso, Maryann. 2004. *Governing NOW*. Ithaca, NY: Cornell University Press.

Baumgardner, Jennifer, and Amy Richards. 2000. *Manifesta: Young Women, Feminism and the Future.* New York: Farrar, Straus and Giroux.

Beder, Sharon. 2002. *Global Spin: The Corporate Assault on Environmentalism*, rev. edn. Totnes, UK: Green Books.

Bégin, Monique. 1992. 'The Royal Commission on the Status of Women in Canada: Twenty Years Later', in Constance Backhouse and David H. Flaherty, eds, *Challenging Times: The Women's Movement in Canada and the United States.* Montreal and Kingston: McGill-Queen's University Press, 21–38.

Benford, Robert D. 1993. 'Frame Disputes within the Nuclear Disarmament Movement', *Social Forces* 71, 3: 677–701.

——— and David A. Snow. 2000. 'Framing Processes and Social Movements: An Overview and Assessment', *Annual Review of Sociology* 26: 611–39.

Bennett, W. Lance. 2003. 'Communicating Global Activism: Strengths and Vulnerabilities of Networked Politics', *Information, Communication & Society* 6, 2: 143–68.

Bernstein, Mary. 1997. 'Celebration and Suppression: The Strategic Uses of Identity by the Lesbian and Gay Movement', *American Journal of Sociology* 103, 3: 531–65.

Black, Naomi. 1993. 'The Canadian Women's Movement: The Second Wave', in Sandra Burt, Lorraine Code, and Lindsay Dorney, eds, *Changing Patterns: Women in Canada*, 2nd edn. Toronto: McClelland & Stewart, 151–75.

Blanding, Michael. 2006. 'The Case against Coca-Cola', *The Nation* 282, 17: 13–17.

Blumer, Herbert. 1951. 'Collective Behavior', in A.M. Lee, ed., *Principles of Sociology.* New York: Barnes and Noble, 166–222.

Bob, Clifford. 2005. *The Marketing of Rebellion: Insurgents, Media, and International Activism.* New York: Cambridge University Press.

Bramble, Tom, and John Minns. 2005. 'Whose Streets? Our Streets! Activist Perspectives on the Australian Anti-Capitalist Movement', *Social Movement Studies* 4, 2: 105–21.

Branch, Taylor. 1988. *Parting the Waters: America in the King Years 1954–63.* New York: Simon & Schuster.

Brodie, Janine, Shelley A.M. Gavigan, and Jane Jenson. 1992. *The Politics of Abortion.* Toronto: Oxford University Press.

Brown, Michael P. 1997. *Replacing Citizenship: AIDS Activism and Radical Democracy.* New York: Guilford Press.

Brown, Michael, and John May. 1991. *The Greenpeace Story.* New York: Dorling Kindersley.

Brulle, Robert J. 2000. *Agency, Democracy, and Nature: The U.S. Environmental Movement from a Critical Theory Perspective.* Cambridge, Mass.: MIT Press.

——— and J. Craig Jenkins. 2006. 'Spinning Our Way to Sustainability', *Organization & Environment* 19, 1: 82–7.

——— and David N. Pellow. 2006. 'Environmental Justice: Human Health and Environmental Inequalities', *Annual Review of Public Health* 27: 103–24.

Brysk, Alison, and Carol Wise. 1997. 'Liberalization and Ethnic Conflict in Latin America', *Studies in Comparative International Development* 32, 2: 76–104.

Buechler, Steven M. 1990. *Women's Movements in the United States.* New Brunswick, NJ: Rutgers University Press.

———. 1995. 'New Social Movement Theories', *Sociological Quarterly* 36, 3: 441–64.

———. 2000. *Social Movements in Advanced Capitalism.* New York: Oxford University Press.

———. 2002. 'Toward a Structural Approach to Social Movements', *Research in Political Sociology* 10: 1–45.

Burstein, Paul, Rachel L. Einwohner, and Jocelyn A. Hollander. 1995. 'The Success of Political Movements: A Bargaining Perspective', in J.C. Jenkins and B. Klandermans, eds, *The Politics of Social Protest*. Minneapolis: University of Minnesota Press, 275–95.

Bush, Evelyn, and Pete Simi. 2001. 'European Farmers and Their Protests', in D. Imig and S. Tarrow, eds, *Contentious Europeans*. Lanham, Md: Rowman & Littlefield, 97–121.

Bush, Rod. 1999. *We Are Not What We Seem: Black Nationalism and Class Struggle in the American Century*. New York: New York University Press.

Buttel, Frederik, and Kenneth Gould. 2005. 'Global Social Movements at the Crossroads: An Investigation of Relations between the Anti-Corporate Globalization and Environmental Movements', in Podobnik and Reifer (2005: 139–55).

Cairns, Alan. C. 2000. *Citizens Plus: Aboriginal Peoples and the Canadian State*. Vancouver: University of British Columbia Press.

Calhoun, Craig. 1993. '"New Social Movements" of the Early Nineteenth Century', *Social Science History* 17, 3: 385–427.

Canadian Press. 1951. 'Calls Indian Bill Dictatorial', *Globe and Mail*, 3 Mar., 8.

———. 1972. 'Iroquois Says Ottawa Seeks to Split Indians', *Globe and Mail*, 27 July, 9.

———. 1974. 'Indians Driven Off in Battle of Parliament Hill', *Globe and Mail*, 1 Oct., 1–2.

———. 1980. 'Violence Is Last thing They Want, Indians Say of Ottawa Journey', *Globe and Mail*, 27 Nov., 12.

———. 1981. 'Native Group Reviewing BNA Stand', *Globe and Mail*, 21 Apr., 8.

Carden, Maren Lockwood. 1974. *The New Feminist Movement*. New York: Russell Sage Foundation.

Cardinal, Harold. 1999. *The Unjust Society*. Vancouver: Douglas & McIntyre.

Carmin, Joann, and Deborah B. Balser. 2002. 'Selecting Repertoires of Action in Environmental Movement Organizations', *Organization & Environment* 15, 4: 365–88.

Carroll, William K., and R.S. Ratner. 1995. 'Old Unions and New Social Movements', *Labour/Le Travail* 35 (Spring): 195–221.

——— and ———. 1996. 'Master Framing and Cross-Movement Networking in Contemporary Social Movements', *Sociological Quarterly* 37, 4: 601–25.

——— and ———. 1999. 'Media Strategies and Political Projects: A Comparative Study of Social Movements', *Canadian Journal of Sociology* 24, 1: 1–34.

Carson, Clayborne. 1981. *In Struggle: SNCC and the Black Awakening of the 1960s*. Cambridge, Mass.: Harvard University Press.

Cassidy, Sean. 1992. 'The Environment and the Media: Two Strategies for Challenging Hegemony', in J. Wasko and V. Mosco, eds, *Democratic Communications in the Information Age*. Toronto: Garamond, 159–74.

Caute, David. 1988. *The Year of the Barricades: A Journey through 1968*. New York: Harper and Row.

Chafetz, Janet S., and Anthony G. Dworkin. 1986. *Female Revolt: The Rise of Women's Movements in World and Historical Perspective*. Totowa, NJ: Rowman & Littlefield.

Chauncey, George. 2004. *Why Marriage?* New York: Basic Books.

Cherniak, Donna, and Allan Feingold. 1972. 'Birth Control Handbook', in *Women Unite!* Toronto: Canadian Women's Educational Press, 109–13.

Coleman, William D. 1984. *The Independence Movement in Quebec: 1945–1980.* Toronto: University of Toronto Press.

Collier, George A., and Jane F. Collier. 2005. 'The Zapatista Rebellion in the Context of Globalization', *Journal of Peasant Studies* 32, 3 and 4: 450–60.

Congress of Aboriginal Peoples. Indian Act/Bill C-31—Part 1. At: <www.abo-peoples.org/programs/C-31/c-31-1.html>.

Connell, Robert W. 1990. 'A Whole New World: Remaking Masculinity in the Context of the Environmental Movement', *Gender & Society* 4, 4: 452–78.

Conway, Janet M. 2004. *Identity, Place, Knowledge: Social Movements Contesting Globalization.* Halifax: Fernwood.

Cornell, Stephen. 1988. *The Return of the Native: American Indian Political Resurgence.* New York: Oxford University Press.

Costain, Anne N. 1992. *Inviting Women's Rebellion: A Political Process Interpretation of the Women's Movement.* Baltimore: Johns Hopkins University Press.

Cravey, Altha J. 2004. 'Students and the Anti-Sweatshop Movement', *Antipode* 36, 2: 203–8.

Cummings, Joan Grant. 2001. 'From Natty Dreads to Grey Ponytails: The Revolution is Multi-generational', in Mitchell et al. (2001: 309–14).

Cuneo, Michael W. 1989. *Catholics against the State: Anti-Abortion Protest in Toronto.* Toronto: University of Toronto Press.

Curtis, Russell L., Jr, and Louis Zurcher Jr. 1973. 'Stable Resources of Protest Movements: The Multi-organizational Field', *Social Forces* 52: 53–61.

Dale, Stephen. 1996. *McLuhan's Children: The Greenpeace Message and the Media.* Toronto: Between the Lines.

Dalton, Russell J. 2005. 'The Greening of the Globe? Cross-national Levels of Environmental Group Membership', *Environmental Politics* 14, 4: 441–59.

Davies, James C. 1962. 'Toward a Theory of Revolution', *American Sociological Review* 27: 5–19.

———. 1971. *When Men Revolt and Why.* New York: Free Press.

Dayan, Daniel, and Elihu Katz. 1992. *Media Events: The Live Broadcasting of History.* Cambridge, Mass.: Harvard University Press.

Decima Research. 2007. 'Environment on the Agenda', press release, 4 Jan.

della Porta, Donatella. 1995. *Social Movements, Political Violence, and the State.* Cambridge: Cambridge University Press.

———, Massimiliano Andretta, Lorenzo Mosca, and Herbert Reiter. 2006. *Globalization from Below: Transnational Activists and Protest Networks.* Minneapolis: University of Minnesota Press.

——— and Olivier Fillieule. 2004. 'Policing Social Protest', in Snow et al. (2004: 217–41).

D'Emilio, John. 1983. *Sexual Politics, Sexual Communities: The Making of a Homosexual Minority in the United States, 1940–1970.* Chicago: University of Chicago Press.

Devall, Bill. 1992. 'Deep Ecology and Radical Environmentalism', in Riley E. Dunlap and Angela G. Mertig, eds, *American Environmentalism: The U.S. Environmental Movement, 1970–1990.* Philadelphia: Taylor and Francis, 51–62.

Diani, Mario. 1992. 'The Concept of Social Movement', *Sociological Review* 40, 1: 1–25.

———. 1997. 'Social Movements and Social Capital: A Network Perspective on Movement Outcomes', *Mobilization* 2, 2: 129–47.

Dickason, Olive Patricia. 2002. *Canada's First Nations: A History of Founding Peoples from Earliest Times*, 3rd edn. Toronto: Oxford University Press.

Doherty, Brian. 1999. 'Paving the Way: The Rise of Direct Action against Road-building and the Changing Character of British Environmentalism', *Political Studies* 47, 2: 275–91.

Dowie, Mark. 1995. *Losing Ground: American Environmentalism at the Close of the Twentieth Century*. Cambridge, Mass.: MIT Press.

Downs, Anthony. 1972. 'Up and Down with Ecology—The "Issue-Attention Cycle"', *Public Interest* 28: 38–50.

Downton, James V., Jr, and Paul E. Wehr. 1991. 'Peace Movements: The Role of Commitment and Community in Sustaining Member Participation', *Research in Social Movements, Conflicts and Change* 13: 113–34.

Duberman, Martin B. 1993. *Stonewall*. New York: Dutton.

Duchen, Claire. 1994. *Women's Rights and Women's Lives in France, 1944–1968*. New York: Routledge.

Dunlap, Riley E. 2006. 'Show Us the Data', *Organization & Environment* 19, 1: 88–102.

Earl, Jennifer. 2004. 'The Cultural Consequences of Social Movements', in Snow et al. (2004: 508–30).

―――― and Alan Schussman. 2003. 'The New Site of Activism: On-Line Organizations, Movement Entrepreneurs, and the Changing Location of Social Movement Decision Making', *Research in Social Movements, Conflicts and Change* 24: 155–87.

Eberts, Mary. 2005. *Aboriginal Women's Rights are Human Rights*. Ottawa: Department of Justice Canada. At: <www.justice.gc.ca/char/en/eberts.html>.

Echols, Alice. 1989. *Daring to Be Bad: Radical Feminism in America, 1967–1975*. Minneapolis: University of Minnesota Press.

Edwards, Bob, and John D. McCarthy. 2004. 'Resources and Social Movement Mobilization', in Snow et al. (2004: 116–52).

Eisinger, Peter K. 1973. 'The Conditions of Protest Behavior in American Cities', *American Political Science Review* 67: 11–28.

Engel, Stephen M. 2001. *The Unfinished Revolution: Social Movement Theory and the Gay and Lesbian Movement*. Cambridge: Cambridge University Press.

Epstein, Barbara. 1991. *Political Protest and Cultural Revolution: Nonviolent Direct Action in the 1970s and 1980s*. Berkeley: University of California Press.

―――― . 2001. 'What Happened to the Women's Movement?', *Monthly Review* 53, 1: 1–13.

Epstein, Steven. 1999. 'Gay and Lesbian Movements in the United States: Dilemmas of Identity, Diversity, and Political Strategy', in B.D. Adam, J.W. Duyvendak, and A. Krouwel, eds, *The Global Emergence of Gay and Lesbian Politics*. Philadelphia: Temple University Press, 30–90.

Erwin, Lorna. 1993. 'Neoconservatism and the Canadian Pro-Family Movement', *Canadian Review of Sociology and Anthropology* 30, 3: 401–20.

Evans, Sara. 1979. *Personal Politics: The Roots of Women's Liberation in the Civil Rights Movement and the New Left*. New York: Vintage Books.

―――― . 2003. *Tidal Wave: How Women Changed America at Century's End*. New York: Free Press.

Eyerman, Ron, and Andrew Jamison. 1989. 'Environmental Knowledge as an Organizational Weapon: The Case of Greenpeace', *Social Science Information* 28, 1: 99–119.

Fairclough, Adam. 1987. *To Redeem the Soul of America: The Southern Christian Leadership Conference and Martin Luther King, Jr.* Athens: University of Georgia Press.

Ferree, Myra Marx, William Anthony Gamson, Jürgen Gerhards, and Dieter Rucht. 2002. *Shaping Abortion Discourse: Democracy and the Public Sphere in Germany and the United States.* Cambridge: Cambridge University Press.

—— and Carol McClurg Mueller. 2004. 'Feminism and the Women's Movement: A Global Perspective', in Snow et al. (2004: 576–607).

Findlen, Barbara, ed. 2001. *Listen Up: Voices from the Next Feminist Generation*, 2nd edn. Emeryville, Calif.: Seal Press.

Fireman, Bruce, and William A. Gamson. 1979. 'Utilitarian Logic in the Resource Mobilization Perspective', in M.N. Zald and J.D. McCarthy, eds, *The Dynamics of Social Movements: Resource Mobilization, Social Control, and Tactics.* Cambridge, Mass.: Winthrop, 8–44.

Flanagan, Tom. 2000. *First Nations? Second Thoughts.* Montreal and Kingston: McGill-Queen's University Press.

Fleras, Augie, and Jean Leonard Elliott. 1992. *The 'Nations Within': Aboriginal–State Relations in Canada, the United States, and New Zealand.* Toronto. Oxford University Press.

—— and ——. 2003. *Unequal Relations: An Introduction to Race and Ethnic Dynamics in Canada*, 4th edn. Toronto: Prentice-Hall.

Francome, Colin. 1984. *Abortion Freedom—A Worldwide Movement.* Winchester, Mass.: Allen and Unwin.

Fraser, Ronald. 1988. *1968: A Student Generation in Revolt.* London: Chatto & Windus.

Freeman, Jo. 1975. *The Politics of Women's Liberation.* New York: Longman.

——. 1979. 'Resource Mobilization and Strategy: A Model for Analyzing Social Movement Organization Actions', in M.N. Zald and J.D. McCarthy, eds, *The Dynamics of Social Movements: Resource Mobilization, Social Control, and Tactics.* Cambridge, Mass.: Winthrop, 167–89.

Gagné, Marie-Anik. 1994. *A Nation within a Nation: Dependency and the Cree.* Montreal: Black Rose Books.

Gamson, Josh. 1989. 'Silence, Death, and the Invisible Enemy: AIDS Activism and Social Movement "Newness"', *Social Problems* 36, 4: 351–67.

Gamson, William A. 1990. *The Strategy of Social Protest*, 2nd edn. Belmont, Calif.: Wadsworth. (First edition 1975.)

——. 1998. 'Social Movements and Cultural Change', in Marco G. Giugni, Doug McAdam, and Charles Tilly, eds, *From Contention to Democracy.* Lanham, Md: Rowman & Littlefield, 57–77.

——. 2004. 'Bystanders, Public Opinion, and the Media', in Snow et al. (2004: 242–61).

—— and David S. Meyer. 1996. 'Framing Political Opportunity', in McAdam et al. (1996: 275–90).

—— and Gadi Wolfsfeld. 1993. 'Movements and Media as Interacting Systems', *Annals, Academy of Political and Social Science* 528: 114–25.

Gans, Herbert J. 1979. *Deciding What's News: A Study of CBS Evening News, NBC Nightly News, Newsweek and Time.* New York: Vintage Books.

Ganz, Marshall. 2000. 'Resources and Resourcefulness: Strategic Capacity in the Unionization of California Agriculture, 1959–1966', *American Journal of Sociology* 105, 4: 1003–62.

Garrow, David J. 1986. *Bearing the Cross: Martin Luther King, Jr. and the Southern Christian Leadership Conference*. New York: Vintage Books.

Gazette (Montreal). 2001. 'Protesters Make Dent in Agenda', 19 July.

———. 2001. 'Unlikely Allies Descend on Italy', 20 July.

———. 2006. 'Proud and Loud in Toronto', 26 June.

Gerhards, Jürgen, and Dieter Rucht. 1992. 'Mesomobilization: Organizing and Framing in Two Protest Campaigns in West Germany', *American Journal of Sociology* 98, 3 (Nov.): 555–95.

Gerlach, Luther, and Virginia H. Hine. 1970. *People, Power, Change: Movements of Social Transformation*. Indianapolis: Bobbs-Merrill.

Gilmore, Stephanie. 2005. 'Bridging the Waves: Sex and Sexuality in a Second Wave Organization', in Reger (2005: 97–116).

Gitlin, Todd. 1980. *The Whole World Is Watching: Mass Media and the Making of the New Left*. Berkeley, Calif.: University of California Press.

———. 1987. *The Sixties: Years of Hope, Days of Rage*. New York: Bantam Books.

Giugni, Marco G. 1998. 'Was It Worth the Effort? The Outcomes and Consequences of Social Movements', *Annual Review of Sociology* 98: 371–93.

Globe and Mail. 1959. 'Secession: Chiefs to Supervise Six Nations Affairs, Form Own Government', 6 Mar., 1.

———. 1972. 'Ontario Group Wants Ottawa to "Live Up to Commitment": Indians Occupy Federal Office to Protest Holding Back of Grants', 18 July, 5.

———. 1990a. 'CBC News/Poll', 9 July, A4.

———. 1990b. 'Ontario Natives Blockade Roads, Rail Line', 6 Sept., A6.

———. 1994. 'Myth of Eternal Forest Toppled', 14 July, A1, A3.

Goddu, Jenn. 1999. '"Powerless, Public-Spirited Women", "Angry Feminists", and "The Muffin Lobby": Newspaper and Magazine Coverage of Three National Women's Groups from 1980 to 1995', *Canadian Journal of Communication* 24: 105–26.

Goodwin, Jeff, and James M. Jasper. 1999. 'Caught in a Winding, Snarling Vine: The Structural Bias of Political Process Theory', *Sociological Forum* 14, 1: 27–54.

———, ———, and Francesca Polletta, eds. 2001. *Passionate Politics: Emotions and Social Movements*. Chicago: University of Chicago Press.

Gould, Deborah B. 2002. 'Life during Wartime: Emotions and the Development of Act Up', *Mobilization* 7, 2: 177–200.

Gould, Kenneth, Tammy Lewis, and J. Timmons Roberts. 2005. 'Blue–Green Coalitions: Constraints and Possibilities in the Post 9/11 Political Environment', in Podobnik and Reifer (2005: 123–38).

Gould, Roger V. 1993. 'Collective Action and Network Structure', *American Sociological Review* 58, 2: 182–96.

Graff, E.J. 1999. 'Same-Sex Spouses in Canada', *The Nation* 269, 2 (12 July): 23–4.

Grand Council of the Crees. 1998. *Never without Consent: James Bay Crees' Stand against Forcible Inclusion into an Independent Québec*. Toronto: ECW Press.

Guillemin, Jeanne. 1978. 'The Politics of National Integration: A Comparison of United States and Canadian Indian Administrations', *Social Problems* 25, 3: 319–32.

Gurney, Joan Neff, and Kathleen J. Tierney. 1982. 'Relative Deprivation and Social Movements: A Critical Look at Twenty Years of Theory and Research', *Sociological Quarterly* 23, 1: 33–47.

Gurr, Ted Robert. 1970. *Why Men Rebel.* Princeton, NJ: Princeton University Press.

Gusfield, Joseph R. 1981. 'Social Movements and Social Change: Perspectives of Linearity and Fluidity', *Social Movements, Conflicts and Change* 4: 317–39.

Habermas, Jürgen. 1984. *The Theory of Communicative Action,* vol. 1, trans. Thomas McCarthy. Boston: Beacon Press.

———. 1987. *The Theory of Communicative Action,* vol. 2, trans. Thomas McCarthy. Boston: Beacon Press.

Hacket, Robert A., and Richard Gruneau. 2000. *The Missing News: Filters and the Blind Spots in Canada's Press.* Aurora, Ont.: Garamond Press.

Hagan, John. 2001. *Northern Passage: American Vietnam War Resisters in Canada.* Cambridge, Mass.: Harvard University Press.

Haig-Brown, Celia. 1988. *Resistance and Renewal: Surviving the Indian Residential School.* Vancouver: Arsenal Pulp Press.

Halleck, DeeDee. 2003. 'Gathering Storm: Cyberactivism after Seattle', in J. Harper and T. Yantek, eds, *Media, Profit, and Politics: Competing Priorities in an Open Society.* Kent, Ohio: Kent State University Press, 202–14.

Hallin, Daniel C. 1989. *The 'Uncensored War': The Media and Vietnam.* Berkeley: University of California Press.

Hartmann, Susan M. 1998. *The Other Feminists: Activists in the Liberal Establishment.* New Haven: Yale University Press.

Hawkesworth, Mary. 2004. 'The Semiotics of Premature Burial: Feminism in a Postfeminist Age', *Signs* 29, 4:961–85.

Heirich, Max. 1968. *The Spiral of Conflict: Berkeley, 1964.* New York: Columbia University Press.

Henry, Astrid. 2004. *Not My Mother's Sister: Generational Conflict and Third-Wave Feminism.* Bloomington: Indiana University Press.

———. 2005. 'Solitary Sisterhood: Individualism Meets Collectivity in Feminism's Third Wave', in Reger (2005: 81–96).

Heywood, Leslie, and Jennifer Drake, eds. 1997. *Third Wave Agenda: Being Feminist, Doing Feminism.* Minneapolis: University of Minnesota Press.

Hoffer, Eric. 1951. *The True Believer.* New York: Harper.

Hole, Judith, and Ellen Levine. 1971. *Rebirth of Feminism.* New York: Quadrangle Books.

Hull, Kathleen E. 2006. *Same-Sex Marriage: The Cultural Politics of Love and Law.* Cambridge: Cambridge University Press.

Hunter, Robert. 2004. *The Greenpeace to Amchitka: An Environmental Odyssey.* Vancouver: Arsenal Pulp Press.

Indian and Northern Affairs Canada. 1996. *Report of the Royal Commission on Aboriginal Peoples.* Ottawa: Indian and Northern Affairs Canada. At: <www.ainc-inac.gc.ca/ch/rcap/sg/sgmm_e.html>.

———. 1996. *Report of the Royal Commission on Aboriginal Peoples,* Section 9.12 (Indian Voting Rights). Ottawa: Indian and Northern Affairs Canada. At: <www.ainc-inac.gc.ca/ch/rcap/sg/sg26_e.html#92>.

———. 1996. *Report of the Royal Commission on Aboriginal Peoples,* Section 9.5 (Attacks on Traditional Culture). Ottawa: Indian and Northern Affairs Canada. At: <www.ainc-inac.gc.ca/ch/rcap/sg/sg25_e.html#85>.

———. n.d. *The James Bay and Northern Quebec Agreement and the Northeastern Quebec Agreement: History*. Ottawa: Indian and Northern Affairs Canada. At: <www.ainc-inac.gc.ca/pr/info/info14_e.html>.

Inglehart, Ronald. 1990. *Culture Shift in Advanced Industrial Society*. Princeton, NJ: Princeton University Press.

———. 1995. 'Public Support for Environmental Protection: Objective Problems and Subjective Values in 43 Societies', *PS: Political Science and Politics* 28, 1: 57–72.

Jasper, James M. 1998. 'The Emotions of Protest: Affective and Reactive Emotions in and around Social Movements', *Sociological Forum* 13, 3: 397–424.

Jenkins, J. Craig. 1981. 'Sociopolitical Movements', in S.L. Long, ed., *Handbook of Political Behavior*, vol. 4. New York: Plenum, 81–154.

———. 1983. 'Resource Mobilization Theory and the Study of Social Movements', *Annual Review of Sociology* 9: 527–53.

———, David Jacobs, and Jon Agnone. 2003. 'Political Opportunities and African-American Protest, 1948–1997', *American Journal of Sociology* 109, 2: 277–303.

——— and Charles Perrow. 1977. 'Insurgency of the Powerless: Farm Workers Movements, 1946–1972', *American Sociological Review* 42: 249–68.

Jenson, Jane. 1992. 'Getting to Morgentaler: From One Representation to Another', in Brodie et al. (1992: 15–55).

——— and Martin Papillon. 2000. 'Challenging the Citizenship Regime: The James Bay Cree and Transnational Action', *Politics & Society* 28, 2: 245–64.

Johnson, Troy R. 1996. *The Occupation of Alcatraz Island: Indian Self-Determination and the Rise of Indian Activism*. Urbana: University of Illinois Press.

Josephy, Alvin M., Jr, Joane Nagel, and Troy Johnson. 1999. *Red Power: The American Indians' Fight for Freedom*, 2nd edn. Lincoln: University of Nebraska Press.

Kaplan, Laura. 1995. *The Story of Jane: The Legendary Underground Feminist Abortion Service*. New York: Pantheon Books.

Katzenstein, Mary Fainsod. 1998. *Faithful and Fearless: Moving Feminist Protest inside the Church and Military*. Princeton, NJ: Princeton University Press.

Keck, Margaret E., and Kathryn Sikkink. 1998. *Activists Beyond Borders: Advocacy Networks in International Politics*. Ithaca, NY: Cornell University Press.

Kennedy, Elizabeth L., and Madeline D. Davis. 1993. *Boots of Leather, Slippers of Gold: The History of a Lesbian Community*. New York: Penguin Books.

Khasnabish, Alex. 2004. 'Moments of Coincidence: Exploring the Intersection of Zapatismo and Independent Labour in Mexico', *Critique of Anthropology* 24, 3: 256–76.

Kielbowicz, Richard B., and Clifford Scherer. 1986. 'The Role of the Press in the Dynamics of Social Movements', *Research in Social Movements, Conflicts and Change* 9: 71–96.

Killian, Lewis M. 1994. 'Are Social Movements Irrational or Are They Collective Behavior?', in R.R. Dynes and K.J. Tierney, eds, *Disasters, Collective Behavior, and Social Organization*. Newark: University of Delaware Press, 273–80.

Klandermans, Bert. 1986. 'New Social Movements and Resource Mobilization: The European and American Approach', *International Journal of Mass Emergencies and Disasters* 4: 13–37.

———. 1992. 'The Social Construction of Protest and Multiorganizational Fields', in A.D. Morris and C.M. Mueller, eds, *Frontiers in Social Movement Theory*. New Haven: Yale University Press.

————. 1997. *The Social Psychology of Protest*. Oxford: Blackwell.

———— and Dirk Oegema. 1987. 'Potentials, Networks, Motivations, and Barriers: Steps towards Participation in Social Movements', *American Sociological Review* 52, 4: 519–31.

Kleidman, Robert. 1993. *Organizing for Peace: Neutrality, the Test Ban, and the Freeze*. Syracuse, NY: Syracuse University Press.

Klein, Naomi. 1999. *No Logo*. New York: Picador.

Kornhauser, William. 1959. *The Politics of a Mass Society*. New York: Free Press.

Kostash, Myrna. 1980. *Long Way from Home: The Story of the Sixties Generation in Canada*. Toronto: James Lorimer.

Krieber, Janine. 1989. 'Protest and Fringe Groups in Québec', in C.E.S. Franks, ed., *Dissent and the State*. Toronto: Oxford University Press, 211–23.

Kriesi, Hanspeter, Rudd Koopmans, Jan Willem Duyvendak, and Marco G. Giugni. 1995. *New Social Movements in Western Europe: A Comparative Analysis*. Minneapolis: University of Minnesota Press.

Kurzman, Charles. 2004. 'The Poststructuralist Consensus in Social Movement Theory', in Jeff Goodwin and James M. Jasper, eds, *Rethinking Social Movements*. Lanham, Md: Rowman & Littlefield, 111–20.

Kutchins, Herb, and Stuart A. Kirk. 1997. *Making Us Crazy*. New York: Free Press.

La Botz, Dan. 2002. 'After a Decade of Antisweatshop Organizing, Activists Say It's Time They Pulled Together', 28 June. At: <www.organicconsumers.org/clothes/sweatshop_movement. cfm>.

Lang, Kurt, and Gladys E. Lang. 1961. *Collective Dynamics*. New York: Thomas Y. Crowell.

Langford, Tom, and J. Rick Ponting. 1992. 'Canadians' Responses to Aboriginal Issues: The Roles of Prejudice, Perceived Group Conflict and Economic Conservatism', *Canadian Review of Sociology and Anthropology* 29, 2: 140–66.

Lawrence, Bonita. 2003. 'Gender, Race, and the Regulation of Native Identity in Canada and the United States: An Overview', *Hypatia* 18, 2: 3–31.

Le Bon, Gustav. 1895. *The Crowd*. New York: Viking.

Leiserowitz, Anthony A., Robert W. Kates, and Thomas M. Parris. 2005. 'Do Global Attitudes and Behaviors Support Sustainable Development?', *Environment* 47, 9: 22–38.

Lent, Adam. 2003. 'The Transformation of Gay and Lesbian Politics in Britain', *British Journal of Politics and International Relations* 5, 1: 24–49.

Levi, Margaret, David J. Olson, and Erich Steinman. 2004. 'Living Wage Movement', in I. Ness, ed., *Encyclopedia of American Social Movements*, vol. 4. Armonk, NY: Sharpe Reference.

Levitt, Cyril. 1984. *Children of Privilege: Student Revolt in the Sixties: A Study of Student Movements in Canada, the United States, and West Germany*. Toronto: University of Toronto Press.

Lichterman, Paul. 1996. *The Search for Political Community: American Activists Reinventing Commitment*. Cambridge: Cambridge University Press.

Lofland, John. 1979. 'White-Hot Mobilization: Strategies of a Millenarian Movement', in M.N. Zald and J.D. McCarthy, eds, *The Dynamics of Social Movements*. Cambridge, Mass.: Winthrop, 157–66.

Long, David. 1992. 'Culture, Ideology, and Militancy: The Movement of Native Indians in Canada, 1969–1991', in W.K. Carroll, ed., *Organizing Dissent: Contemporary Social Movements in Theory and Practice*. Toronto: Garamond Press, 118–34.

Lowe, Philip, and Jane Goyder. 1983. *Environmental Groups in Politics.* London: George Allen & Unwin.

McAdam, Doug. 1983. 'Tactical Innovation and the Pace of Insurgency', *American Sociological Review* 48, 6: 735–54.

———. 1986. 'Recruitment to High-Risk Activism: The Case of Freedom Summer', *American Journal of Sociology* 92, 1: 64–90.

———. 1988. *Freedom Summer.* New York: Oxford University Press.

———. 1994. 'Culture and Social Movements', in E. Larana, H. Johnston, and J.R. Gusfield, eds, *New Social Movements: From Ideology to Identity.* Philadelphia: Temple University Press, 36–57.

———. 1995. '"Initiator" and "Spin-off" Movements: Diffusion Processes in Protest Cycles', in M. Traugott, ed., *Repertoires and Cycles of Collective Action.* Durham, NC: Duke University Press, 217–39.

———. 1996. 'The Framing Function of Movement Tactics: Strategic Dramaturgy in the American Civil Rights Movement', in McAdam et al. (1996: 338–55).

———. 1999. *Political Process and the Development of Black Insurgency*, 2nd edn. Chicago: University of Chicago Press. (First edition 1982.)

——— and Debra Friedman. 1992. 'Collective Identity and Activism: Networks, Choices, and the Life of a Social Movement', in Aldon D. Morris and Carol M. Mueller, eds, *Frontiers in Social Movement Theory.* New Haven: Yale University Press, 156–73.

———, John D. McCarthy, and Mayer N. Zald. 1988. 'Social Movements', in J.S. Neil, ed., *Handbook of Sociology.* Newbury Park, Calif.: Sage, 695–737.

———, ———, and ———, eds. 1996. *Comparative Perspectives on Social Movements.* New York: Cambridge University Press.

——— and Dieter Rucht. 1993. 'The Cross-National Diffusion of Movement Ideas', *Annals, American Academy of Political and Social Science* 528: 56–74.

——— and William Sewell Jr. 2001. 'It's About Time: Temporality in the Study of Social Movements and Revolutions', in R. Aminzade, J. Goldstone, D. McAdam, E. Perry, W. Sewell, S. Tarrow, and C. Tilly, eds, *Silence and Voice in Contentious Politics.* Cambridge: Cambridge University Press, 89–125.

———, Sidney Tarrow, and Charles Tilly. 2001. *Dynamics of Contention.* Cambridge: Cambridge University Press.

McCammon, Holly J. 2001. 'Stirring Up Suffrage Sentiment: The Formation of the State Women's Suffrage Organizations, 1866–1914', *Social Forces* 80, 2: 449–80.

McCarthy, John D., and Mayer N. Zald. 1973. *The Trend of Social Movements in America: Professionalization and Resource Mobilization.* Morristown, NJ: General Learning Press.

——— and ———. 1977. 'Resource Mobilization and Social Movements: A Partial Theory', *American Journal of Sociology* 82, 6: 1212–41.

——— and ———. 2002. 'The Enduring Vitality of the Resource Mobilization Theory of Social Movements', in H.T. Jonathan, ed., *Handbook of Sociological Theory.* New York: Kluwer Academic/Plenum, 533–65.

McCloskey, Michael. 1992. 'Twenty Years of Change in the Environmental Movement: An Insider's View', in Riley E. Dunlap and Angela G. Mertig, eds, *American Environmentalism: The U.S. Environmental Movement, 1970–1990.* Philadelphia: Taylor and Francis, 77–88.

McComas, Katherine, and James Shanahan. 1999. 'Telling Stories about Global Climate Change', *Communication Research* 26, 1: 30–57.

McKenzie, Judith I. 2002. *Environmental Politics in Canada: Managing the Commons into the Twenty-First Century*. Toronto: Oxford University Press.

McRoberts, Kenneth. 1993. *Quebec: Social Change and Political Crisis*, 3rd edn. Toronto: Oxford University Press.

Mansbridge, Jane J. 1986. *Why We Lost the ERA*. Chicago: University of Chicago Press.

Maracle, Lee. 1992. *Sundogs*. Penticton, BC: Theytus Books.

Marwell, Gerald, and Pamela Oliver. 1984. 'Collective Action Theory and Social Movements Research', *Research in Social Movements, Conflicts and Change*, 7: 1–27.

———— and ————. 1993. *The Critical Mass in Collective Action: A Micro-Social Theory*. Cambridge: Cambridge University Press.

Marwick, Arthur. 1998. *The Sixties: Cultural Revolution in Britain, France, Italy, and the United States*. New York: Oxford University Press.

Marx, Gary T., and James L. Wood. 1975. 'Strands of Theory and Research in Collective Behavior', *Annual Review of Sociology* 1: 363–428.

Matthews, J. Scott. 2005. 'The Political Foundations of Support for Same-Sex Marriage in Canada', *Canadian Journal of Political Science* 38, 4: 841–66.

Mayo, Marjorie. 2005. *Global Citizens: Social Movements and the Challenge of Globalization*. New York: Zed Books.

Meier, August, and Elliott Rudwick. 1973. *CORE: A Study of the Civil Rights Movement, 1942–1968*. Urbana: University of Illinois Press.

Melucci, Alberto. 1988. 'Getting Involved: Identity and Mobilization in Social Movements', *International Social Movement Research* 1: 329–48.

————. 1989. *Nomads of the Present: Social Movements and Individual Needs in Contemporary Society*, ed. John Keane and Paul Mier. Philadelphia: Temple University Press.

————. 1996. *Challenging Codes: Collective Action in the Information Age*. Cambridge: Cambridge University Press.

Meyer, David S. 2004. 'Protest and Political Opportunities', *Annual Review of Sociology* 30: 125–45.

———— and Suzanne Staggenborg. 1996. 'Movements, Countermovements, and the Structure of Political Opportunity', *American Journal of Sociology* 101, 6: 1628–60.

———— and ————. 1998. 'Countermovement Dynamics in Federal Systems: A Comparison of Abortion Politics in Canada and the United States', *Research in Political Sociology* 8: 209–40.

———— and Nancy Whittier. 1994. 'Social Movement Spillover', *Social Problems* 41, 2: 277–98.

Miller, James R. 1989. *Skyscrapers Hide the Heavens: A History of Indian–White Relations in Canada*. Toronto: University of Toronto Press.

Mitchell, Allyson, Lisa Bryn Rundle, and Lara Karaian, eds. 2001. *Turbo Chicks: Talking Young Feminisms*. Toronto: Sumach Press.

Mitchell, Robert Cameron. 1979. 'National Environmental Lobbies and the Apparent Illogic of Collective Action', in C.S. Russel, *Collective Decision Making: Applications from Public Choice Theory*. Baltimore: Johns Hopkins University Press, 87–136.

———. 1984. 'Public Opinion and Environmental Politics in the 1970's and 1980's', in J.V. Norman and M.E. Kraft, eds, *Environmental Policy in the 1980's: Reagan's New Agenda*. Washington: Congressional Quarterly Press, 51–74.

———, Angela G. Mertig, and Riley E. Dunlap. 1992. 'Twenty Years of Environmental Mobilization: Trends among National Environmental Organizations', in Riley E. Dunlap and Angela G. Mertig, eds, *American Environmentalism: The U.S. Environmental Movement, 1970–1990*. Philadelphia: Taylor and Francis, 11–26.

Moghadam, Valentine M. 2005. *Globalizing Women*. Baltimore: Johns Hopkins University Press.

Morgan, Rhiannon. 2004. 'Advancing Indigenous Rights at the United Nations: Strategic Framing and Its Impact on the Normative Development of International Law', *Social and Legal Studies* 13, 4: 481–500.

Morris, Aldon D. 1981. 'Black Southern Student Sit-In Movement: An Analysis of Internal Organization', *American Sociological Review* 46, 4: 744–67.

———. 1984. *The Origins of the Civil Rights Movement: Black Communities Organizing for Change*. New York: Free Press.

———. 2000. 'Reflections on Social Movement Theory: Criticisms and Proposals', *Contemporary Sociology* 29: 445–54.

——— and Cedric Herring. 1987. 'Theory and Research in Social Movements: A Critical Review', *Annual Review in Political Science* 2: 137–98.

——— and Suzanne Staggenborg. 2004. 'Leadership in Social Movements', in Snow et al. (2004: 171–96).

Morris, Stephen D. 2001. 'Between Neo-Liberal and Neo-Indigenismo: Reconstructing National Identity in Mexico', *National Identities* 3, 3: 239–55.

Morris, William. 1969a. 'Chretien Capitulates to Indians' Demands, Backs Panel to Probe Treaty, Related Rights', *Globe and Mail*, 3 May, 10.

———. 1969b. 'Ottawa Plans to Abolish Treaties, Move Out of Indian Affairs in 5 Years', *Globe and Mail*, 26 June, 1–2

Morton, F.L. 1992. *Morgentaler v. Borowski: Abortion, the Charter, and the Courts*. Toronto: McClelland & Stewart.

Mueller, Carol McClurg. 1987. 'Collective Consciousness, Identity Transformation, and the Rise of Women in Public Office in the United States', in M. Mary Fainsod Katzenstein and Carol McClurg, eds, *The Women's Movements in the United States and Western Europe: Consciousness, Political Opportunity and Public Policy*. Philadelphia: Temple University Press, 89–108.

———. 1994. 'Conflict Networks and the Origins of Women's Liberation', in E. Laraña, H. Johnston, and J.R. Gusfield, eds, *New Social Movements*. Philadelphia: Temple University Press, 234–63.

Myers, Daniel J. 1994. 'Communication Technology and Social Movements: Contributions of Computer Networks to Activism', *Social Science Computer Review* 12, 2: 250–60.

Nagel, Joane. 1994. 'Constructing Ethnicity: Creating and Recreating Ethnic Identity and Culture', *Social Problems* 41, 1: 152–76.

———. 1995. 'American Indian Ethnic Renewal: Politics and the Resurgence of Identity', *American Sociological Review* 60, 6: 947–65.

———. 1996. *American Indian Ethnic Renewal: Red Power and the Resurgence of Identity and Culture*. New York: Oxford University Press.

New York Times. 1999. 'Loggers Find Canadian Rain Forest Flush with Foes', 22 Oct.

Niezen, Ronald. 2000. 'Recognizing Indigenism: Canadian Unity and the International Movement of Indigenous Peoples', *Comparative Studies in Society and History* 42, 1: 119–48.

Noonan, Rita K. 1995. 'Women against the State: Political Opportunities and Collective Action Frames in Chile's Transition to Democracy', *Sociological Forum* 10, 1: 81–111.

Oberschall, Anthony. 1973. *Social Conflict and Social Movements.* Englewood Cliffs, NJ: Prentice-Hall.

———. 1978. 'The Decline of the 1960s Social Movements', *Research in Social Movements, Conflicts, and Change* 1: 257–89.

Obonsawin, Roger, and Heather Howard-Bobiwash. 1997. 'The Native Canadian Centre of Toronto: The Meeting Place for the Aboriginal Community for 35 Years', in Frances Sanderson and Heather Howard-Bobiwash, eds, *The Meeting Place: Aboriginal Life in Toronto.* Toronto: Native Canadian Centre of Toronto.

Office of the High Commission of Human Rights. *Fact Sheet No. 9 (Rev. 1), The Rights of Indigenous Peoples.* New York: Office of the High Commission of Human Rights. At: <www.unhchr.ch/html/menu6/2/fs9.htm>.

Oliver, Pamela E., Jorge Cadena-Roa, and Kelley D. Strawn. 2003. 'Emerging Trends in the Study of Protest and Social Movements', *Research in Political Sociology* 12: 213–44.

Olson, Mancur. 1965. *The Logic of Collective Action: Public Goods and the Theory of Groups.* Cambridge, Mass.: Harvard University Press.

Owram, Doug. 1996. *Born at the Right Time: A History of the Baby-Boom Generation.* Toronto: University of Toronto Press.

Paehlke, Robert. 1997. 'Green Politics and the Rise of the Environmental Movement', in Thomas Fleming, ed., *The Environment and Canadian Society.* Scarborough, Ont.: ITP Nelson, 252–74.

Park, Robert E., and Ernest W. Burgess. 1921. *Introduction to the Science of Sociology.* Chicago: University of Chicago Press.

Peckham, Michael. 1998. 'New Dimensions of Social Movement/Countermovement Interaction: The Case of Scientology and Its Internet Critics', *Canadian Journal of Sociology* 23, 4: 317–47.

Perrow, Charles. 1979. 'The Sixties Observed', in Mayer N. Zald and John D. McCarthy, eds, *The Dynamics of Social Movements.* Cambridge, Mass.: Winthrop, 192–211.

Pianta, Mario. 2003. 'Democracy vs Globalization. The Growth of Parallel Summits and Global Movements', in D. Archibugi, ed., *Debating Cosmopolitics.* London: Verso, 232–56.

Pichardo, Nelson A. 1997. 'New Social Movements: A Critical Review', *Annual Review of Sociology* 23: 411–30.

Pierceson, Jason. 2005. *Courts, Liberalism, and Rights: Gay Law and Politics in the United States and Canada.* Philadelphia: Temple University Press.

Piven, Frances Fox, and Richard A. Cloward. 1977. *Poor People's Movements: Why They Succeed, How They Fail.* New York: Vintage Books.

Platiel, Rudy. 1970. 'Indians Warn Battles Over Treaties May Fill the Courts', *Globe and Mail,* 15 Apr., 5.

Podobnik, Bruce. 2005. 'Resistance to Globalization: Cycles and Trends in the Globalization Protest Movement', in Podobnik and Reifer (2005: 51–68).

——— and T. Reifer, eds. 2005. *Transforming Globalization.* Leiden, Netherlands: Brill.

Poirier, Patricia. 1990. 'Mohawks Prepared for Talks to Resume: Hint at Proposals to Reopen Bridge', *Globe and Mail*, 27 Aug., A1, A3.

Polletta, Francesca. 1997. 'Culture and Its Discontents: Recent Theorizing on the Cultural Dimensions of Protest', *Sociological Inquiry* 67, 4: 431–50.

———. 2002. *Freedom Is an Endless Meeting*. Chicago: University of Chicago Press.

———. 2004. 'Culture in and Outside of Institutions', *Research in Social Movements, Conflicts and Change* 25: 161–83.

——— and M. Kai Ho. 2006. 'Frames and Their Consequences', in R.E. Goodin and C. Tilly, eds, *The Oxford Handbook of Contextual Political Analysis*. Oxford: Oxford University Press, 187–209.

——— and James M. Jasper. 2001. 'Collective Identity and Social Movements', *Annual Review of Sociology* 27: 283–305.

Ponting, J. Rick. 2000. 'Public Opinion on Canadian Aboriginal Issues, 1976–98: Persistence, Change, and Cohort Analysis', *Canadian Ethnic Studies* 32, 3: 44–75.

Pride, Richard A. 1995. 'How Activists and Media Frame Social Problems: Critical Events versus Performance Trends for Schools', *Political Communication* 12, 1: 5–26.

Raeburn, Nicole C. 2004. *Changing Corporate America from Inside Out: Lesbian and Gay Workplace Organizing*. Minneapolis: University of Minnesota Press.

Ramos, Howard. 2004. 'Divergent Paths: Aboriginal Mobilization in Canada, 1951–2000', Ph.D. thesis, McGill University.

———. 2006. 'What Causes Canadian Aboriginal Protest? Examining Resources, Opportunities and Identity, 1951–2000', *Canadian Journal of Sociology* 31, 2: 211–34.

Rayside, David. 1998. *On the Fringe: Gays and Lesbians in Politics*. Ithaca, NY: Cornell University Press.

Rebick, Judy. 2005. *Ten Thousand Roses: The Making of a Feminist Revolution*. Toronto: Penguin Canada.

Reger, Jo, ed. 2005. *Different Wavelengths: Studies of the Contemporary Women's Movement*. New York, Routledge.

——— and Lacey Story. 2005. 'Talking about My Vagina: Two College Campuses and *The Vagina Monologues*', in Reger (2005: 139–60).

Ricard, François. 1994. *The Lyric Generation: The Life and Times of the Baby Boomers*, trans. Donald Winkler. Toronto: Stoddart.

Rimmerman, Craig A. 2002. *From Identity to Politics: The Lesbian and Gay Movements in the United States*. Philadelphia: Temple University Press.

Rome, Adam. 2003. '"Give Earth a Chance": The Environmental Movement and the Sixties', *Journal of American History* 90, 2: 525–54.

Rootes, Christopher. 1999. *Environmental Movements: Local, National and Global*. London: Frank Cass.

———. 2004. 'Environmental Movements', in Snow et al. (2004: 608–40).

Rosen, Ruth. 2000. *The World Split Open: How the Modern Women's Movement Changed America*. New York: Penguin Books.

Ross, Robert J.S. 2005. 'From Anti-Sweatshop, to Global Justice, to Anti-War: Student Participation in Globalization Protests', in Podobnik and Reifer (2005: 112–21).

Roth, Benita. 2004. *Separate Roads to Feminism: Black, Chicana, and White Feminist Movements in America's Second Wave*. Cambridge: Cambridge University Press.

Rucht, Dieter. 1988. 'Themes, Logics, and Arenas of Social Movements: A Structural Approach', *International Social Movement Research* 1: 305–28.

———. 1995. 'Ecological Protest as Calculated Law-breaking: Greenpeace and Earth First! in Comparative Perspective', in R. Wolfgang, ed., *Green Politics Three*. Edinburgh: Edinburgh University Press, 66–89.

———. 2004. 'Movement Allies, Adversaries, and Third Parties', in Snow et al. (2004: 197–216).

———. 2005. 'The Internet as a New Opportunity for Transnational Protest Groups', in M. Kousis and C. Tilly, eds, *Economic and Political Contention in Comparative Perspective*. Boulder, Colo.: Paradigm, 70–85.

——— and Jochen Roose. 1999. 'The German Environmental Movement at a Crossroads?', *Environmental Politics* 8, 1: 59–80.

——— and ———. 2001. 'Neither Decline nor Sclerosis: The Organizational Structure of the German Environmental Movement', *West European Politics* 24, 4: 55–81.

Rupp, Leila J. 1997. *Worlds of Women: The Making of an International Women's Movement*. Princeton, NJ: Princeton University Press.

——— and Verta Taylor. 1987. *Survival in the Doldrums: The American Women's Rights Movement, 1945 to the 1960s*. New York: Oxford University Press.

——— and ———. 1999. 'Forging Feminist Identity in an International Movement: A Collective Identity Approach to Twentieth-Century Feminism', *Signs* 24, 2: 363–86.

Saad, Lydia. 2006. 'Americans Still Not Highly Concerned about Global Warming', *The Gallup Poll* (Apr.): 20–2.

Sale, Kirkpatrick. 1973. *SDS*. New York: Random House.

———. 1993. *The Green Revolution*. New York: Hill and Wang.

Schudson, Michael. 2003. *The Sociology of News*. New York: Norton.

Schulz, Markus S. 1998. 'Collective Action across Borders: Opportunity Structures, Network Capacities, and Communicative Praxis in the Age of Advanced Globalization', *Sociological Perspectives* 41, 3: 587–616.

Seidman, Gay W. 2000. 'Adjusting the Lens: What Do Globalizations, Transnationalism, and the Anti-apartheid Movement Mean for Social Movement Theory?', in J.A. Guidry, M.D. Kennedy, and M.N. Zald, eds, *Globalizations and Social Movements*. Ann Arbor: University of Michigan Press, 339–57.

Shaw, Randy. 1999. *Reclaiming America: Nike, Clean Air, and the New National Activism*. Berkeley: University of California Press.

Shellenberger, Michael, and Ted Nordhaus. 2004. 'The Death of Environmentalism: Global Warming Politics in a Post-Environmental World'. At: <www.thebreakthrough.org/images/Death_of_Environmentalism.pdf>.

Shorter, Edward. 1975. *The Making of the Modern Family*. New York: Basic Books.

Sigal, Leon V. 1973. *Reporters and Officials: The Organization and Politics of Newsmaking*. Lexington, Mass.: D.C. Heath.

Simpson, Jeffrey. 1999. 'The Cost of Expectations', *Globe and Mail*, 29 Oct, A19.

Skrentny, John D. 1998. 'The Effect of the Cold War on African-American Civil Rights: America and the World Audience, 1945–1968', *Theory and Society* 27: 237–85.

Smelser, Neil J. 1962. *Theory of Collective Behavior*. New York: Free Press.

———. 1970. 'Two Critics in Search of a Bias: A Response to Currie and Skolnick', *Annals, American Academy of Political and Social Science* 391: 46–55.

Smith, Jackie. 2001. 'Globalizing Resistance: The Battle of Seattle and the Future of Social Movements', *Mobilization* 6, 1: 1–19.

Smith, Miriam. 1998. 'Social Movements and Equality Seeking: The Case of Gay Liberation in Canada', *Canadian Journal of Political Science* 31, 2: 285–309.

———. 1999. *Lesbian and Gay Rights in Canada*. Toronto: University of Toronto Press.

———. 2005. 'The Politics of Same-Sex Marriage in Canada and the United States', *PS: Political Science and Politics* 38, 2: 225–8.

Snow, David A. 2001. 'Collective Identity', in Neil J. Smelser and Paul B. Baltes, eds, *International Encyclopedia of the Social and Behavioral Sciences*. London: Elsevier, 2212–19.

———. 2004. 'Social Movements as Challenges to Authority: Resistance to an Emerging Conceptual Hegemony', *Research in Social Movements, Conflicts and Change* 25: 3–25.

——— and Robert D. Benford. 1992. 'Ideology, Frame Resonance and Participant Mobilization', *International Social Movement Research* 1: 197–217.

———, E. Burke Rochford Jr, Steven K. Worden, and Robert D. Benford. 1986. 'Frame Alignment Processes, Micromobilization, and Movement Participation', *American Sociological Review* 51, 4: 464–81.

———, Sarah A. Soule, and Hanspeter Kriesi, eds. 2004. *The Blackwell Companion to Social Movements*. Malden, Mass.: Blackwell.

———, Louis A. Zurcher Jr, and Sheldon Ekland-Olson. 1980. 'Social Networks and Social Movements: A Microstructural Approach to Differential Recruitment', *American Sociological Review* 45, 5: 787–801.

Snyder, David, and William R. Kelley. 1979. 'Strategies for Investigating Violence and Social Change: Illustrations from Analyses of Racial Disorders and Implications for Mobilization Research', in M.N. Zald and J.D. McCarthy, eds, *The Dynamics of Social Movements: Resource Mobilization, Social Control, and Tactics*. Cambridge, Mass.: Winthrop, 212–37.

Soule, Sarah A., and Susan Olzak. 2004. 'When Do Movements Matter? The Politics of Contingency and the Equal Rights Amendment', *American Sociological Review* 69: 473–97.

Speed, Shannon, and Jane F. Collier. 2000. 'Limiting Indigenous Autonomy in Chiapas, Mexico: The State Government's Use of Human Rights', *Human Rights Quarterly* 22: 877–905.

Springer, Kimberly. 2005. *Living for the Revolution: Black Feminist Organizations, 1968–1980*. Durham, NC: Duke University Press.

Staggenborg, Suzanne. 1986. 'Coalition Work in the Pro-Choice Movement: Organizational and Environmental Opportunities and Obstacles', *Social Problems* 33, 5: 374–90.

———. 1988. 'The Consequences of Professionalization and Formalization in the Pro-Choice Movement', *American Sociological Review* 53: 585–605.

———. 1989. 'Stability and Innovation in the Women's Movement: A Comparison of Two Movement Organizations', *Social Problems* 36, 1: 75–92.

———. 1993. 'Critical Events and the Mobilization of the Pro-Choice Movement', *Research in Political Sociology* 6: 319–45.

———. 1995. 'Can Feminist Organizations Be Effective?', in Myra Marx Ferree and Patricia Yancey Martin, eds, *Feminist Organizations: Harvest of the New Women's Movement*. Philadelphia: Temple University Press, 339–55.

———. 1998. 'Social Movement Communities and Cycles of Protest: The Emergence and Maintenance of a Local Women's Movement', *Social Problems* 45, 2: 180–204.

———. 2001. 'Beyond Culture versus Politics: A Case Study of a Local Women's Movement', *Gender & Society* 15, 4: 507–30.

——— and Verta Taylor. 2005. 'Whatever Happened to the Women's Movement?', *Mobilization* 10, 1: 37–52.

Starr, Amory. 2005. *Global Revolt: A Guide to the Movements against Globalization*. New York: Zed Books.

Steinberg, Marc W. 1998. 'Tilting the Frame: Considerations on Collective Action Framing from a Discursive Turn', *Theory and Society* 27, 6: 845–72.

Steinhart, Peter. 1987. 'The Longer View', *Audubon* 89, 2: 10–13.

Stewart, Keith. 2003. 'If I Can't Dance: Reformism, Anti-Capitalism and the Canadian Environmental Movement', *Canadian Dimension* 37, 5: 41–3.

Swerdlow, Amy. 1993. *Women's Strike for Peace*. Chicago: University of Chicago Press.

Switzer, Jacqueline Vaughn. 1997. *Green Backlash: The History and Politics of Environmental Opposition in the U.S.* Boulder, Colo.: Lynne Rienner.

Szasz, Andrew. 1994. *Ecopopulism: Toxic Waste and the Movement for Environmental Justice*. Minneapolis: University of Minnesota Press.

Taras, David. 1990. *The Newsmakers: The Media's Influence on Canadian Politics*. Scarborough, Ont.: Nelson.

Tarrow, Sidney. 1989. *Democracy and Disorder: Protest and Politics in Italy, 1965–1975*. Oxford: Oxford University Press.

———. 1998. *Power in Movement: Social Movements and Contentious Politics*, 2nd edn. Cambridge: Cambridge University Press.

———. 2005. *The New Transnational Activism*. New York: Cambridge University Press.

Taylor, Verta. 1989. 'Social Movement Continuity: The Women's Movement in Abeyance', *American Sociological Review* 54: 761–75.

——— and Leila J. Rupp. 1993. 'Women's Culture and Lesbian Feminist Activism: A Reconsideration of Cultural Feminism', *Signs* 19, 1: 32–61.

——— and Nancy E. Whittier. 1992. 'Collective Identity in Social Movement Communities: Lesbian Feminist Mobilization', in A.D. Morris and C.M. Mueller, eds, *Frontiers in Social Movement Theory*. New Haven: Yale University Press, 104–29.

Tennant, Paul. 1990. *Aboriginal Peoples and Politics: The Indian Land Question in British Columbia, 1849–1989*. Vancouver: University of British Columbia Press.

Tierney, Kathleen J. 1982. 'The Battered Women Movement and the Creation of the Wife Beating Problem', *Social Problems* 29, 3: 207–20.

Tilly, Charles. 1978. *From Mobilization to Revolution*. Reading, Mass.: Addison-Wesley.

———. 1984. 'Social Movements and National Politics', in H. Charles Bright and Susan Harding, eds, *Statemaking and Social Movements*. Ann Arbor: University of Michigan Press, 297–317.

———. 1986. 'European Violence and Collective Action Since 1700', *Social Research* 53, 1: 159–84.

———. 1988. 'Social Movements, Old and New', *Research in Social Movements, Conflicts and Change* 10: 1–18.

———. 1995. *Popular Contention in Great Britain, 1758–1834*. Cambridge, Mass.: Harvard University Press.

———. 2004a. *Contention and Democracy in Europe, 1650–2000*. New York: Cambridge University Press.

————. 2004b. *Social Movements, 1768–2004*. Boulder, Colo.: Paradigm.

Tindall, David B. 2002. 'Social Networks, Identification and Participation in an Environmental Movement: Low-medium Cost Activism within the British Columbia Wilderness Preservation Movement', *Canadian Review of Sociology and Anthropology* 39, 4: 413–52.

Toronto Star. 1999. 'Logging on to Protest', 29 Nov.

Touraine, Alain. 1971. *The May Movement: Revolt and Reform*. New York: Random House.

Tuchman, Gaye. 1978. *Making News: A Study in the Construction of Reality*. New York: Free Press.

Turner, Ralph. 1981. 'Collective Behavior and Resource Mobilization as Approaches to Social Movements: Issues and Continuities', *Social Movements, Conflicts and Change* 4: 1–24.

———— and Lewis M. Killian. 1957. *Collective Behavior*. Englewood Cliffs, NJ: Prentice-Hall.

———— and ————. 1972. *Collective Behavior*, 2nd edn. Englewood Cliffs, NJ: Prentice-Hall.

———— and ————. 1987. *Collective Behaviour*, 3rd edn. Englewood Cliffs, NJ: Prentice-Hall.

Useem, Michael. 1975. *Protest Movements in America*. Indianapolis: Bobbs-Merrill.

Van Deburg, William L. 1992. *New Day in Babylon: The Black Power Movement and American Culture, 1965–1975*. Chicago: University of Chicago Press.

Van Dyke, Nella. 2003. 'Crossing Movement Boundaries: Factors that Facilitate Coalition Protest by American College Students, 1930–1990', *Social Problems* 50, 2: 226–50.

Vickers, Jill, Pauline Rankin, and Christine Appelle. 1993. *Politics as if Women Mattered: A Political Analysis of the National Action Committee on the Status of Women*. Toronto: University of Toronto Press.

Vipond, Robert. 2004. 'The Civil Rights Movement Comes to Winnipeg: American Influence on "Rights Talk" in Canada, 1968–71', in S.L. Newman, ed., *Constitutional Politics in Canada and the United States*. Albany: State University of New York Press, 89–107.

Voss, Kim, and Rachel Sherman. 2000. 'Breaking the Iron Law of Oligarchy: Union Revitalization in the American Labor Movement', *American Journal of Sociology* 106, 2: 303–49.

Walker, Gillian A. 1990. *Family Violence and the Women's Movement*. Toronto: University of Toronto Press.

Walker, Rebecca, ed. 1995. *To Be Real: Telling the Truth and Changing the Face of Feminism*. New York: Anchor Books.

Wall, Derek. 1999. *Earth First! and the Anti-Roads Movement: Radical Environmentalism and the Comparative Social Movements*. London: Routledge.

Walsh, Edward J. 1988. *Democracy in the Shadows: Citizen Mobilization in the Wake of the Accident at Three Mile Island*. Westport, Conn.: Greenwood Press.

Warner, Tom. 2002. *Never Going Back: A History of Queer Activism in Canada*. Toronto: University of Toronto Press.

Webster, Norman. 1979. 'Indians to Petition the Queen on Constitution', *Globe and Mail*, 2 July, 4.

Werum, Regina, and Bill Winders. 2001. 'Who's "In" and Who's "Out": State Fragmentation and the Struggle over Gay Rights, 1974–1999', *Social Problems* 48, 3: 386–410.

Weyler, Rex. 2004. *Greenpeace: How a Group of Ecologists, Journalists and Visionaries Changed the World*. Vancouver: Raincoast Books.

Wilkes, Rima. 2004a. 'First Nation Politics: Deprivation, Resources, and Participation in Collective Action', *Sociological Inquiry* 74, 4: 570–89.

————. 2004b. 'A Systematic Approach to Studying Indigenous Politics: Band-Level Mobilization in Canada, 1981–2000', *Social Science Journal* 41: 447–57.

————. 2006. 'The Protest Actions of Indigenous Peoples: A Canadian–U.S. Comparison of Social Movement Emergence', *American Behavioral Scientist* 50, 4: 510–25.

Wilson, Jeremy. 1992. 'Green Lobbies: Pressure Groups and Environmental Policy', in R. Boardman, ed., *Canadian Environmental Policy: Ecosystems, Politics, and Process*. Toronto: Oxford University Press, 109–25.

————. 2001. 'Continuity and Change in the Canadian Environmental Movement: Assessing the Effects of Institutionalization', in D.L. VanNijnatten and R. Boardman, eds, *Canadian Environmental Policy: Context and Cases*. Toronto: Oxford University Press, 46–65.

Wilson, John. 1973. *Introduction to Social Movements*. New York: Basic Books.

Wood, Lesley J. 2005a. 'Taking to the Streets against Neoliberalism: Global Days of Action and Other Strategies', in Podobnik and Reifer (2005: 69–81).

————. 2005b. 'Bridging the Chasms: The Case of Peoples' Global Action', in J. Bandy and J. Sith, eds, *Coalitions Across Borders: Transnational Protest and the Neoliberal Order*. Lanham, Md: Rowman & Littlefield, 95–117.

Young, Scott. 1969. 'A Strange Feeling at the Centre of Indian Discontent', *Globe and Mail*, 11 July, 7.

Zald, Mayer N. 2000. 'Ideologically Structured Action: An Enlarged Agenda for Social Movement Research', *Mobilization* 5, 1: 1–16.

———— and Bert Useem. 1987. 'Movement and Countermovement Interaction: Mobilization, Tactics, and State Involvement', in M.N. Zald and J.D. McCarthy, eds, *Social Movements in an Organizational Society*. New Brunswick, NJ: Transaction Books, 247–72.

Zogby International. 2006. 'Zogby Post-Election Poll: Dems Gained from Global Warming Debate', press release, 16 Nov.

Index

Themes in Canadian Sociology Series

Scott Davies and Neil Guppy
The Schooled Society: An Introduction to the Sociology of Education (2006)
ISBN 9780195421088

Maureen Baker
Choices and Constraints in Family Life (2007)
ISBN 9780195421057

Vic Satzewich and Nikolaos Liodakis
'Race' and Ethnicity in Canada: A Critical Introduction (2007)
ISBN 9780195421316

William O'Grady
Crime in Canadian Context: Debates and Controversies (2007)
ISBN 9780195422955

Suzanne Staggenborg
Social Movements (2008)
ISBN 9780195423099

Ludmilla.voitkovska
@usask.ca